DATE DUE

DEMCO 38-296

NARRATIVE AND GENRE

Any life story, whether a written autobiography or an oral testimony, is shaped not only by the reworkings of experience through memory and re-evaluation, but also by art. Any communication has to use shared conventions not only of language itself but also the more complex expectations of 'genre': of the forms expected within a given context and type of communication.

This collection of essays by international academics draws on a wide range of disciplines in the social sciences and the humanities to examine how far the expectations and forms of genre shape different kinds of autobiography and influence what messages they can convey. After investigating the problem of genre definition, and tracing the evolution of genre as a concept, contributors explore such issues as:

- how far can we argue that what people narrate in their autobiographical stories is selected and shaped by the repertoire of genre available to them?
- to what extent is oral autobiography shaped by its social and cultural context?
- what is the relationship between autobiographical sources and the ethnographer?

Narrative and Genre presents exciting new debates in an emerging field and will encourage international and interdisciplinary debate. Its authors and contributors are scholars from the fields of anthropology, cultural studies, literary analysis, psychology, psychoanalysis, social history and sociology.

Mary Chamberlain is Professor of Modern Social History at Oxford Brookes University. **Paul Thompson** is Research Professor at the University of Essex and Director of Qualidata.

ROUTLEDGE STUDIES IN MEMORY AND NARRATIVE
Edited by Mary Chamberlain and Paul Thompson

I. NARRATIVE AND GENRE
Edited by Mary Chamberlain and Paul Thompson

EDITORIAL STATEMENT

Memory and Narrative is a new series of volumes published at least twice yearly and exploring how personal and collective memory is shaped and represented in different cultures, contexts and forms. Each volume will examine the relation between remembering and forgetting, forms of narrative communication and social practice in diverse social contexts and parts of the world. These forms of communication will range from oral reminiscence and life stories, to autobiography, imaginative literature and written history: and from monuments or museums to television and CD-Rom. By contrasting the functions of the varied forms of reminiscence, the series will promote a fuller understanding of the role of each in structuring and presenting personal and collective identity, experience and knowledge of the past. The series aims to stimulate debate by drawing on a wide range of disciplines in the social sciences and the humanities, including anthropology, cultural studies, literary analysis, psychology, psychoanalysis, social history and sociology. Each volume will normally be organized around a single theme and will include book reviews and a section on methods and new technologies. There will be no limit as to time period or geography. The volumes will be edited alternately from Europe and North America, with the support of an international network of associate editors to encourage contributions from all parts of the world.

Principal editors Mary Chamberlain, Paul Thompson, Selma Leydesdorff, Kim Lacy Rogers
Consulting editors Alessandro Portelli, Daniel Bertaux, Homi Bhabha
Editors Timothy Ashplant, Natasha Burchardt, Susan Condor, Graham Dawson, Brian Elliott, Arthur A. Hansen, Steve Hussey, Nina Kidron, Eva McMahan, Laura Marcus, Judith Modell, Charles Morissey, Daphne Patai, Susannah Radstone, Michael Roper, Linda Shopes, Richard Candida Smith, Elizabeth Tonkin, David Vincent, Jerry W. Ward Jr
Principal review editor Selma Leydesdorff
Review editors Timothy Ashplant, Elizabeth Tonkin (English), Annemarie Granet-Abisset (French), Helma Lutz (German), Karen Fog Olwig

NARRATIVE AND GENRE

*Edited by Mary Chamberlain
and Paul Thompson*

London and New York

First published 1998
by Routledge
11 New Fetter Lane, London EC4P 4EE

Simultaneously published in the USA and Canada
by Routledge
29 West 35th Street, New York, NY 10001
Reprinted 2000 (twice), 2001

Routledge is an imprint of the Taylor & Francis Group

Typeset in Garamond by RefineCatch Limited, Bungay, Suffolk

Printed and bound in Great Britain by
T.J.I. Digital, Padstow, Cornwall

British Library Cataloguing in Publication Data
A catalogue record for this book is available from the British Library

Library of Congress Cataloguing in Publication Data
A catalogue record for this book has been requested

ISBN 0–415–15198–8

We
dedicate this first volume
to the memory of
RAPHAEL SAMUEL
1934–1996
historian and socialist
colleague in oral history and popular memory
dearly loved friend

CONTENTS

NOTES ON CONTRIBUTORS

Rosilene Alvim is an anthropologist at the Institute of Social Sciences of the Federal University of Rio de Janeiro and has written about craftsmanship in a pilgrimage city in the Brazilian North East, the working-class family and, most recently, working-class childhood.

T. G. Ashplant teaches cultural history at Liverpool John Moores University and is currently researching masculinity, class and politics in life narratives.

Mary Chamberlain is Professor of Modern Social History at Oxford Brookes University and author of *Fenwomen*, *Old Wives' Tales*, *Growing Up in Lambeth* and *Narratives of Exile and Return*, and editor of *Writing Lives*. She is a trustee of the National Life Story Collection, and was reviews editor of *Oral History* from 1977 to 1987.

Kathryn Marie Dudley is a cultural anthropologist researching with the American Studies Program at Yale University.

Stephan Feuchtwang is an anthropologist researching on China and Professor of Sociology at the City University, London. His books include *An Anthropological Analysis of Chinese Geomancy* and *The Imperial Metaphor: Popular Religion in China*.

Diana Gittins is a social historian and a poet, whose previous books include *Fair Sex* and *The Family in Question*.

Yvette J. Kopijn is researching on women in Surinam at the Belle van Zuylen Instituut, University of Amsterdam.

José Sérgio Leite Lopes is an anthropologist who has researched for many years based in the Museu Nacional in Rio de Janeiro. His books include *O Vapor do Diabo* on the sugar plantations of the North East of Brazil. Most recently he has been writing on the culture of Brazilian football.

Orvar Löfgren is Professor of European Ethnology at Lund. He has researched on the relationships between the economy and culture, and especially on changes in the Swedish family. His books include *Culture Builders: A Historical Anthropology of Middle Class Life*. His current research interests focus on Swedish consumption and tourism and on national identities.

Chris Mann is researching on gender differences in degree results at the University of Cambridge.

Alessandro Portelli teaches American studies at the University of Rome, La Sapienza. He was founder editor of a journal of popular culture and song, *I giorni cantati*, and his books include an oral history of Terni, *Biografia di una città*, and two collections of essays, *The Death of Luigi Trastulli and Other Stories* and *The Battle of Valle Giulia*.

Paul Thompson is Research Professor at the University of Essex and Director of Qualidata. He is founder of the National Life Story Collection and founder editor of *Oral History*. His books include *The Voice of the Past*, *The Work of William Morris*, *The Edwardians* and (with Raphael Samuel) *The Myths We Live By*.

Jerry White is a former editor of *History Workshop Journal* and the author of *Rothschild Buildings* (1980), *The Worst Street in North London* (1986) and (with Michael Young) *Governing London* (1996). He is currently the Local Government Ombudsman for Central and South-West England and Visiting Professor in the School of History and Politics, Middlesex University.

INTRODUCTION TO THE SERIES

Memory and narrative have long been central concerns, although in different ways, for a wide range of academic disciplines: from literature and history in the humanities, through ethnology to social anthropology, sociology, psychology and psychoanalysis in the social and behavioural sciences. Two hundred years ago there were of course no such academic disciplines with their self-conscious boundaries: in Enlightenment Edinburgh, for instance, a philosopher could without comment write history or practise politics, a historical novelist could be a ballad collector, or a national statistical survey could comprehend both antiquarian notes and contemporary economic and demographic information. The subsequent rise of sharply demarcated different perspectives, protected by those rising disciplinary walls, has made it increasingly difficult to see any common ground between the preoccupations of a behavioural psychologist, a specialist in the poetry of William Wordsworth, or an anthropologist in the tropics. Nevertheless all of them, in one way or another, were preoccupied with the role of memory in shaping a narrative, and narrative in shaping memory. In recent years, however, a reversal of the earlier distancing has begun. Prompted partly by the growing use of life story interviews by oral historians and sociologists, partly by the revived literary interest in both written and spoken autobiography, there has been a new recognition that autonomous disciplinary endeavours can be greatly enriched through exchange of ideas, approaches and insights across the boundaries.

Those who work with memory in the shape of the interview have come to acknowledge their role in, and contribution to, the process of recall and recount. It is no longer sufficient to present memory as innocent empirical evidence, but to see it, necessarily, as a multi-authored, textual and contextual event. Memories contain and are contained by a narrative which orders, links and makes sense of the past, the present and the future. At the same time they contain para-narratives, which weave in and out offering a counterpoint here, a substance there. Placing memory, in all its multifaceted and multilayered dimensions, within the *longue durée* of a narrative suggests more an act of creativity than a finite text, where the process of recall is as vital as the substance remembered.

Unravelling the meanings and construction of narrative has long been a preoccupation of literary scholars. The richness and power of oral sources, whether in song or tradition, lore or memory, in informing and inspiring novelists and poets, from Sir Walter Scott to Thomas Hardy or, more recently, Toni Morrison or Derek Walcott, has been well acknowledged. At the same time, a renewed interest in autobiography, as a literary form and as a structure for the novel, has focused attention on the process and representation, as well as the content, of recall. With this has come an understanding that memories are rarely 'raw' but shaped in and by social and historical narrative, reflected in, but also living beyond, the literature it has inspired.

Disparate disciplines thus prove to be linked by common interests and preoccupations, so that historians as well as social and behavioural scientists now are concerned with searching for the narrative structures which inform the memories they seek to analyse, while literary scholars seek out the meanings of the memories which have inspired and driven their narrative texts. It is for these reasons, a vital and exciting convergence of interests, that we consider it appropriate to launch this series, to provide a regular inter-disciplinary forum for exchange of approaches and ideas in the analysis and uses for, and of, memory and narrative.

We have, therefore, chosen for our first book the theme of genre and narrative, the cultural and imaginative constructions which shape perception and memory, recall and recount, which describe and interpret, argue and explain. We have chosen this theme for three reasons. First, all scholarly disciplines may be seen at one level as narrative, as ways of explaining and interpreting. Narrative and genre, therefore, is a useful way of spanning the disciplines represented in the series, as well as highlighting their arbitrariness. Second, notions of narrative and genre are used as principles of both organization and interpretation *within* the disciplines, and to focus on their different uses within a variety of disciplines serves as a way of linking them. Finally, it points to the centrality and vitality of memory – that seemingly most idiosyncratic and individual function of the brain – in the transmission and transformation of culture and of the self within it.

This first book is deliberately broad. Our second book focuses on a more urgent and immediate question, that of trauma and the uses to which memory is put in understanding and negotiating it, and how narrative is employed in explaining it. Book number three has the environment as its theme, and a following one will be on public commemorations. A call for proposals on both these themes is included at the end of this volume.

The broad aim of Memory and Narrative is to stimulate debate and encourage fresh research. In many ways, however, Memory and Narrative will be breaking new ground. Some of our publications will be closer to the multi-theme format of a traditional journal; others will be dedicated anthologies; others monographs. Along with the books mentioned above, we shall be publishing anthologies on nineteenth-century memory and history, and on living through the Soviet period in Russia, and a monograph on the social history and memories of a mental hospital. Along with contributions to collections, the editors also welcome proposals for anthologies and for monographs which would fit within the broad aims of the series.

It is not, however, the variable format which differs. We hope that our broad theme of memory and narrative will appeal to a wide range of scholars and practitioners across a number of disciplines. Our aim is to hold a continuing conversation, using a variety of voices, interests and approaches.

Finally, our publications alternate between an editorial group based in the United States and one based in Europe. Both these groups are supported by a world-wide network of associate editors who represent every continent, a wide range of cultures and our interdisciplinary profile. Although we publish in English, so that authors must submit final manuscripts in English only, we shall be glad to give initial opinions on proposals, and early draft manuscripts can be sent in French, German, Italian, Portuguese or Spanish.

ACKNOWLEDGEMENTS

Chapter 2, 'Oral history as genre' by Alessandro Portelli, is also published in 1997 in his book *The Battle of Valle Giulia: Oral History and the Art of Dialogue*, and is included here by kind permission of the University of Wisconsin Press.

Page 48, extract reprinted by permission of the publishers and the Trustees of Amherst College from *The Poems of Emily Dickinson*, Thomas H. Johnson (ed.), Cambridge, Mass.: The Belknap Press of Harvard University Press, copyright © 1951, 1955, 1979, 1983 by the President and Fellows of Harvard College.

1

INTRODUCTION
Genre and Narrative in Life Stories
Mary Chamberlain and Paul Thompson

Any life story, whether a written autobiography or an oral testimony, is shaped not only by the reworkings of experience through memory and re-evaluation but also always at least to some extent by art. Any communication has to use shared conventions not only of language itself but also the more complex expectations of 'genre': of the forms expected within a given context and type of communication. How far do the expectations and forms of genre shape different kinds of autobiography and influence what messages it can convey?

Genre is not an easy matter to discuss; on the one hand the term is relatively new for social scientists, while on the other it has a very long and at times confusing history in literature and the visual arts, which continues to yield many helpful insights on autobiography. Our objective in this volume has been to encourage a creative interdisciplinary approach to genre issues which brings together current thinking in both the humanities and social sciences. But because the use of genre as a concept goes back much further in literature and the visual arts, yet has undergone a somewhat tortuous history, it will be most helpful to start by briefly clarifying the evolution of this thinking.

There have certainly been some fundamental difficulties with the traditional conceptualization of genre in the humanities. The first is a surprising confusion in the meaning of the word 'genre' itself. The concept goes back to the basic distinction made by the Greeks between the dramatic, epic and lyrical forms of literature: that is, a distinction made partly in terms of mood and theme, and partly of mode of presentation and the relationship with the audience. And although later genre came to be applied almost entirely to written forms of literature – thus from our perspective seriously reducing its value for understanding autobiography – we may note that for the Greeks the three major forms were all primarily expressed in their spoken form.

The current meaning of 'genre', which dates from the nineteenth century, is 'a style or category of painting, novel, film, etc., characterized by a particular form or purpose'. In the visual arts, however, its use later became more narrowly confined to a style of painting depicting scenes from everyday life.

1

However, in practice, historians of art and architecture have nevertheless focused – some would say overfocused – on developing, although without using generic terms, an elaborate and agreed taxonomy of styles, formulaic elements and elements of design, of precisely the kind which is so strikingly absent in literature. Of course, too rigid a taxonomy, which does not allow room for the evolution of forms in changing historical contexts, becomes a straitjacket in itself: but with literature the problem with genre categorization was not so much of overprecision as of vague generality. A further impediment has been that in literature a genre can be defined by form (such as drama, poetry, proverbs, letters), by mood (as comedy, tragedy) or by content (as history, memoirs, autobiography); even though certainly these are usually closely tied together.[1] Genre may also refer either to a type of text , or to an element within that text. Because all these definitions cut across each other, it has been impossible to agree on any settled definitions of genres, or to group them convincingly as major and minor genres and subgenres.

The problem of definition has indeed seriously concerned some of the most influential literary critics. Thus Northrop Frye wrote in 1957 in his classic *Anatomy of Criticism* that 'the critical theory of genres is stuck precisely where Aristotle left it.' Contemporary critics had neither standards nor even a name equivalent to 'drama' or 'poetry' with which to identify prose art:

> Thanks to the Greeks, we can distinguish tragedy from comedy in drama . . . [But] when we come to deal with such forms as the masque, opera, movie, ballet, puppet-play, mystery-play, morality, *commedia dell'arte*, and *zauberspiel*, we find ourselves in the position of the Renaissance doctors who refused to treat syphilis because Galen said nothing about it. The Greeks hardly needed to develop a classification of prose forms. We do, but have never done so. . . . The circulating-library distinction between fiction and non-fiction, between books which are about things admitted not to be true and books which are about everything else, is apparently exhaustive enough for critics.[2]

Yet paradoxically the important new perspectives which Frye himself heralded did not lead to an elaboration of genre analysis. This was because, although there was to be a radical new use of genre by 'structuralists' – who emphasized the importance of the form rather than the individual creativity of the author – which in itself constituted an attack on the high literary tradition, concepts of genre in the main continued to be associated with old-fashioned conservative formalism. Hence the focus of critical innovation was much more on new attempts to break beyond its conventional boundaries of genre and to reject the constrictions of focusing on a 'canonic literature' of great works and old-fashioned generic typologies.[3] Settled definitions and agreed taxonomies thus became taboo. Genre now seemed to many radical critics an unacceptably superficial and external way of categorizing works of literature, especially for 'phenomologists', with their concern for what they called 'deconstruction' and 'theory', for exploring ideology, values, individual 'subjectivity', feelings, the subconscious and the irrational. Turning their backs on genre was helpful in allowing them to extend the whole arena of literary criticism and to analyse numerous texts which until then would not have been considered works of literature at all. On the other hand, perhaps more surprisingly, even those who still concentrated on major creative works had become uncomfortable with genre, for it seemed increasingly clear that the less original a work the more likely it was to fit comfortably into a genre category, while the greatest creative works defied such easy formal categorization.

A second difficulty arises from the anomalous position of autobiography within traditional genres. How far should it be read as a narrative of real experience, and how far as a form of fiction? Traditional literary criticism of autobiography did reach a position which seems on the surface to accord reasonably well with that of current researchers using oral life stories. Thus Roy Pascal wrote in 1960 that autobiography is indeed a story, but 'the story of a life in the world'. But a good narrative 'has to have a shape, an outward shape in the narrative, and this shape is the outcome of an interpenetration and collusion of inner and outer life, of the person and society. The shape interprets both. This is the decisive achievement of autobiography.'[4] Ironically, however, just at the moment at the end of the 1970s when oral historians and life story sociologists were accepting that interviews were as interesting for their subjective as for their informational content, the main current of literary criticism was dividing, and some of the paths taken then looked much less helpful to sociologists or historians. Perhaps the least rewarding perspective proved to be that of the small but – at least until the late 1980s – influential group of radical critics who moved from 'deconstruction' towards a 'postmodernism' in which there was no longer a biographical self capable of reflection, or a biographical reality upon which to reflect. Hence reflection itself was merely ideology; and autobiography totally fictional.

There were, however, more positive ways of getting out of an increasingly arid debate about the differences between fiction and non-fiction. It was evident that other literary forms besides autobiography, and most notably the novel, also drew on a mixture of experience, observation and imagination. For many critics indeed, it seems better to treat both autobiography and the novel, alongside biography and other types of historical works, as particular forms of the major genre of narrative. From this perspective the study of 'the narrative construction of reality' has been a sustained concern of the influential Chicago literary review *Critical Inquiry*, and it is an approach which has brought literature increasingly close to history.[5] A different path, but again a fruitful one, has been taken by the 'reader response' school, which took special account of audience perceptions, and the 'cultural materialists', who sought to examine texts within their cultural context. Most recently, all these groups have converged into the cultural studies approach.

Under these influences genre has come increasingly to be understood not as a rigid form of classification but more akin to language, with its fundamental flexibility, but at the same time its common assumptions between writer, speaker and audience of conventions, manner and tone, forms of delivery, timings, settings, shapes, motifs and characters.

An equally serious difficulty has been that until the early 1980s most literary discussion of genre in autobiography was conducted from a very exclusive perspective.[6] Autobiography was conceived in terms of a high literary tradition of the lifetime reflections of great men, from 'the first great autobiography' by Saint Augustine, through Benvenuto Cellini to Benjamin Franklin, Gibbon, Rousseau, Goethe, John Henry Newman and Edmund Gosse, mirroring the classic concerns of Western conscience and individualism. Inclusion in the canon and exclusion from it were primarily questions of art;[7] but almost equally strongly, of class and gender prejudice.

As a result, even the published autobiography of the lower classes was almost entirely ignored. Despite the pioneering lead given by David Vincent,[8] there has been little more recent work addressing the genres of or within European working-class autobiography. Most historians have been too preoccupied with questions of factual accuracy. One suggestive exception, however, is the work of Mark Traugott on nineteenth-century French workers' autobiographies, which he divides into five 'common conventional forms' or subgenres: the legacy to posterity, the picaresque adventure, the success story, the plea for defence and the conversion experience.[9]

Equally seriously, the canon had no place at all either for the unwritten oral recollections of the majority of the population. Nor, despite the usual inclusion of religious conversion narratives within the genre, was there space within the canon for less total forms of private written reflection which lacked an explicit relationship between autobiographer and audience – and indeed, were sometimes addressed to God, or a rich patron, rather than to the public. These excluded autobiographical forms, which included diaries, spiritual journals of confession or conscience, travel journals, or letters, were also precisely those most likely to be used by women.[10] Breaking out from this straitjacket has proved a long and slow process.

In winning this change, perhaps the most persistent influence has been that of feminist criticism. The beginnings of a shift can already be seen in Robert Fothergill's study of diaries, *Private Chronicles* (1974), where selection is still canonical, but three women's diaries are included.[11] Meanwhile leading feminist critics such as Ellen Moers and Elaine Showalter in the United States and Juliet Mitchell in Britain were re-examining the lives of famous women novelists and showing how they responded to the constraints of patriarchal ideology by using their fiction to express their own personal experiences and to provide exemplary tales of women's suffering and defiance. This approach continues to be vigorously pursued.[12] And in the 1980s Julia Swindells and Liz Stanley have broadened the focus through in-depth

4

examinations of the diaries of nineteenth-century working-class women in Britain. Swindells in particular shows how her diarists borrowed from popular genres such as romance and melodrama in order to express personal feelings on 'women's issues' which could not otherwise be addressed.[13]

An especially striking contribution has come from a cluster of studies, initially emanating from the Centre for Contemporary Cultural Studies in Birmingham in the late 1970s with Angela McRobbie's essay on schoolgirls' comics,[14] in which the focus has been on popular forms of romantic story-telling and their meaning in the everyday lives of women. The central issue here has been how 'the formulaic elements of popular culture' shape women's consciousness, and so their lives: how women are socialized into femininity, their own real lives squeezed into the genre of fiction through their identification with fictional heroines.[15] The concern is as much with what audiences make of communications and how they identify with and use stories as with literary form. However, the range of forms considered is extremely wide: from Virago fiction, popular romantic novels and girls' comics, to talking, kissing, dancing . . .[16] And we should note too that at this important moment of innovation the structural analysis drew not only on literary conventions, but also on ethnographic and folklore forms of analysis, and in particular the much earlier Russian work of Vladimir Propp.[17] A particularly good example of this approach at its best, intertwining fantasy with autobiography, fiction with poetry, the contexts of home and school, is Valerie Walkerdine's *Schoolgirl Fictions*.[18]

Feminist critics early pointed out how story forms are gendered, and while women prefer to read love stories or – as Alessandro Portelli suggests, tell hospital stories – men go for adventure, science fiction, thrillers, or war stories. Some of the earliest studies of these formulaic male stories – although without any explicit awareness of gender issues – are by John Cawelti, whose background was in American folklore and literature: he published on the Western and the detective story.[19] More recently, studies of masculinity influenced by the feminist work have begun to explore the relationship between fictional genres and auto/biographical accounts of men's lives and identities, as in Graham Dawson's *Soldier Heroes*. However, partly because not so much suitable material has been identified, the range of masculine life stories covered by critics remains much more restricted in scope.[20]

It is also from the United States that the first studies have come of 'black English' in storytelling and also in vernacular preaching, although there is still a need for more specific study of forms of black autobiography.[21] Hence much closer to our concerns here has been the important literary critical interest, again chiefly in the Americas, in the Latin American *testimonio*. This is an autobiographical form which coalesced as a recognized radical narrative genre in the 1960s, partly through official encouragement in Cuba. Later it was used in refugee politics in the United States. It is typically a spoken autobiography in book form, and although it draws on some traditional Latin American literary devices and also on anthropological life stories, its key feature, as the name *testimonio* indicates, is as a secular spiritual testimony, telling a life as a left-wing moral with the overt intention of raising consciousness. That is what makes *I, Rigoberta Menchù*, edited by the Venezuelan social scientist Elisabeth Burgos-Debray, a *testimonio*, while Oscar Lewis's *Pedro Martinez* is not.[22]

Again outside Europe, and this time also outside the Americas, it is significant that there was an early recognition of the formal literary character of spoken oratory, poetry and life stories in West Africa through the work of Ruth Finnegan.[23] The implications of such genre contexts for spoken autobiography have, however, only been taken up much more recently through anthropology, in the work of Elizabeth Tonkin.

With European autobiography, however, the influence of the classic literary conventions remained strong for much longer. For the mainstream perhaps the most crucial break has come through the work of Philippe Lejeune from the late 1970s. Lejeune had written a series of studies on classic autobiography, of which the best known, *Le Pacte autobiographique*, explores the basis of confidence between author and reader.[24] His turning point was reached with *Je est un autre*. Here he deliberately begins with autobiographies by great authors, but shows how even these reveal a series of subgenres, including writing in the third person, or from the 1940s the radio interview. Lejeune then turns to the more recent fashion for the 'document vécu', published in series such as 'Témoignages', 'Elles-mêmes' or 'En direct', the candid autobiography typically of an unlettered and unknown underdog whose strength is presented as a naive honesty of feeling and description rather than the classical sophistication of self-reflection. They thus tend to be written in the present tense, with much dialogue. Lejeune also shows, however, how despite their apparent spontaneity some in fact draw closely on previous narrative models, such as prisoners' stories, or the reversing of them, a nurse's autobiography in *Moi, une infirmière* being a deliberate counterfoil to a doctors' romance like *Les Hommes en blanc*.

Lejeune goes still further: *Je est un autre* ends with discussions of 'The autobiography of those who do not write', including both oral history and the ethnographic life stories of Oscar Lewis. In this, however, his main concern is with how the process of editing reduces the original oral dialogue to a printed monologue. More importantly from our perspective here, he has returned to the question of the influence of genre in the autobiography of the obscure in his recent *Le Moi des demoiselles*. Here he takes an early nineteenth-century subgenre of French autobiography which would never have been included in the classic tradition, for the authors were unknown adolescent girls who were writing confessional diaries rather than restrospective autobiography. Lejeune shows that the few examples which were published are misleadingly atypical, for they were by girls who had died, so that their parents only selected extracts which suggested their goodness and piety. The full diaries are quite different, full of challenging self-analysis and often of rebellion against both school and family. But although they are overlong and repetitious to the point of boredom, it would be very mistaken to understand them as naive. Lejeune shows how the diaries were deliberately encouraged by parents, schools and convents, and the girls were shown models to follow such as the *Journal de Marguerite*.[25] At the start they would be corrected by the mother, and girls also showed their diaries to each other. It was only when they grew a little older that they became more secretive; and more interesting. Confronted with the richness of insights which Lejeune can offer here on a single autobiographical written subgenre, one can only regret that he has not returned to discuss similar issues in oral autobiography.

*   *   *

In the meantime, however, there have been equally important influences from other directions on thinking about genre in life stories and auto-biography. The spread of these new approaches has undoubtedly been very much helped forward by the breaking down of traditional academic disciplinary boundaries. The present-day walls between academic disciplines result from the gradual development over the last two hundred years of a self-defensive disciplinary autonomy, which has cut off the social and behavioural sciences from literary and art criticism, and encouraged each discipline to develop separate interpretative tools and its own exclusive technical jargon. More recently, however, there has been an increased sensitivity, with on the one hand literature responding not only to history but also to the social sciences, and on the other, a recognition of the relevance of literary insights to social science research. This volume is itself an expression of a new interdisciplinary convergence which it would have been difficult to imagine even ten years ago. And the present closely comparable prestige of cultural studies in literature and cultural history in history is another indication of this sea change. On the one hand, literature must inevitably be an important aspect of cultural history; while on the other, through cultural studies literature has become engaged with travel, anthropology, landscape, scientific drawing and visual representation.

This breaking down of barriers has made it easier for some of the most recent impetus to come from the social sciences. There are two roots to this. The first, which is still at a relatively early stage of development, concerns various types of psychological and psychoanalytical writing and research.

Thus in terms of child development, there is a well-established current of thinking in linguistics, which has already influenced oral historians, showing the importance from a very early age of gender in shaping both what is remembered and the telling of memories: questions which were particularly important in *Gender and Memory*, the 1996 volume of the *International Year-book*.[26] At the same time, psychological research on the consequences of successful or unsuccessful attachment in infancy has suggested that the ability to form a coherent narrative at all is shaped by the social experience of parents or other crucial adult figures very early in life.[27] This suggests that the shaping of autobiographical narrative, and particularly of oral remembering, is a basic part of cultural learning in childhood. There are clearly implications of fundamental importance here for our understanding of the functions of form and genre in autobiography, and indeed for narrative remembering as such.

There is a more developed autobiographical tradition in psychoanalysis, which is clearly an autobiographical genre in itself, and, as we shall see, it has been used as such by some recent autobiographers. On reflection, however, it seems clear that therapeutic sessions are likely to generate a number of autobiographical forms. Thus the encounter between client and therapist is likely to be governed, as with all types of therapy, by definite formal rules: there is a strict time limit, and depending on what type of therapy is felt to be taking place – in the mode of psychoanalysis, psychotherapy, counselling, family therapy – the client may either sit facing the therapist or lie flat gazing into space, while the therapist may comment and intervene, respond only briefly, or remain largely silent. Probably the most dramatically interactive form is with family therapy, in which the clients are a group, often vociferously interrupting each other, so that single life story accounts are impossible to sustain, while the therapists typically work as a pair, at intervals retreating behind a one-way screen and re-emerging to make deliberately challenging interventions.

The stories recounted by the clients may also centre on a number of possible themes, which will no doubt strongly influence its character: suffering, loss, abuse, frustration, confusion and so on. But the themes are equally likely to be influenced by the preoccupations of the therapist, who, if inclined to classic Freudianism, is most likely to concentrate on the relationship with the father, or if a Kleinian with the mother, and so on. Some accounts may be close to the illness stories recounting physical ill-health and suffering which have concerned some anthropologists.[28] In psychoanalysis, however, the therapist's aim will be to draw out not so much a well-constructed story, as the 'deconstructed' elements behind it: the raw memories and dreams. The dreams, as Freud showed in his earliest work, may be 'screen memories' which serve to conceal unacceptable recollections such as those of sexual encounters and desire: clues to the decoding of the unconscious. This is the purpose of free association. It is then the task of the analyst to help the client towards a new reconstruction of the story.

More than this, with psychoanalysis there may also be another account in the patient's diary for recording dreams and other thoughts. And particularly significant, there is the form in which the 'case' is written up. Scientific discourse had developed by the later nineteenth century into a new genre in itself, a way of explaining, constructing and presenting human experience. But paradoxically this meant that the significances of the rhetorical forms and storytelling devices in an original spoken life story collected for social or scientific investigation were lost from sight. Was it Henry Mayhew or the watercress girl who told her story when his stenographer had recorded it? And similarly, when Freud had completed Dora's narrative, was it hers, or Freud's?[29]

In retrospect we might feel that there could have been a choice in this, for there is a very strong literary tradition in psychoanalytic writing. Indeed Donald Spence has emphasized how one of Freud's key skills was his mastery of 'the narrative tradition', his ability to construct a pattern out of the often apparently random memories he had heard.

> Freud made us aware of the persuasive power of a coherent narrative . . . [to] make sense out of nonsense. There seems to be no doubt that a well-constructed story possesses a kind of narrative truth that is real and immediate and carries an important significance for the process of therapeutic change.[30]

But paradoxically, Freud's concern to relate his findings as a literary narrative made it no less difficult for him to allow that the memories he had heard might bear a variety of interpretations, or indeed that his own interpretation of them might change. And still more important, he seems to have been unwilling to tolerate a possible rival voice from the client whose memories he was now recounting. He had in the end to remain the scientist, recording his findings as a decisive judgement. 'Because the raw data have no secure place in this tradition, they tend to be left out. . . . Streamlined case reports have tended to take the place of the original data.' Thus psychoanalysis, despite being based on the hearing of life stories, contrived to suppress the voices of patients as effectively as did conventional medicine. It was not until the 1960s that R. D. Laing and his followers began to call for the voices of the mentally ill to be heard, and taken more seriously.[31]

It should be added, of course, that the convention of reinterpreting the story of an informant or patient to the point of losing the original voice was not an invention of psychoanalysis. It is a longstanding, and indeed continuing, legal tradition, in that witness statements were taken down by the police in paraphrase, reported in the third person, rather than in the witness's own words. Even the speeches of Members of Parliament have always been officially recorded in the third person rather than direct speech. And it was also the normal convention of doctors in taking a patient's history, 'clerking the patient', cutting out the ramblings of the oral vernacular and reducing the discourse to the bare medical details. Psychoanalysis was in fact an important step forward simply in allowing much more genuine listening to the client.

9

All this discussion amounts to a series of promising but still tentative leads. By contrast a much more sustained and innovative discussion of genre, this time based on the experience of anthropological research in West Africa, and indeed the original stimulus for the workshop which proceeded this volume, has come from Elizabeth Tonkin's *Narrating our Pasts*.[32] Her underlying aim has been a reintegration of literary perception and social scientific research on the basis that 'facts and opinions do not exist as freestanding objects, but are reproduced through grammar and larger conventions of discourse. . . . Meanings exist because people mean and others believe they understand.' Genres are the 'conventions of discourse' which signal how the reader or listener should interpret the words. But there is a crucial difference in this respect between literary genres, where the author and reader do not have to have any direct social connection, and oral genres, in which the time, the place, the occasion, the accompaniments such as music, the audience and the status of the teller are all essential to the genre. Oral genres have to be understood as 'purposeful social actions', and Tonkin's purpose is to show how the tellers, audiences and narrative structures connect.[33]

In *Narrating our Pasts* the detailed discussion is largely in terms of Tonkin's own anthropological fieldwork with the Jlao in and around Sasstown on the tropical coast of Liberia. She shows how – contrary to the impressions given by many earlier studies in Africa – the Jlao talk about history not only in formal genres, such as praise poems and proverbs, folk tales and myths, epics, and heroic narratives, but also informally in daily conversation. What is conveyed about the past can differ between the genres. And they may give yet another version as court witnesses in a legal dispute. So even to begin to interpret these different accounts, it is necessary to understand the genres which help to shape them. 'Oracy implies skilled production, and its messages are transmitted through artistic means. An oral testimony cannot be treated only as a repository of facts and errors of fact.' And in this vital way, Tonkin sees the now common distinction between 'oral literature' and 'oral history', the one a field for literary analysis and the other not, as profoundly misleading. Indeed we need to pay much more attention 'to the rhetorical skills of ordinary speakers'. And Tonkin's belief is that we have as much need to look at the whole range of genres in Western as in 'traditional' cultures. We should be looking much more closely at how we know to laugh at a joke or to dismiss a 'sob-story'; how pub storytellers or academic lecturers seek to hold their audiences; how radio announcers use different styles to cue their audiences; or what are the significant subgenres of the interview.[34]

Her call remains still largely unanswered. Apart from the earlier work of Lejeune and of David Vincent, there are still surprisingly few studies of the non-classical written autobiographical genre, and still fewer on oral narrative. We see the chapters in this volume as an important step into largely uncharted territory. They confront broadly three issues: the complexity of indentifying genre; the shaping of meaning by genre; and the influence of social and cultural context on form and meaning.

$*$ $*$ $*$

We have so far considered genre as if each form were distinct. But in fact, not only can autobiography itself be broken down into a series of genres, but each of them is likely to draw on other genres: both in the sense of major genres, and also of generic motifs and devices. Lejeune points out how Sartre incorporates the interview form in his published autobiography. In his published autobiography *In Search of a Past* Ronald Fraser brings together recorded oral history interviews with the former servants of his childhood home, his own remembered conversations with his own father on the way to an old people's home presented as dialogue, and a diary of his own encounters with his psychoanalyst.[35] Carolyn Steedman similarly invokes fairy stories, psychoanalysis, literary and historical narrative in her story of her mother and herself in *Landscape for a Good Woman*.[36] We might say that these last two examples not only draw on a variety of autobiographical genres – interviews, documents, the psychoanalytic consultation – but also, by bringing together personal life stories with accounts of parents and others, constitute in themselves a new subgenre of autobiography.[37] Indeed Luisa Passerini has entitled her own closely comparable Piedmontese reflections a 'group autobiography'.[38]

Portelli in chapter 2 below argues that oral history itself is by definition 'a composite genre of discourse', for it is both a genre in its own right within history and narrative, and also 'a cluster of genres, some shared with other forms, some peculiar to itself'. He also illustrates elements of this cluster at a series of different levels: story types in terms of subject matter, such as war stories and hospital stories, or of moral outcome, such as the worker standing up to the big boss; or five subgenres of publication, ranging from the edited transcript which foregrounds the original speaker to the historian's argument illustrated only by brief quotations.

In a more detailed way the same point is made by Timothy Ashplant's sensitive elucidation in chapter 6 of the narrative skills of the former unskilled building labourer George Hewins in *The Dillen*.[39] He shows how Hewins's apparently spontaneous oral narrative is a complex construction, using specific formal devices, such as anecdote and parody, which he drew partly from the contemporary music-hall, and from pub entertainers. His narrative also displays modes of irony – and the accompanying literary devices of quotation and parody – which are parallel to the devices of more self-consciously political 'proletarian' writing.

Anecdote, the story within the story, is probably in most life stories the element most immediately recognizable as having formal literary qualities. Twenty years ago Robert Fothergill in discussing diaries remarked how

11

anecdote was 'a human titbit, a bite-sized morsel of the human comedy, to be relished by the connoisseur . . . [which] presupposes a selectively structured observation of behaviour'.[40] But as Ashplant shows, Hewins was no ordinary storyteller, but a skilled and practised oral artist drawing on a wide repertoire of sources and devices.

An equally remarkable example is provided by the discovery of a rare workers' autobiography in the form of a novel written by Adauto Machado, one of his own informants, by José Sérgio Leite Lopes during his anthropological fieldwork in a textile factory town in north-east Brazil (see chapter 4). The novel itself in part takes the form of interview testimonies, presenting three different accounts of the same story from different characters, each in the first person. It thus borrowed the features of anthropological fieldwork which the author had observed as an interviewee. At the same time, the structure of the novel and its images bears recognizable features of the traditions of *cordel* literature and oral storytelling which the author had himself practised. It seems also to have been influenced by the few other published testimonies of working-class peoples in Brazil, in its marked emphasis on particular themes which characterize this genre: on education and self-instruction, on travel and adventure, on survival and self-improvement, and especially on individuality.

Adauto Machado recounts his autobiographical novel in ways which reflect his desires and aspirations so as to conform to a broader narrative which equates his migration from village to town as a story of progress, success and modernity, and which highlights the cleverness and singularity of the actor. It is, perhaps, a narrative peculiar to the New World, a narrative carved out of, and making sense of, the experience of migration itself. But the ideology of making good, of material success, of social mobility is not confined to the New World. The material culture which surrounds and reflects society itself enters into and shapes the imaginative forms through which we construct an image, an identity of self, with all its dreams, hopes and aspirations. It thus leads to many other types of story.

One of these Western story genres is explored by Orvar Löfgren in chapter 7. Perhaps nothing characterizes contemporary material culture so vividly as consumption itself, arguably one of the drives, and certainly the expression, of capital and modernity. From studies of the early nineteenth-century department stores to research into the semiotics of advertising, patterns of consumption and the social uses to which consumption has been put have been a legitimate area not only of economic but also of sociological and even psychological theory. Although often critical, such studies have packaged capital, consumption and advertising in a single bag and cast it into the role of insidious manipulator, held responsible for hooking generations on to Marlboro, for causing anorexia in teenage girls, and malnutrition in developing countries. Advertising creates desires and needs, creates an enviable world, through the promotion of consumption. That is its function. But, as modern communications theory also suggests, messages are not received transparently. Whether in words or images or both, they speak in forms, genres, which carry implicit meanings, expectations and associations; and at the same time their significance, meaning and impact are mediated and transformed by the values, predispositions and social world of the receivers themselves.

Contemporary Western society does not consume merely to survive. What we wear or eat, what we discard, how we decorate our homes, the consumer choices we make, or do not make, or would wish to make, give off signs, articulate aspects of our personality, with all its complexities of dreams, and aspirations, as well as status and position, wealth and class. Such choices also convey a relationship with both the present and the past, embrace or reject new ideologies, reconstruct and deconstruct the material world in an image of the self, as Raphael Samuel so vividly explores in *Theatres of Memory*.[41] Rather than regarding consumption behaviour as a passive response to the rhetoric of advertising, it can be used to provide particular insights into life choices, the life course and the life cycle. These insights come not merely from what has been consumed, but from how people talk about the things they have bought or own, their relationship to their possessions, to changes in the material culture which surrounds them and to shifts in their own sense of identity: from the stories which they tell about their lives.

Orvar Löfgren's life story interviews on the 'biography of things' thus suggest new meanings in the relationship between self and the material culture. Consumption is learned behaviour and it implies notions of value, worth and morality. It can thus become a battleground not only of taste and style but also of ideology. Equally, notions of taste and style conform to genres of material representation. IKEA's recent advertising campaign in Britain – 'throw out your chintz' – is nothing more than an appeal to genre, in direct opposition to what Raphael Samuel characterized as the retrochic 'genre' of Laura Ashley. It is precisely this unspoken, but not unrecognized, notion of genre which advertising exploits so successfully, providing it with short cuts to convey a far wider vision.

But if things conform to genre, how people relate to their possessions can also be classified by genre. Löfgren's life stories of consumption can, he argues, be categorized into moral genres, and these can help us to identify the key values which drive a culture. Thus one moral genre conveys a strong if implicit condemnation of a supposedly affluent, and by implication, spoilt (younger) generation. Another moral evaluation attempts to measure the distance between naivety and sophistication. Consumption brings out strikingly issues of authority and independence, of class, and gender. There are times too when the moral intensity of consumption battles can reach a dramatic pitch. Families may split and not speak for months over where to go at Christmas, or who precisely to invite for Christmas lunch, or – especially if Muslim or Jewish or atheist – over whether to buy a Christmas tree. Consumption stories are thus a genre providing an especially rich 'cultural prism' through which to examine the microcultures of social conflict, consensus and change.

* * *

We can see therefore how the development of genre itself depends on changes in both the material and the cultural context. But how far can we argue that what people narrate in their autobiographical stories is selected and shaped by the repertoire of genre available to them? An especially suggestive exploration of this question was made by Stefan Bohman, who heads the autobiography section of the Nordic Archive in Stockholm. He compared diaries collected by the archive with the memoirs sent to auto-biographical competitions and subsequent oral interviews with the same authors, all Swedish working men. The diaries are unreflective journals of events, mainly about work and the weather. The memoirs and interviews were more reflective, and often alike, using the same stories and phrases, but with important differences. The written memoirs focus much more on early life, and they tend to use a more formal abstract language, even when dealing with highly emotional events like the death of a parent. Thus one man, who in his later interview vividly described his feelings about his father's bloody suicide in the face of poverty and depression, in his memoir simply borrowed the formula of public obituary announcements, calling his death stoic, 'after a long illness patiently borne'. Here it was clear that the message had been fundamentally reshaped by the genre chosen.[42]

One can see how the assumptions of a genre operate in everyday life by considering the end-of-the-year circulated letters which are a common practice with North American and migrant English families. In contrast to the intimacy possible in face-to-face conversation, or a phone call, or even a private letter, these mass-produced letters are addressed to a public audience, and hence seem determined to present everything in the best of all possible lights. They are full of boasting about the character and skills of the author and spouse, and above all about their children's achievements. Even when a serious setback or illness is introduced, it is in terms of a triumphant ability to cope with the worst trials: 'she took it all stoically and recovered quickly,' or, after a drastic amputation, 'I took on the insurance company and won full compensation.' Weeping is rarely heard here. One of this year's crop sums up the constricting mode of the genre by concluding: 'Every year I tell you how marvellous my husband was to insist that I have a child . . . I am the luckiest wife and mother ever! I could gush on forever . . .'

A very similar conclusion on how context and genre shape autobiographical accounts is reached by Chris Mann, who has been researching with young English women aged seventeen to eighteen, who are preparing to move out of home and into the world (see chapter 5). At this crucial stage in their lives they volunteered to take part in a project investigating their perspectives of family life as manifested in three kinds of life stories: oral performance in groups, written autobiographies, and oral life histories. In these different contexts, the family stories told by the girls varied in syntax, terminology, content and emphasis. For example, in the group sessions the girls were deliberately theatrical in telling their stories, using dialogue, humour and timing, consciously aware of the giggles and exclamations of their audience. In the written accounts many of them tried to use a literary style, and this form also allowed them to interpret their lives as a whole, within a social context, and to raise issues such as race, religion, family secrets, and especially the girls' own insecurities. The content of the oral interviews varied very much depending on how they felt their relationship with the interviewer. Some told deeply private stories which they had not brought forward in the other two contexts, while others remained from start to finish eager to show their best behaviour. The differences in content thus reflected not only the three formal genres, of which two included audience, but also the interaction between speaker and audience on the occasion itself.

*   *   *

Oral autobiography in all its forms must be partly shaped by its social and cultural context: not only by the intentions of the speaker, but by the customs, wishes, whims and thoughts which together shape the imagination of the audience. But while in Western cultures understanding and reading form and genre may be relatively easy, interviewing cross-culturally raises much more difficult issues. In many ways, the practice of interviewing, one to one, question and answer, has within itself an implicit cultural bias. Quite apart from issues of power and authority, it presupposes first that the individual, and individual memory, is paramount, and second that the appropriate context of communication is at an individual, one on one, level. The primacy given to the individual was refined in Europe as part of the post-Enlightenment endeavour, and is central to Western rationalist and romantic thought. But recording individual memories to use as exemplars of the whole may not appear meaningful to someone raised in cultures beyond (or despite) the tentacles of modern European thought and its emphasis on individualism. Equally, the use of metaphor, of images, as expressions of meaning in one culture could be missed by an emissary from another; and so, at a more basic level, could ways of recounting, explaining, prioritizing which reflect the myriad subcultures (of gender, of generations, of status and position) which structure experience and consciousness. How can a researcher attempt to resolve such problems which are posed precisely by the crossing of cultural assumptions and behaviour?

For all that oral sources convey an illusion of agency and an aura of authenticity, they can no longer be considered transparent. Few scholars now are unaware of their role in shaping the sources and framing the study. Few would innocently claim to be the conduit for the voice of the 'other', or that the voice of the 'other' is itself raw and unadulterated. The methods and skills of interpretation are now far too sophisticated for the historian, sociologist or anthropologist to rely on the simple claims of being the mouthpiece for the dispossessed. It is no longer history (or sociology, anthropology) 'from below', but history (or sociology) from within. The problem, however, is to unravel the complex layers of construction and meaning in the sources, to show in the words of John and Jean Cormaroff 'how realities become real, how essences become essential, how materialities materialize'.[43] In many ways, these concerns echo the relativist insights (or doubts) of postmodernism.

Of course, such questions are not new. Anthropologists have long grappled with the issues of cross-cultural interpretation and representation. Nor is the problem unfamiliar to historians: they too must learn to deal with the 'strangeness' of the past. Each discipline developed its own parallel methodological solutions. Immersion in the sources, whether archival or ethnographic, could in principle result in showing, in Ranke's words, 'how things actually were'. The practice of participant-observation served to immerse the anthropologist within the society and culture under scrutiny, and cautioned against giving priority, and therefore bias, to any one individual over another, preferring to substitute what Lévi-Strauss called the 'anonymity of numbers' over the immediacy of the personal record.[44]

It is precisely this debate over the cross-cultural construction of meaning which both Yvette Kopijn and Stephan Feuchtwang address, though in different ways. Both were confronted with ambiguous memories which required interpretation. Kopijn in chapter 9 questions whether oral historians are fully equipped to interview cross-culturally, for their training imposes a particular pattern on the interview which may well vary from the communicative styles of the interviewee. In so doing, oral historians may unwittingly impose an order on the interview which reflects their own assumptions rather than those of the interviewee, thus distorting not only the interview as event, but also the evidence and necessarily the interpretation. She uses as illustration an interview with an elderly Javanese-Surinamese woman for whom communicating – storytelling, recalling and recounting – is primarily a collective, communal event governed by particular norms and practices (including gender) which govern the content and the context of the communication. It is the antithesis of the one-to-one interview, for which that society has no cultural precedent. As a result, many of the conventions of the formal interview had to be abandoned so as to accommodate these local cultural practices, and the memories recounted only became meaningful when situated within these practices.

The emphasis within Kopijn's article is on form, on the cultural structures which govern communication and on the individual structures which governed experience. In the case of the Javanese-Surinamese community it was only through an awareness of these structures that any understanding could be had. But they were intertwined with the interviewee's own experiences in migrating as a young child from Java to Surinam, where poverty became the single most important leitmotif. To a Western-trained historian, the interview appeared disjointed and hesitant, running not in a linear pattern but on topic-association, returning constantly to the theme of food. Once the dialectic between the cultural practices of communication and the personal experiences – in this case of hunger – which had structured this particular memory were recognized, however, then the 'meaning' of these memories, and these accounts, could be drawn out.

Stephan Feuchtwang shifts the argument to another dimension, speculating in chapter 8 not so much on how to make our sources meaningful, but on the nature of the relationship between those sources and the ethnographer. He compares our work in selecting and representing the lives of otherwise unknown individuals to the process of the canonization of the obscure by the medieval church. But for an anthropologist the issue is not just what and how to interpret, whom to select, but to what purpose and with what effect.[45] Anthropology is as tribalized, as regional or parochial, as the subjects it purports to study, and anthropology is as vulnerable to its own genres of explication as those whom it studies. The avenues for error in interpretation are therefore legion, and the dangers of squeezing distant cultures into home categories or genres ever-present. Fortunately any anthropological endeavour can always be questioned, re-examined and ultimately challenged. Moreover, precisely because its presentation is always provisional, always relative, because it foregrounds human agency, human interpretation, the content and form of self and other's memory, because it reads back to us the genres of explanation and recall which shape and guide other cultures, it challenges the 'ethnocentricity and prejudice' of both the anthropologist and the anthropologized. It forces respect, and forces us to question and revise our own assumptions, beliefs, heresies, our own ethnocentricity. That, Feuchtwang argues, is the final value of ethnography.

Entering into another culture clearly requires knowledge of the forms and genres through which and in which memories are constructed and revealed. In different cultures, autobiography, even a sense of the past, of history, whether personal, family or social, may assume different forms and different meanings. For Kopijn, autobiography was antithetical to the gender and culture of her subject. Autobiography, self-expression, centering the 'I' as the agent in the narrative was not part of the communicative code. For Feuchtwang, history itself, for the Chinese village he studied, was a tale of destiny, not agency. Local heroes and villains were deified and demonized, translated into the genres of religious or mystical iconography. Memories revealed the empirical data; but the collective forms and genres through which life experience was narrated also provided the vital clues for interpreting what was told.

* * *

In seeking this interpretation it is crucial to remember not only that audience plays a necessary role in oral although not in written autobiography, but also that the audience is unlikely to be merely passive. This is true even in the fine arts. Ruth Finnegan's recent study of amateur music in an English midland town not only reveals an extraordinary amount of performance of many varieties of music, but also of extensive composition and reinterpretation.[46] And a National Gallery exhibition in 1996 of popular reproductions of Constable's famous East Anglian painting *The Cornfield* not only revealed a host of images of the picture in materials ranging from pottery to embroidery, but also showed through interviews with their owners that the picture was read by them in ways so extraordinarily diverse that it becomes clear that even with such a well-known masterpiece there is creativity not only in the hand of the artist but also in the eye of the beholder. Thus while for several people the painting evokes memories of 'the English countryside as I knew it', or 'an England that is threatened', 'very English', one woman says that 'it reminds me very much of my childhood in Jamaica. In rural Jamaica you have rivers and cornfields. I remember playing in a stream with my younger brother.' Similarly, one man imagined that the boy lying on the grass might be his elder brother, and others that he was drinking from an unpolluted stream, 'symbolic of innocence', while for one woman the scene was sinister and eerie, the shepherd boy 'lying dead' and his hysterical sheepdog 'running wild' with grief.[47] The possibilities for an interactive relationship between author and audience have – at least in principle – been further opened up by the new technologies, including multimedia, which Paul Thompson discusses in chapter 11.

These are positive instances of the influence of audience on autobiography. But even in our own societies there are many other contexts in which the telling of stories is on the contrary actively discouraged. Diana Gittins describes vividly in chapter 3 the culture of secrecy and silences of the traditional mental hospital, behind whose high walls madness was 'shut up'. But as she eloquently recounts, there are enormous variations within silence, even within a single mental hospital. The written record was purged of scandal, and in the same spirit some people refused to speak about their memories altogether, while others censored them. Yet others – usually those who left long ago – were much more candid. But there were not only variations in silence within the culture of the mental hospital. Silence, as Gittins reminds us, is itself a genre with many variations: from the reflective silence of the Quakers, to the conspiratorial silence of the Mafia and the punitive silence of the prison. Here too, as in its converse, narrative testimony, the genre is a key to opening the meaning.

Silence may perhaps be the most difficult of all the multiple forms of genre to grasp, but there are plenty of easier challenges awaiting us. We hope that this volume will prove a stimulus to the further work which is needed in many directions. We see it too as an especially good starting point for this series. For the concepts of genre and narrative both grew within literary criticism, but with the coming together of literature, history and the social sciences they have taken on new and suggestive meanings, meanings full of promise.

NOTES

We should like to give our special thanks for comments on earlier drafts of this introduction to Timothy Ashplant, Marilyn Butler, Graham Dawson, Karl Figlio, Peter Hulme, Laura Marcus, Elizabeth Tonkin and Steve Wilson. The volume as a whole owes a fundamental debt to the contribution of Sandro Portelli in conceiving the call for papers for the fifth (unpublished) volume of *The International Yearbook of Oral History and Life Stories*, and for his editorial work on the papers which resulted, four of which – including his own – are included in this first volume of the Memory and Narrative series.

1 Similarly Portelli's definition of genre here as 'a verbal construct shaped by shared, if often unrecognized, structures, traits and rules' emphasizes form, but he also distinguishes stories by theme, such as war stories and hospital stories.
2 Northrop Frye, *The Anatomy of Criticism* (Princeton, 1957), pp. 13–14.
3 Particularly in Britain there was one radical current, especially associated with Raymond Williams, of critics who accepted neither, on the one hand, the traditional high literary approach nor, on the other, the deconstruction of the author and exclusive focus on the structures of discourse. Instead they developed a cultural materialism in which writers were seen as real people grappling with historical conditions and articulating their own and shared experiences.
4 Roy Pascal, *Design and Truth in Autobiography* (London, 1960), p. 185.
5 Jerome Bruner, 'The narrative construction of reality', *Critical Inquiry* 18 (1991): 1–21.
6 The moment of change is indicated by comparing James Olney's *Metaphors of Self: The Meaning of Autobiography* (Princeton, 1973), which discusses only the classics, with his edited volume *Autobiography: Essays Theoretical and Critical* (Princeton, 1980), which offers a much broader canvas now including black and women writers.
7 This was why the autobiographies of middle-class industrialists were ignored, see Philippe Lejeune, 'Autobiography and social history in the nineteenth century', in Lejeune, *On Autobiography*, ed. Paul John Eakin, trans. K. Leary (Minneapolis, 1989), pp. 163–84.
8 David Vincent, *Bread, Knowledge and Freedom: A Study of Nineteenth-Century Working-Class Autobiography* (London, 1981).
9 Mark Traugott (ed.), *The French Worker: Autobiographies from the Early Industrial Era* (Berkeley, 1993), pp. 27–8. Luisa Passerini has also noted the conversion experience as a life story form among industrial workers in Turin: Luisa Passerini, *Torino operaia e fascismo* (Rome, 1984), pp. 17, 22, 33.
10 Pascal, *Design and Truth*, p. 10; Laura Marcus, *Auto/biographical Discourses: Theory, Criticism, Practice* (London, 1994), pp. 1, 229–73 ('The law of genre').

11 Robert Fothergill, *Private Chronicles: A Study of English Diaries* (London, 1974): he included only personal diaries, excluding public memoirs, journals of consciences, travel journals and writers' notebooks.

12 Margaret Walters, 'Mary Wollstonecraft, Harriet Martineau, and Simone de Beauvoir', in Juliet Mitchell and Ann Oakley, *The Rights and Wrongs of Women* (Harmondsworth, 1976), pp. 304–78. The journal *Tulsa Studies* from the University of Minnesota at Minneapolis is directed towards women's writing and focuses especially on such themes.

13 Julia Swindells, *Victorian Writing and Working Women: The Other Side of Silence* (Cambridge, 1985), pp. 137–61; Liz Stanley, *The Diaries of Hannah Culwick, Victorian Maidservant* (London, 1984).

14 Angela McRobbie, *Jackie: An Ideology of Adolescent Femininity* (CCCS, Birmingham, 1978), reprinted in B. Waites, T. Bennet and G. Martin, *Popular Culture* (London, 1982).

15 Janet Batsleer, *Rewriting English: Cultural Politics of Gender and Class* (London, 1985), pp. 70–106 ('Gender and genre: men's stories/women's stories').

16 Rosalind Coward, *Female Desire* (London, 1984); Janice Radway, *Reading the Romance* (Chapel Hill, 1984).

17 Vladimir Propp, *The Morphology of the Folk Tale* (Austin, 1968); Radway, *Reading the Romance*; cf. Raphael Samuel and Paul Thompson (eds), *The Myths We Live By* (London, 1990), p. 11.

18 Valerie Walkerdine, *Schoolgirl Fictions* (London, 1990).

19 John Cawelti, *The Six-Gun Mystique* (Bowling Green, 1970); John Cawelti, *Adventure, Mystery and Romance: Formula Stories as Art and Popular Culture* (Chicago, 1976).

20 Graham Dawson, *Soldier Heroes: British Adventure, Empire and the Imagining of Masculinities* (London, 1994); cf. David Jackson, *Unmasking Masculinity: A Critical Autobiography* (London, 1990).

21 William Labov, *Language in the Inner City: Studies in the Black English Vernacular* (Philadelphia, 1972).

22 John Beverley, 'The margin at the center: on *testimonio*', *Modern Fiction Studies* 25 (1989): 11–28; Rigoberta Menchù with Elisabeth Burgos-Debray, *I, Rigoberta Menchù: An Indian Woman in Guatemala* (London, 1984); Oscar Lewis, *Pedro Martinez: A Mexican Peasant and his Family* (London, 1964); William Westerman, 'Central American testimonies and performed life stories in the sanctuary movement', in Rina Benmayor and Andor Skotnes (eds), *Migration and Identity*, vol. 3 of *International Yearbook of Oral History and Life Stories* (Oxford, 1994), pp. 167–82.

23 Ruth Finnegan, *Oral Literature in Africa* (Oxford, 1970) and *Oral Traditions and the Verbal Arts: A Guide to Research Practices* (London, 1992).

24 His works include Philippe Lejeune, *L'Autobiographie en France* (Paris, 1971); *Lire Leiris, autobiographie et langage* (Paris, 1975); *Le Pacte autobiographique* (Paris, 1975); *Je est un autre. L'autobiographie, de la littérature aux médias* (Paris, 1981); *Le Moi des demoiselles. Enquête sur le journal de jeune fille* (Paris, 1993). Extracts from some of these books have been translated into English in Lejeune, *On Autobiography*, ed. Eakin: 'The autobiographical pact', pp. 3–30; 'Autobiography and social history in the nineteenth century', pp. 163–84; and 'The autobiography of those who do not write', pp. 185–215.

25 The use of models in English confessional diaries goes back to the seventeenth century, when John Beadle's *Diary of a Thankful Christian* (1656) became a recommended exemplar, see Fothergill, *Private Chronicles*.

26 Selma Leydesdorff, Luisa Passerini and Paul Thompson (eds), *Gender and Memory*, vol. 4 of *International Yearbook of Oral History and Life Stories* (Oxford, 1996), including esp.: 'Introduction', pp. 1–17; Richard Ely and Alyssa McCabe, 'Gender

differences in memory for speech', pp. 17–30; Adriana Piscitelli, 'Love and ambition: gender, memory, and stories from Brazilian coffee plantation families', pp. 89–104; and Gwyn Daniel and Paul Thompson, 'Stepchildren's memories of love and loss: men's and women's narratives', pp. 165–85.

27 Mary Main and Ruth Goldwyn, 'Predicting rejecting of her infant from mother's representation of her own experience: implications for the abused–abusing intergenerational cycle', *International Journal of Child Abuse and Neglect* 8 (1994): 203–17.

28 Arthur Kleinman, *Illness Narratives: Suffering, Healing and the Human Condition* (New York, 1988); a personal sickness story by a paralysed anthropologist is Robert Murphy, *The Body Silent* (New York, 1987).

29 John Forrester and Lisa Appignanesi in *Freud's Women* (London, 1996) have juxtaposed Freud's case histories of women patients with other biographiocal evidence about them.

30 Donald E. Spence, *Narrative Truth and Historical Truth: Meaning and Interpretation in Psychoanalysis* (New York, 1982); an earlier recognition of the importance of narrative in therapy is Roy Schafer, *A New Language for Psychoanalysis* (New Haven, 1976).

31 Jeffrey Masson, *The Assault on Truth: Freud and Child Sexual Abuse* (London, 1992) (which documents not only Freud's own concealment of his doubts and different earlier views on child sexual abuse, but also the maintenance of this concealment by Anna Freud in her editing of her father's letters); R. D. Laing and Aaron Esterson, *Sanity, Madness and the Family* (London, 1964).

32 Elizabeth Tonkin, *Narrating our Pasts: The Social Construction of Oral History* (Cambridge, 1992). At the workshop on 'Autobiography, oral history and social history' held at the University of Essex on 9 May 1992 one main session was on 'Forms of autobiography: genre, narrative and their analysis', with contributions by Philippe Lejeune, Sandro Portelli, Kim Lacy Rogers, Liz Stanley, Elizabeth Tonkin and David Vincent. Subsequently volume 5 of the *International Yearbook* was planned to be on genre and narrative, with Portelli as its special editor. The present volume has grown from this basis.

33 Tonkin, *Narrating our Pasts*, pp. 2–3.

34 Ibid., pp. 12, 14, 54. On oral literaure see especially Ruth Finnegan's pioneering work mentioned above, *Oral Literature in Africa*.

35 Ronald Fraser, *In Search of a Past* (London, 1984). For a literary analysis of Fraser, see Paul John Eakin, *Touching the World* (Princeton, 1992).

36 Carolyn Steedman, *Landscape for a Good Woman* (London, 1986).

37 A less self-conscious instance is Blake Morrison, *And When Did You Last See Your Father?* (London, 1993).

38 Luisa Passerini, *Autoritratto di gruppo* (Florence, 1988), combining her own childhood reminiscences of Asti with 68 interviews on the 1968 student rebellion in Turin, another diary of psychoanalysis, and her own reflections as a historian; translated as *Autobiography of a Generation: Italy 1968* (Middletown, Conn., 1996).

39 Angela Hewins, *The Dillen: Memories of a Man of Stratford-on-Avon* (Oxford, 1981), recorded from George Hewins (1879–1977).

40 Fothergill, *Private Chronicles*, p. 26.

41 Raphael Samuel, *Theatres of Memory* (London, 1994).

42 Stefan Bohman, 'The people's story: on the collection and analysis of autobiographical materials', paper to conference on working-class culture, Nörrkoping, Sept. 1986.

43 John and Jean Cormaroff, *Ethnography and the Historical Imagination* (Boulder, Colo. 1992), p. 20.

44 Claude Lévi-Strauss, *Structural Anthropology* (New York, 1963).

45 See James Clifford and George E. Marcus, *Writing Culture: The Poetics and Politics of*

Ethnography (Berkeley, 1986), including Clifford, 'On ethnographic allegory', pp. 98–121.

46 Ruth Finnegan, *The Hidden Musicians: Music-Making in an English Town* (Cambridge, 1989).

47 Colin Painter, *At Home with Constable's Cornfield* (London: National Gallery, 1996), pp. 10–44.

2

ORAL HISTORY AS GENRE

Alessandro Portelli

A CLUSTER OF GENRES: GENRE IN ORAL HISTORY, ORAL HISTORY AS GENRE

As the term itself implies, oral history is a specific form of discourse: history evokes a narrative of the past, and oral indicates a medium of expression. In the development of oral history as a field of study, much attention has been devoted to its linguistic and narrative dimensions. Most of this work, however, has been concerned with the analysis of the source, that is, of the speech and performance of the interviewees. Research, in other words, has focused mostly on genre in oral history: the use of folklore and anecdote; the influence of other oral or written forms of discourse such as epic, the novel or mass media; the analogies and differences between orality and writing, and so on.[1]

On the other hand, oral historians have become increasingly aware that oral history is a dialogic discourse, created not only by what the interviewees say, but also by what we as historians do – by the historian's presence in the field, and by the historian's presentation of the material. The expression *oral history* therefore contains an ambivalence that I will intentionally retain in this paper: it refers both to what the historians *hear* (the oral sources) and to what the historians *say* or *write*. On a more cogent plane, it refers to what the source and the historian do *together* at the moment of their encounter in the interview.

The complexity of oral history as a sequence of verbal processes and constructs generated by cultural and personal encounters in the context of fieldwork between the narrator(s) and the historian derives to a large extent from the rich heteroglossia resulting from a dialogic shaping of discourse.[2] Oral history is therefore a composite genre, which calls for a stratified critical approach: in addition to the uses of genre in the collected discourse of the narrator(s), we need also to recognize genre in the public discourse of the historian, and genre in the space between them. If we define genre as a verbal construct shaped by shared verbal devices – whether conventionally established or not – oral history is then both a genre of narrative and

23

historical discourse, and a cluster of genres, some shared with other types of discourse, some peculiar to itself. In this chapter, therefore, I will begin with a few preliminary comments on aspects of genre *in* oral history, and then go on to oral history *as* genre and to genres *in* oral history.

UNTOLD STORIES, TWICE-TOLD TALES

I remember sitting in Santino Cappanera's parlour in Terni, Italy, taping an interview about his life as a steelworker and political activist.[3] His teenage daughter was in the next room, doing her homework. After about twenty minutes, she had moved her chair to the hall, outside the parlour; a little while later, she was standing by the door; about one hour into the interview, she came and sat next to us, listening.

What is spoken in a typical oral history interview has usually never been told *in that form* before. Most personal or family tales are told in pieces and episodes, when the occasion arises; we learn even the lives of our closest relatives by fragments, repetitions, hearsay. Many stories or anecdotes may have been told many times within a narrator's immediate circle, but the whole story has hardly ever been told in sequence as a coherent and organized whole. The grandparent who takes a grandchild on his or her knee and tells the story of his or her life is a literary fiction.[4] The life story as a full, coherent oral narrative does not exist in nature; it is a synthetic product of social science – but no less precious for that. No wonder Santino Cappanera's daughter listened. Her father's boring anecdotes were becoming 'history' before her eyes.

Cappanera's narrative also acquired status and importance, in his own eyes as well as his daughter's, because of the interview itself. In fact, even when stories have been told before, they have never been told to that special listener and questioner who is the oral history interviewer. The interview implicitly enhances the authority and self-awareness of the narrator, and may raise questions about aspects of experience that the speaker has never spoken or even seriously thought about.

Thus an oral history interview tends to be a story untold, even if largely made up of twice-told tales, and the speaker tends to strive for the best possible diction. The novelty of the situation and the effort at diction accentuate a feature of all oral discourse – that of being a 'text'[5] in the making, which includes its own drafts, preparatory materials and discarded attempts. There will be gradual approaches in search of a theme, not unlike musical glissando; conversational repairs and after-the-fact corrections, for the sake either of accuracy or of pragmatic effectiveness; incremental repetitions for the sake of completeness and accuracy, or of dramatic effect. This personal effort at composition in performance[6] is supported by the use of socialized linguistic matter (clichés, formulas, folklore, frozen anecdotes, commonplaces) and by the example of genres derived from writing (the novel, autobiography, history books) or mass media. These established blocks of discourse define secure paths in the uncharted territory of discourse, much like the invisible but rigid airways that guide airplanes in the fluid territory of the sky: I remember the story (a legend, perhaps) about a dock worker in Civitavecchia (near Rome) who was speechless in front of the intellectuals in his party meetings until he realized he could speak in rhymes, and found his voice.

Between the fluid textual experiments and the frozen formulaic material, the 'achieved' discourse breaks through and floats like a moving island, the tip of an iceberg. In order to understand how the narrative is shaped, we must not limit ourselves to these moments of fulfilment; we need to consider also the formulaic materials, the apparently formless connecting and supporting matter, and the dialogic and directive role of the historian.

Though oral history may avail itself of all other recognized and unrecognized genres of oral discourse, from the proverb to the epic poem, yet it is distinct from them all, both for its composite internal structure (a genre of genres), and for its peculiar cultural positioning. While the genres of oral expression and cultures serve their function within the world of orality, oral history begins in the orality of the narrator but is directed towards (and concluded by) the written text of the historian. Oral narrators are aware of this written destination, and bear it in mind as they shape their performance; on the other hand, the task of the oral historian is to write in such a way that readers are constantly reminded of the oral origins of the text they are reading. In the end, we might define oral history as the genre of discourse which orality and writing have developed jointly in order to speak to each other about the past.

HISTORY-TELLING: WHAT IS ORAL HISTORY ABOUT?

As Jean-Marie Schaeffer notes, the classification of speech acts, and of genres of discourse in particular, depends on a fivefold question: *Who says what in which channel to whom with what effect?*[7] Taking this phrase as my pattern, I will begin with *what*.

In theory (and in practice), oral history can be about anything; open-endedness at all levels is one of its distinctive formal characteristics. I believe, however, that at the core of oral history, in epistemological and in practical terms, lies one deep thematic focus which distinguishes it from other approaches and disciplines also based on interviewing and fieldwork, such as anthropology, sociology and folklore: the combination of the prevalence of the narrative form on the one hand, and the search for a connection between biography and history, between individual experience and the transformations of society, on the other. Elsewhere, I describe this genre of discourse as *history-telling*: a cousin of storytelling, but distinct from it because of its broader narrative range and dialogic formation.[8]

25

The questions 'How historical is private life?' and 'How personal is history?' may be asked by the narrator, by the historian, or by both; indeed, the issue of what is private and what is public in a person's narrative is often uncertain, especially if we are after the elusive theme of the history of private life. For instance, listening to Maggiorina Mattioli, an old seamstress in Terni, I realized that there was more history in her personal love story than in her reminiscences about the anti-Fascist underground.[9] However that may be, oral history expresses the awareness of the historicity of personal experience and of the individual's role in the history of society and in public events: wars, revolutions, strikes, floods (as in the work of Selma Leydersdorff) and earthquakes (as in the work of Eugenia Meyer).[10]

A by-product of this generic focus is that oral history is more intrinsically itself when it listens to speakers who are not already recognized protagonists in the public sphere. An interview with a head of state about her political career is, of course, very legitimate oral history, but veers towards more established genres of historical writing.[11]

Genre, then, depends to a large extent on the shifting balance between the personal and the social, between biography and history. *Life and times* is a cliché definition of biography and autobiography in general (*Life and Times of Frederick Douglass*, for one);[12] according to where the scales tip between the *life* and the *times*, oral history shifts between performance-oriented *narrative* and content-oriented *document*, between subject-oriented *life* story and theme-oriented *testimony*. In practice, oral history stays mostly in-between: its role is precisely to connect life to times, uniqueness to representativeness, as well as orality to writing. The key word in *life and times* is the one in the middle.

At the core of the narrative created by the classic oral history interview and by the classic oral history text, therefore, we find motifs and themes that insist on the relationship of the individual and public. For instance, narrators everywhere relish narratives of 'standing up to the big man', theatrical anecdotes of personal confrontations with figures of institutional authority in which workers stand up to bosses (especially in stories of union negotiations), rank and file to leaders, students to teachers, soldiers to officers, in complex representations of personal courage, professional pride or political resistance.[13]

The most common narrative of this kind, of course, is the war narrative. As we know, it is hard to keep any (male) informant from expounding about what he did in the war (or in the service). War embodies history in the most obvious schoolbook sense of the word; having been in the war is the most immediately tangible claim for having been in history. Even in peacetime, the military is the most immediately accessible experience of the public sphere. As Antonio Gibelli points out, participation in the military institution and in war is a crucial passage in the life of the rural masses, marking their entrance into the public sphere and contact with the organization and technology of the modern state.[14] Since the era of air-raids, civilians have their own war tales, too: as an old woman explained to me once, in World War I 'they fought among themselves out there,' but in World War II 'we all were involved.'[15]

For these reasons, war stories are a recognized thematic genre, with specific formal characteristics, in literature, history, autobiography and film.[16] Oral history, however, features other narratives that play a similar role but are less commonly recognized. For instance, while I was working on my oral history of Terni, I realized that there were two types of stories that seemed so commonplace that I did not even bother to transcribe them from the tapes: men's stories about war and military service, and women's stories about health and hospitals. It was only later that I began to wonder whether a functional analogy lay behind this parallel exclusion – if, in other words, the genre of the hospital tale may be for women what the genre of the war story is for men.

Hospital tales – especially about assisting hospitalized family members – are in fact one way for women to talk about their effect on the public sphere. Like men at war, they leave their homes to deal with death (playing the mythic roles, respectively, of healers and warriors); like the draftees, they face the state in its bureaucratic and technological aspects; they deal with hierarchies, machinery and science; and they 'stand up to the big man': to doctors, administrators and their own relatives – usually males. As Prue Chamberlaine and Annette King put it, in West German women's narratives, 'Hospitals form a politically salient meeting ground of public authority and personal intimacy'; narrators often confront this authority structure – 'Here the theme is how, an uneducated nobody, encouraged by women in my neighbourhood, I gained the determination and confidence to confront the negligence and high-handedness of the doctors.'[17]

Hospital tales, then, constitute a coherent, if largely unrecognized, narrative genre, found with little variation across national, cultural and linguistic boundaries. While the tellers of military tales relish the use of technical language about weaponry and ranking, women struggle with the esoteric language of the medical environment: Giuseppina Migliosi, a seamstress from Terni, has a hard time articulating *commozione cerebrale* (concussion of the brain); Appalachian women in Eastern Kentucky pronounce *autopsy* as *artòpsy* and naturalize *Alzheimer's disease* as *old timer's disease*. Migliosi hitches a ride to leave home to go to see her husband in the hospital after a motorcycle accident; Debbie Spicer, a coal-miner's wife in Harlan, Kentucky, hires an ambulance to take her husband to a better hospital in a city where she has never been. Spicer contends with the incompetence and carelessness of the medical staff, and Migliosi fights the bureaucracy in the hospital and in the war office in Rome in order to obtain her husband's X-rays, have his disability recognized and get his pension released. Both graphically represent the ambiguous relationship between the powerlessness of their hospitalized husbands and their own empowerment. Spicer handles her husband like a baby:

They just had him on the table for a long time, and didn't do anything and he had trouble with his bowels and they didn't know it, so his bowels moved. ... And I washed him, cleaned him up, and spread some towels over him so he wouldn't get too cold till I came back with his pyjamas, and when I came back I put his pyjamas on.

Migliosi is forced, and enabled, to take control after the accident turns her husband from an authoritarian male (a policeman and a militant Fascist) to a vegetating body ('concussion of the brain, fractured skull, all bandaged over, his arms, his head, everything, only his nose and mouth were [in sight]') and a dependent brain- and speech-impaired invalid.[18]

Perhaps war stories are a universally recognized genre and hospital stories are not because wars are 'events', while nurturing in hospitals is a continuing function. This fact tells us, however, a great deal about established and gender-determined definitions of what is history and what is not, who is in it and who is not. By enabling us to hear both genres and to identify their relationship, oral history helps us to overcome these prejudices.

WHO SPEAKS TO WHOM? INTERROGATION AND THICK DIALOGUE

There is no oral history before the encounter of two different subjects, one with a story to tell and the other with a history to reconstruct. We tend to forget, however, that the first person who speaks in an oral history interview is usually not the interviewee, but the interviewer.[19] In a very concrete sense, the source's narrative can be seen always as a response to the historian's initial questions: 'When were you born?' 'Tell me about your life' 'Who was the union secretary at that time?'

By opening the conversation, the interviewer defines the roles and establishes the basis of narrative authority. In fact, although an oral auto-biographical narrative may look on the surface very much like any other autobiographical *text*, it constitutes a very different autobiographical *act*, because the basis of authority is different. Autobiography (especially if written for publication) begins with a person's decision to write about herself or himself, but in the interview, the initiative is taken by the interviewer, from whom the legitimacy to speak is ostensibly derived. The right to speak, especially about oneself, is not automatically assumed, especially among the socially disadvantaged groups to which oral historians most frequently address themselves. In folklore, authority is derived mainly from tradition; in literary or historical autobiography, it is derived from the person's sense of her or his own importance or ability, which justifies the implicit breach of modesty. In oral history, however, the process of legitimation is more complex. Typical beginnings, such as 'I have nothing to say', or even 'What do you want me to say',[20] may be coy manoeuvrings, but they may also indicate that the narrator feels entitled to speak only because of a mandate from the interviewer: I only speak because you ask me to (and, often, I will say what you want to hear).

Thus, first-person narratives beginning with 'I was born' belong in fact to very different genres, because they are the result of very different processes of authorization.[21] When we compare Benjamin Franklin's 'I have ever had a pleasure in obtaining any little anecdotes of my ancestors . . . ' with Giuseppina Migliosi's 'To begin with everything I know: my folks moved from Cesena to Terni,' we cannot ignore that the former is a statesman and scientist who has spoken in public all his life (and coyly pretends to be writing a private letter to his son), while the other is ostensibly speaking, in her private parlour, only because her niece and a polite visitor have insisted that she do so. When we take this aspect into account, we recognize the import of the fact that Franklin begins with 'I', while Migliosi begins with 'my folks': the basis of legitimation is different. Consider the following examples also:

I was born in the city of Cork, Ireland, in 1830. My people were poor. For generations they had fought for Ireland's freedom. Many of my folks have died in that struggle.

Let us begin with this business. Well, I was born in Terni. Son of a railroad man; son of a railroad man. And – I lost my father at the age of ten.

In the former example (an as-told-to autobiography), the great radical Irish-American unionist, Mary 'Mother' Jones, boldly talks about herself because she feels that her long and brave life entitles her to do so. In the second example, as the deictic expression 'this business' suggests, the anarchist factory worker Riziero Manconi is responding to an external stimulus, namely, my request: 'We would like you to tell us about your life, your personal and political development, what the environment in which you were born and grew up was like, and then go on to your working life and your political activity.'[22]

Requests like these set the agenda for the interview and begin to shape its form: the chronological order, the relevant themes (work, politics), the interaction of individual and society ('the environment in which you . . . grew up'). Of course, a political activist and class-conscious worker like Manconi would have spoken about these things anyway (he also talked about things I had not asked about, such as his literary efforts). But – and this is the point – if a different person had opened the conversation with a different question, Manconi would have spoken different words and in a different order.

Both subjects bring to the interview an agenda of their own, which is constantly renegotiated in the course of the conversation. In the case of Giuseppina Migliosi, for instance, I did not want to hear her hospital story, but she felt that, history or not, it had to be told. Maggiorina Mattioli wanted to talk about her love story and I wanted to hear about anti-Fascism; and, once again, she was right. Of course, interviewees *will* talk about really irrelevant private matters, but we should listen and wait before we judge. For the oral historian, an interview is always a learning experience.

This negotiation, in turn, generates formal variations. In order to retain the floor and have their say, speakers may (like Migliosi) ignore the interviewers' lack of interest, and launch into a straight monologue,[23] or try to win their listeners' attention by dialogic narrative techniques, as Mattioli did by telling her love story with anxious and skilful incremental repetition.[24]

The exchange of questions and answers defines generic variations in several other ways. An interview can shift from a one-way *questionnaire* to *thick dialogue*, according to how much space questions allow for the answers, and to the way in which the answers act upon the questions. In a judicial interrogation or a sociological questionnaire, the informant's answer to a given question may not influence either the form or the order of the questions to follow, but in a thick dialogue, questions arise dialectically from the answers. Once again, it is important to state that neither form is 'better' than the other; rather, they are suited to different ends: comparability and factuality in the questionnaire, individuality and subjectivity in the thick, open-ended dialogue. The point here is that different forms of exchange generate different genres of discourse.[25]

The social and personal relationship between the two speaking subjects also plays a role. While interviewing coal-miners in Kentucky, I was a 'furriner' from 'across the waters'; when interviewing the students of my own department in Rome, I was a part of the environment I was investigating. One consequence is that the Kentucky interviews emphasize storytelling and history-telling, with a great deal of straight information and narrative, while the Rome interviews read like tentative essays, replete with commentary, evaluation and analysis (one verbal clue of this generic difference is the higher density of deixis and allusion, and the diminished attention to chronology in the student interviews). While this has something to do with intrinsic cultural differences (the Appalachian habit of couching concepts in narrative, versus the abstract training of philosophy majors), it also shows that the form of the interview depends on the extent to which the interviewer belongs to the reality under investigation: narrators will assume that a 'native' historian already knows the fact, and will furnish explanations, theories and judgements instead.

Now, as Dennis Tedlock noted, Franz Boas used to warn his students precisely against this type of interview: beware, he taught, of 'intelligent Indians' who may have 'formed a theory' about the research in progress. Tedlock juxtaposes this injunction against theorizing informants to Margaret Mead's intimation against interfering researchers: 'The fieldworker is not in the field to talk but to listen' and should never 'express complicated ideas of his own that will muddle the natives' accounts'.[26] A fearful symmetry structures this hierarchic separation between the interviewer's *ideas* and the informant's *account*. The fiction of non-interference turns the dialogue into two monologues: informants supply a monologue of brute facts, while historians and anthropologists will supply – later, from the safety of their desks – a monologue of sophisticated ideas that the informant never hears about.

However, human beings, including 'native informants', never speak without attempting to form an idea, a theory, of what they are speaking about, to whom, and why. The stereotype of the 'dumb Indian' at least exists in the hegemonic imagination, but the concept of a 'dumb philosopher' sounds like a contradiction in terms – if not necessarily in fact. A student reversed the flow of discourse by asking a question: 'Can I ask a question, too? How did you become a professor, anyway?'[27] A folk singer near Rome formed an opinion about me by noticing the newspaper I had on the back seat of my car. The less the historians reveal about their identity and thoughts, the more likely informants are to couch their testimony in the broadest and safest terms, and to stick to the more superficial layers of their conscience and the more public and official aspects of their culture.[28]

This, of course, is perfectly legitimate if it is what we are looking for. What a culture will most readily tell about itself, what people feel to be the safest form of self-presentation, can be very revealing. On the other hand, a critical, challenging, even a (respectfully) antagonistic interviewer may induce the narrator to open up and reveal less easily accessible layers of personal knowledge, belief and experience. An informant's dissent from his or her own culture is more likely to emerge when speaking to a dissenting interviewer. One cannot expect informants to tell the truth about themselves if we start out by deceiving them about ourselves. Fascists and capitalists who knew which side I was on often gave me much more vivid and motivated accounts and explanations than if they had blandly assumed I shared their party or class line. Thus what the interviewer reveals about him or herself is ultimately relevant in orienting the interview towards monologue or self-reflexive thick dialogue.

The myth of non-interference concerns one of the most delicate turns in the passage from field testimony to published text: transforming the informants' speech from one directed to a *determined* addressee, the fieldworker, to one addressed to an *undetermined* and multiple one, the historian's audience. In the opening page of Zora Neale Hurston's *Mules and Men*, her account of a folklore-gathering expedition to her native village of Eatonville, the narrators ask: 'Who you reckon want to hear all them old-time tales about Brer Rabbit and Brer Bear?' While they recognize the person who *is listening* ('Well, if it ain't Zora Hurston!'), they don't know who *will read*: the shift from empirical addressee to undetermined implied audience is reiterated by Hurston's vague answer: 'Plenty of people.'[29]

Hurston chooses to retain the traces of the dialogic experience and the personal addressee by foregrounding her presence throughout the book. In more standard works of folklore, anthropology, sociology, and in much oral history, however, the tendency prevails to efface the historian's presence both from the field situation and from the published text, in the attempt to create the fiction that the informant is speaking directly to the reader, and – just like a book – would have spoken in the same way to anyone. Thus a *personal exchange* becomes a *public statement*, which may be a perfectly legitimate process when this is the effect both parties are looking for (as in the case of 'as-told-to' autobiographies of politicians or movie stars).[30] In this case, the writer acts as hired medium through which the speaker writes; in scholarly work, however, the historian speaks through the sources, quoting their words to make a point, and using their artificial textuality to enhance the authority of historical discourse.

Ultimately, in fact, the shift from determined to undetermined addressee is part of the process by which a *performance* is turned into a *text*: a legitimate, indeed necessary process, which begins when the speaker's ephemeral words are fixed on tape or film, to be later transcribed, edited and published. This brings us to the next question.

THROUGH WHAT CHANNELS? BIOGRAPHY AND MONTAGE

The most immediate difference between a field interview and any other conversation is that in the interview the voices go through some kind of machine: a tape recorder, a camera, or at least a notebook. This acts as a moderating influence on the narrator's perception of the interviewer: the presence of the machine indicates that these words will be repeated, elsewhere, to an absent undetermined audience (hence the ethical requirement always to display the equipment). Technical aspects – the placing of a microphone, the lighting used for video – may incline the interview towards the genre of personal dialogic exchange or that of monologic public statement; in turn, the channels through which this dialogue is made available to the public (akin to Northrop Frye's 'radical of presentation') orient the generic definition of the historians' discourse.

In 1972, during a train trip, I turned my tape recorder on in the midst of informal talk with Amerigo Matteucci, a construction worker, mayor of the village of Polino (near Terni), and extraordinary history-teller. Twenty years later, a local film group taped a video interview with him. The stories and the words were surprisingly consistent (in part because since our interview he had repeated them in public many times), but the shift from personal exchange to public statement was clear.[31] In the videotape, Matteucci wore his best clothes, sat at his mayor's desk, and spoke into the camera a monologue to an invisible audience. His voice was flatter; his body language (lost to my audio tape, but vivid in my memory) stiffer. On the other hand, *some* body language and facial expression were at least visible. Because he was much more aware of speaking in public, and because the fact of filming implies more preparation, he was more coherent and clear, and the video was a nearly finished product, while my tape required much editing. Once again, my purpose is not to claim that one form is better than another. A conscious public presentation of self is as much a part of a culture as a spontaneous, unguarded utterance, but they are different genres of discourse, and are better served (or more actively stimulated) by different channels of collection and transmission.

It is beyond the scope of this chapter to delineate a theory of oral history on video or film.[32] I have neither the data nor the competence; besides, I feel that, since *oral* history implies a centrality of language and sound, audio tape is closer to its semantic focus. I would like, however, to make some tentative remarks for future research, based on the video interviews I have seen.

- The camera has more impact on the interviewer than on the interviewee. While the interviewee may shift genres, the interviewer tends to disappear altogether. Audio picks up both voices more or less equally, but the camera does not dwell equally on both subjects (often, the fiction of non-interference induces the interviewer to stay out of range entirely).[33]
- There is less time. The visual forms of publication, cinema or TV documentary, are usually more compressed than books. While visual information is enhanced, verbal space is reduced. It takes more courage on the film-maker's part to include in the finished product what I have called the 'preparatory materials' of the oral performance and to retain the tempo of the narrators. The temptation of selecting the 'achieved' conclusions, the brief, effective statement – the sound bite – is very strong. This reinforces the drift from personal exchange to public statement.
- Rather than through the historian's voice, the meaning is transmitted mostly through montage (for some reason, voice-over in visual presentations is thought to be more authoritarian than the historian's voice in books). The result is both more pluralistic (sources seem to speak for themselves, and all on the same plane) and more authoritarian (the hand that coordinates and pieces them together remains invisible). Which aspect prevails depends, to a great extent, on the sensitivity and professional skill of the film-maker.[34] As Paula Rabinowitz has put it in a different context, 'Documentaries that repress the presence of the documentarian's voice or body posit a natural truth captured at random in words or images and seemingly open to direct consumption by the audience.'[35]

Ultimately, as far as I have been able to see, we have failed to consistently develop an *analytical*, let alone a *scholarly* form of video presentation, which would necessarily include such devices as stopped frames, slow motion, repetition, electronic elaboration of images, and, yes, the historian's taking responsibility to speak and interpret in an open, if not authoritarian, manner, as one voice and presence among others in the visual text. Multimedia approaches are likely to generate the same problems (and some possible solutions) in the near future.

Oral history, however, circulates most often in writing (an irony which is not lost on its critics, and on most of its practitioners). There are as many ways of translating orality into writing – transcribing, editing, writing, publishing oral history – as there are ways of collecting it, and their generic variety also shifts from project to project, from one disciplinary area to another. There is no all-purpose transcript; rather, there are many specialized transcripts for different subgenres of oral history discourse. It is one thing to transcribe for a linguistic study of phonetics, and another to transcribe for a project of narrative history. The same applies to editing: is it intended to reproduce as carefully as possible the actual sounds of the spoken word, or to make the spoken word accessible to readers through the written medium? 'Accuracy' is recognized unanimously as the aim of all transcribing and editing, but the term is not easy to define univocally: a transcript so minutely faithful to sounds that it turns a beautiful speech into an unreadable page can hardly be described as 'accurate'. Perhaps the old pun – *traduttore traditore*, 'translator traitor' – also applies to the creative job of translating words from speech through tape to page, by exercising selection, choice, even artistic judgement, in harmony with our interpretation of what we hear and with our strategy of presentation. Perhaps nowhere more than in transcription (and editing) is the correlation of form to aim and genre so stringent.

I will consider here three major genre-defining parameters in the publication of oral history: (1) the scope of the narrative; (2) the representation and continuation of the dialogic experience and of the oral performance; and (3) the intended audience. One other parameter – the intended effect on the reader – will be considered in the final paragraph.

Although oral history is often associated with 'microhistory' because of its focus on individual lives and its mode of transmission,[36] the work of oral historians varies widely. The range of characters may go from an individual's life story to the choral reconstruction of a process involving millions of people;[37] the geographic scope may be a workplace, a neighbourhood, a town, an international phenomenon;[38] the time period may vary from thirty minutes to one or two centuries.[39] An in-depth life story, a collection of interviews, an interpretative essay on a historical period[40] are all *oral history*, but they are not the same thing; rather, they represent different genres with very different rhetorical strategies.

The most immediately visible generic consequence of the scope of the research concerns the presentation of voice. Who speaks in these books? How many voices are included, and how are they broken down and put together? A work of oral history may be concerned with one voice (an individual's life story) or with many; in the latter case, these may be presented as a series of monologues, or intertwined into a thematic or chronological montage.[41] The shift between monologue and polyphony also changes the interpretative approach. An individual life story is a different genre from a book in which a number of interviewees are presented one after the other as a series of monologues (with or without a general introduction, or introductory sketches to each piece), and both are different from a chronological or thematic montage of interview excerpts.

Thus two apparently similar books on the same topic, the Vietnam War, may display very different strategies of presentation and interpretation. Both Mark Baker's *Nam* and Wallace Terry's *Bloods: An Oral History of the Vietnam War by Black Veterans* present the interviews as distinct monologues; however, while *Bloods* retains the integrity of the individual life stories, *Nam* subdivides the narratives into thematic sections. Thus *Bloods* places the Vietnam experience in each individual's life cycle, while *Nam* attempts the reconstruction of a collective, and therefore anonymous, experience. While both display a strategy of objectivity (the interviewer's voice is silenced), the voices of the sources interact in different ways with that of the historian through the form of the presentation and the paratext.[42]

Which leads us to the second parameter: the relationship of these voices to the voice of the historian. To what extent does the publication continue or represent the dialogue and the performance? What is, in each case, the balance between *oral* and *history*, the mode of transmission and factual reconstruction?

If we take five examples from Italy we can see that, while they are all legitimate forms of historical work, the ways of handling the source's speech and the historian's voice are so different that they define very different genres of oral history. Nuto Revelli's books – *Il mondo dei vinti* and *L'anello forte* – are based on a rigorous distinction of voices: the historian writes rich, informative, sensitively self-reflexive introductions, after which we read the edited testimony of the informants, one after the other, individually. The narrators are allowed to speak at length about themselves, and the interpretation is left to the reader, within the framework designed in the introduction. Documentary objectivity in the arrangement of voice is displayed in order to enhance the subjective pathos of each narrative.[43]

Luisa Passerini's *Torino operaia e il fascismo* is an example of how oral history can be used to produce excellent history without adjectives.[44] Passerini performs a sophisticated reading of the testimony as well as of written archival sources, framed in a tight historical narrative. The interviews are quoted in the same way as historical documents: as textual verifications of a historical interpretation. The book's approach, however, is specific to oral history because it is centred on the reconstruction of subjectivity. While the orality of the sources is scarcely thematized, and little advantage is taken of the possibilities of narrative and linguistic analysis, the 'oral' remains essential to the success of this book as 'history', through the category of subjectivity.

In Maurizio Gribaudi's *Mondo operaio e mito operaio*,[45] the opposition between 'world' and 'myth', the effort to bring out factual reality and dispel ideological delusions, leads to an ancillary use of a limited number of oral sources as repositories of mainly factual information about economic strategies and demographic trajectories. The words of the interviewees are hardly quoted at all, and are interpreted rather cursorily, with scarcely any attention to the language, the narrative form, and their less explicit meanings. The balance between 'oral' and 'history' leans heavily towards the more established forms of the latter. Indeed, this book has been described as a case of 'total devaluation of any significance of oral sources'.[46]

My *Biografia di una città* is perhaps at the opposite end of the spectrum. An intense use of montage and bricolage of sources (including archival ones) foregrounds polyphony and dialogue. The historian ostensibly speaks as little as possible – providing connections, briefly suggesting ways of reading – yet is very much in control, and at key moments enters the stage to include the experience of the interview as a key to its meaning.[47] The minute fragmentation and recomposition of the voices (and their interaction with other sources) is re-created to convey the dialogic experience of a town's story told by many voices, less as objective reproduction than as creative representation. The models are derived less from history and sociology than from literature (Dos Passos, Conrad, Faulkner), cinema, music (the alternation of solos, arias, recitativo, choral, and orchestral pieces of the baroque oratory). While factual events of history provide the skeleton of the narrative, its meaning lies almost entirely in the lower frequencies of the oral communication.

The most intense and self-reflexive dialogue between the sources and the historian, finally, is represented in another work by Luisa Passerini, *Autoritratto di gruppo*.[48] Weaving oral histories of the student movement of 1968 with the history of her research and the analysis of the interviews, as well as with her own autobiography and psychoanalysis, Passerini creates an original synthesis of autobiography and historiography, psychoanalysis, social history and literature, which is a new genre altogether. No wonder that this book has also inspired a form of presentation to which oral history seems to lend itself very successfully: a theatre performance.[49]

This raises the final question: to whom do these texts speak? Again, the generic spectrum ranges from collections of interviews intended for a broad audience (such as Studs Terkel's excellent books) to scholarly papers meant for selected groups of colleagues at international conferences, or for publication in academic journals with a specialized audience. Another parameter concerns the question of 'restitution': does the intended audience include the social circle of the narrators, and what responsibility does the text take on their behalf?

The latter question has been mostly discussed in ethical terms;[50] however, as in the rest of this paper, I am interested here in the linguistic and formal consequences. Speaking to specialists implies the use of a more rigorously technical language (including bibliographies, footnotes, etc.); speaking to the community or to the general public requires a more pointed effort towards communication; the former will be more interpretative, the latter more narrative. Ironically, the originary orality of the sources tends to be retained much more extensively in works not intended primarily for a scholarly audience.

Speaking to the community, or targeting a broad, non-academic audience, then, does not necessarily subtract from the quality of the work. One of the things that make oral history different is its democratic potential, which can make an oral history project academically relevant at the same time that it is accessible to the general public, not only through readable books, but also through community projects, exhibits and – as already noted – film, video and theatre.[51] Rhetorical strategies vary significantly, however. An academic audience is almost a captive one: its attention is assumed for professional reasons. In the case of the community or the general public, attention must be gained and retained – or, if the word does not offend – *entertained*. This opens the question on which I would like to end this discussion: what is the intended effect of oral history on its listeners and readers? In other words, is there an aesthetics of oral history, and what does it mean?

TO WHAT EFFECT? BEAUTY AND TRUTH

In his autobiography, the American writer Paul Bowles recalls meeting in Tangiers a local person, a guard, with whom he struck up an acquaintance: 'A few anecdotes he told about his life impressed me deeply, not with their unusual content, but because of the way in which he recounted them. His rhetorical sense was extraordinary; he knew exactly which nuances and details to include in order to make a tale complete and convincing.'[52]

It seems, then, that there are two bases for legitimation in telling a life story: either the life is meaningful, or the story is well told (the ideal, of course, is to combine both). The distinction is recognizable in the field of written autobiography: Mother Jones and Big Bill Haywood, historic leaders of labour, publish the stories of their lives as straight autobiography, based on the importance of their achievements and the documentary truth of their testimony. Jack Conroy and Woody Guthrie, rank-and-file workers, also write the stories of their lives, but publish them as fiction, because the basis of legitimation, their most important achievement, is their ability as storytellers.[53] Paul Bowles planned to publish his friend's stories as oral history, but he found a publisher only when he agreed to let them be labelled as a novel. Though they were true stories, what was valuable in them was less the truth than the beauty.

Genre distinctions, as we know, are often blurred in oral performance: narrators do not always stick to a rigid distinction between a true story or a good story; they may be after narrative pleasure while the historian is after hard facts. What do we, as historians, do with the aesthetic project of many narrators, with the beauty incorporated in so many of the stories we hear?

Do we, as purveyors of truth, expunge these features from our work (thus, of course, maiming the authenticity of the document), or do we recognize them as also *facts* in their own right, to be acknowledged and used? The way in which the narrators' voices are included in the historian's book also depends on whether the effect that the book is striving for is one of material factuality, or whether the aesthetic value of a good story, invented or not, is taken as a sign of cultural or individual subjectivity, and whether the historian attempts to convey to the reader also some of the aesthetic revelations or pleasures experienced in listening to oral history. In the apparent opposition of truth and beauty, perhaps beauty can be, rather than superfluous ornament, another – and perhaps the only possible – way of telling other truths.

In his autobiography, narrated through the poet John Neihardt, the Sioux holy man Black Elk makes this point several times: 'Whether it happened so or not I do not know; but if you think about it you can see that it is true'; or 'Watanye said the story happened just as he told it, and maybe it did. If it did not, it could have, just as well as not.'[54] Just as in many of the stories we hear, Black Elk heard in these tales not the truth of material events, but the truth of religious symbol and the truth of possibility: in other words, the special truth of the work of art. Sometimes, this truth told in beauty can also illuminate through symbol and feeling our understanding of history. I will close with one such example.

Dante Bartolini was a singer, a poet and a storyteller; his work has been an inspiration to me since our first encounter, and is featured at several points in my writings. He had been a factory worker and a guerrilla fighter in the anti-Fascist resistance; he was also a herb doctor, a barman, a farmer and a killer and dresser of hogs. The day I first met him, he introduced the singing of his partisan songs with a brief historical narrative. The hieratic tones, the carefully timed pauses, the solemn rhythm, conveyed to the story the quality of epic poetry. The facts, however, were all wrong.

> The eighth of September, nineteen hundred and forty-three
> the armistice was announced
> the defeat of Fascism and Nazism.
> The battle of Stalingrad
> was the end for the Germans.
> Von Paulus, the commander of the German army
> surrendered after a month of fighting.
> And the war ended.
>
> However,
> [the Fascists] reorganized their little republic in the North.
> And we
> anti-Fascists
> immediately arranged to take up arms.

The weapons factory in Terni.
We went
thousands of workers
we broke through the gates
thrust them wide open
we seized the weapons
some of them
and then we left
for the mountains.[55]

The 8th of September 1943 is not the date of the German surrender at Stalingrad, but of Italy's separate peace with the allies and of the dissolution of the Italian army and state. Although the Resistance struggle began immediately after that date, the partisans did not obtain their weapons by breaking into factories. If all we were looking for was factual information, this interview would be useless (it would be so even if it was accurate: we don't need Bartolini's testimony to know about Stalingrad). On the other hand, we stand to learn a great deal if we listen to it as the poetic, ritual representation of the meaning of a historical experience, based on the materialization of two metaphors.

The first metaphor is 'taking up arms', repeated as 'We seized the weapons' (the two sound the same in Italian). The beginning of the partisan movement after 8 September can indeed be described as an act of *taking up arms*: the scene described by Bartolini substantiates a linguistic formula. Yet it is not invented outright: Bartolini was one of the workers (a small group, not 'thousands') who broke into the guard rooms at the steelworks and raided the guns, not in 1943, but in 1949, in the nearly insurrectional mood that followed the attempted murder of Palmiro Togliatti, national secretary of the Communist Party. By merging the two events, the narrator establishes a symbolic but real continuity between the Resistance of 1943–4 and the mass protest of 1949: maybe the Resistance was not finished yet, and the wounding of Togliatti demonstrated that armed struggle was still necessary; or, conversely, maybe the Resistance was over, and any episode of armed struggle had to be pushed back in memory to a time when it was legitimate.

In the second place, by setting the beginning of the struggle in the factory, Bartolini underlines the class nature of the anti-Fascist movement in Terni: even if the struggle was fought in the mountains, the partisans derived their 'weapons' – especially their conscience and solidarity – from the factory, the space where their class consciousness was formed and the continuity of anti-Fascism secured.

The second metaphor is a complex, two-sided one: 'We broke through the gates / Thrust them wide open.' Breaking the gates is a standard image of liberation; it is, however, most frequently represented as breaking *out*, from prison to freedom. In this case, instead, Bartolini describes the workers breaking *in* to the factory. In the former sense, then, the metaphor describes the Resistance as liberation from political oppression; in the latter, as economic liberation, the workers repossessing the nation's wealth: the epic of the Bastille (prisoners breaking out) combines with the epic of the Winter Palace (revolutionaries breaking in). Freedom and socialism are but two sides of the same metaphor: this is the poetic/political meaning we can *feel* in Dante Bartolini's narrative, if we only listen.

The way we perceive this passage depends on the way we hear it, and the way we hear it and interpret it shapes the way we represent it on the written page. Following Dennis Tedlock's instructions, I have transcribed it so as to follow the rhythmic quality of the voice: if it looks like a poem on the page, it is because, as Tedlock has shown, there is a close relationship between oral history and poetry.[56] This transcription, then, draws our attention both to the sound quality of the performance, and to its poetic, metaphoric implications.

On the other hand, the deeper theme of the performance is memory: it preserves and conveys an image of the past, and in order to do so, freezes it somewhat by the very solemnity of the words and the tone. At one level, Bartolini declares that the Resistance is unfinished, and suggests we should continue it; at another, he projects it into a special epoch in the past, and suggests we commemorate it. If we wished to underscore the latter aspect, we could do so by transcribing it as follows:

> The eighth of September, nineteen hundred and forty-three
> The armistice was announced
> The defeat of Fascism and Nazism.
> The battle of Stalingrad
> Was the end for the Germans . . .

Merely shifting the disposition of the words on the page turns Bartolini's narrative from poem to epigraph: a monument, a verbal icon to the Resistance (I have been tempted to write the date, a typical incipit in commemorative epigraphs, in Roman numerals). The passage hesitates between historical statement, epic poem and monument; the way readers understand it depends to a large extent on the historian's decision to transcribe it, respectively, as linear prose, verse or epigraph. That these genres coexist in mutual tension in the same words is a tribute to the creative complexity of oral narrative; that we must choose among them as we transcribe is a sign of the responsibilities we take upon ourselves as historians.

NOTES

This chapter is based on a paper presented at the international workshop 'Methodology and methods of oral history and life stories in social research', L'viv, Ukraine, 5–7 Sept. 1994.

1 Elizabeth Tonkin, *Narrating our Pasts: The Social Construction of Oral History* (Cambridge: Cambridge University Press, 1992). Among the papers presented at the L'viv conference, this approach is brilliantly illustrated in Hana Hlosková's 'Oral history and folklore studies', which classifies oral history, within the system of oral literature, as a type of 'legend narrative', based on the belief in the veracity of the narrative.

2 Mikhail Bakhtin, 'Discourse in the novel', in *The Dialogic Imagination* (Austin: University of Texas Press, 1984), pp. 259–422; Eva McMahan and Kim Lacy Rogers (eds), *Interactive Oral History Interviewing* (Hillsdale, N.J.: Lawrence Erlbaum, 1994).

3 Excerpts from this interview are included in 'Absolutely nothing: wartime refugees', in A. Portelli, *The Battle of Valle Giulia: Oral History and the Art of Dialogue* (Madison: University of Wisconsin Press, 1997), ch. 8.

4 See my '*Absalom, Absalom!* Oral history and literature', in *The Death of Luigi Trastulli: Form and Meaning in Oral History* (Albany, N.Y.: State University of New York Press, 1991), pp. 270–2.

5 I use *text* here to indicate the words that make up the discourse. Strictly speaking, of course, there is no such thing as an oral text; see Walter J. Ong, *Orality and Literacy: The Technologizing of the Word* (London and New York: Methuen, 1982), p. 13, and '*Maranatha*: death and life in the text of the book', in *Interfaces of the Word* (Ithaca and London: Cornell University Press, 1977), pp. 230–71.

6 I borrow this expression from Albert Lord, *The Singer of Tales* (Cambridge, Mass.: Harvard University Press, 1960), who uses it to describe the work of oral epic poets. In less formalized terms, it applies to all unrehearsed forms of discourse. On incremental repetition, see Gordon Hall Gerould, *The Ballad of Tradition* (1932; repr. New York: Oxford University Press, 1957), pp. 105–10.

7 Jean-Marie Schaeffer, *Qu'est-ce qu'un genre littéraire?* (Paris: Seuil, 1982); I am quoting from the Italian translation, *Che cos'è un genere letterario?* (Parma: Pratiche, 1992), p. 73, trans. Ida Zaffagnini. Both in the French original and in the translation, the sentence quoted here is in English.

8 See 'There's gonna always be a line: history-telling as a multivocal art', in *The Battle of Valle Giulia*, ch. 2.

9 See Portelli, '*Absalom, Absalom!* Oral history and literature'.

10 Eugenia Meyer, Elena Poniatowska and Eva Salgado Andrade, 'Documenting the earthquake of 1985 in Mexico City', *Oral History Review* 16(1) (Spring 1988): 1–31. A number of papers presented at the L'viv conference exemplify this approach in their very titles: e.g. Katia Foteeva, 'Well-to-do families meet the challenge of revolution'; Daniel Bertaux, 'From families' case histories to the understanding of social-historical processes'.

11 This is not to belittle the work of elite oral historians, but rather to point out that, as oral historians, they are after the distinctive individual personality of their narrators as well as their public role. For a discussion based on elite oral history projects at the CEPEDOC (Documentation Centre) of the Fundaçao Getulio Vargas in Rio de Janeiro, see Marieta de Moraes Ferriera et al., *Entre-vistas: abordagens e usos da história oral* (Rio de Janeiro: Fundaçao Getulio Vargas, 1994).

12 Published in 1881, rev. 1891; repr. New York: Collier's, 1962.

13 Some examples of this motif appear in *The Death of Luigi Trastulli*, pp. 102–3, 134–5.

14 Antonio Gibelli, 'Per una storia dell'esperienza di guerra dei contadini', in *La cultura delle classi subalterne fra tradizione e innovazione*, proceedings of the conference on 'Subaltern cultures between innovation and tradition', Alessandria, 14–16 May 1985 (Alessandria: Edizioni dell'Orso, 1988), pp. 85–102.

15 Irene Guidarelli, born in 1896, interviewed in Terni, 16 July 1980; quoted in

A. Portelli, *Biografia di una città. Storia e racconto: Terni 1831–1985* (Turin: Einaudi, 1985), p. 247.

16 Eric Leed, *No Man's Land: Combat and Identity in World War I* (Cambridge: Cambridge University Press, 1979); Paul Fussell, *The Great War and Modern Memory* (Oxford: Oxford University Press, 1975); Nuto Revelli, *La guerra dei poveri* (Turin: Einaudi, 1962); Alistair Thomson, *Anzac Memories: Living with the Legend* (Melbourne: Oxford University Press, 1994); Gabriele Rosenthal, 'Narración y significado biográfico de las experiencias de guerra', *História y fuente oral* 4 (1990): 119–28; John Limon, *Writing after War: American War Fiction from Realism to Postmodernism* (New York: Oxford University Press, 1994).

17 Prue Chamberlaine and Annette King, 'Carers' narratives as genre: an East-West German comparison', unpubl. paper. Kristine Popova and Peter Vodenicharov's 'The stories of death in the stories of life: corporality and individuality in the narratives of Bulgarian Moslems', presented at the L'viv conference, shows in fascinating detail the continuity between war and hospital stories in the narrative of one (male) informant.

18 Giuseppina Migliosi, b. 1900, interviewed in Terni, 17 October 1980; Debbie Spicer, b. 1907, interviewed in Blackbottom, Harlan County, Kentucky, 10 October 1988.

19 Even in this chapter, I have always used the term *speaker* to refer to the interviewee, not the interviewer. See Ronald J. Grele, 'History and the languages of history in the oral history interview: who answers whose questions and why?', in McMahan and Rogers, *Interactive Oral History Interviewing*, pp. 1–17, and his afterword, ibid., pp. 163–4. On interviewing and fieldwork, see also Elliot G. Mishler, *Research Interviewing: Context and Narrative* (Cambridge, Mass.: Harvard University Press, 1993); Bruce Jackson, *Fieldwork* (Urbana: University of Illinois Press, 1987), pp. 79–101; Sidney W. Mintz, 'The sensation of moving while standing still', *American Ethnologist* 16(4) (Nov. 1989): 786–96; Kathryn Anderson and Dana C. Jack, 'Learning to listen: interview techniques and analyses', in Sherna Berger Gluck and Daphne Patai (eds), *Women's Words: The Feminist Practice of Oral History* (New York: Routledge, 1991), pp. 11–26.

20 Michael Palmer et al., '"I haven't anything to say": reflections of self and community in collecting oral histories', in Ronald J. Grele (ed.), *International Annual of Oral History 1990* (New York: Greenwood, 1990), pp. 167–90.

21 The distinction between self-authorization and authorization from others is especially important in the genre of slave narratives, some of which are taken down by white editors while others are written directly by the ex-slaves themselves. See John W. Blassingame, 'Using the testimony of ex-slaves: approaches and problems', and Robert B. Stepto, 'I rose and found my voice: narration, authentication, and authorial control in four slave narratives', both in Charles T. Davis and Henry Louis Gates Jr. (eds), *The Slaves' Narrative* (Oxford: Oxford University Press, 1985), pp. 78–98 and 225–42.

22 Mary Jones, *The Autobiography of Mother Jones* (Chicago: Charles H. Kerr, 1972); Riziero Manconi, b. 1894, Terni, 7 July 1980.

23 '[The interviewer] spoke only once or twice while she talked. Margaret Jones didn't need him, care for him. She was permitting him to overhear what she told the machine.' See John Wideman, *Philadelphia Fire* (1990; repr. London: Picador, 1995), p. 9.

24 Maggiorina Mattioli's narrative technique is discussed in Portelli, '*Absalom, Absalom!* Oral history and literature'.

25 Most projects, of course, use intermediate techniques, or both. See Dean Hommer and Aaron Wildavsky, 'La entrevista semi-estructurada de final abierto.

Aproximación a una guía operativa', *História y fuente oral* 4 (1990): 23–77; William Cutler III, 'Accuracy in oral history interviewing', in David K. Dunaway and Willia K. Baum (eds), *Oral History: An Interdisciplinary Anthology* (Nashville, Tenn.: American Association for State and Local History, 1984), pp. 79–106.

26 Dennis Tedlock, 'The analogical tradition and the emergence of a dialogical anthropology', in *The Spoken Word and the Work of Interpretation* (Philadelphia: University of Pennsylvania Press, 1983), p. 334.

27 Annamaria Di Marco, b. 1964, interviewed in Rome, 16 July 1992. See 'Deep exchange: roles and gazes in multivocal and multilateral interviewing', in Portelli, *The Battle of Valle Giulia*, ch. 5.

28 See 'Research as an experiment in equality', in Portelli, *The Death of Luigi Trastulli*, pp. 29–44.

29 Zora Neale Hurston, *Mules and Men: Negro Folklore and Voodoo Practices in the South* (1935; repr. New York and Evanston: Harper and Row, 1970), p. 24.

30 A classic of the form, of course, is *The Autobiography of Malcolm X*, written by Alex Haley. In most cases, the actual writers tend to be journalists (paid for the task), rather than historians; professional attitudes and power relationships play an important role in shaping the genre.

31 In fact, the main difference was that, though he repeated his mythic version of the death of Luigi Trastulli (see 'The death of Luigi Trastulli: memory and the event', in Portelli, *The Death of Luigi Trastulli*, pp. 1–36), he was now aware through contact with me that it was factually 'wrong'.

32 See Joel Gardner, 'Oral history and video in theory and practice', *Oral History Review* 12 (1984): 105–11; Silvia Paggi, 'A proposito de la entrevista filmada en la investigación antropologica', *História y fuente oral* 12 (1994): 163–71; Giovanni Contini and Alfredo Martini, *Verba Manent. L'uso delle fonti orali per la storia contemporanea* (Rome: La Nuova Italia Scientifica, 1993), pp. 23–7.

33 There is a justifiable reason for this: the *linguistic* aspect of the interview is usually perceived to pertain more directly to the linguistic and verbal behaviour of the speakers, rather than to the visual and gestural exchange; also, appearing in video tends to be perceived as a more narcissistic act on the part of the interviewer than reporting the questions in a paper. Whether these perceptions are correct is another question.

34 These remarks also apply to various aspects of aural media; in fact, they are in part derived from my experience in documentary records and radio broadcasts. I skip here the discussion of another visual means of presentation, photography. Michael Frisch discusses 'the picture book genre' in 'Get the picture? A review essay', in *A Shared Authority: Essays on the Craft and Meaning of Oral and Public History* (Albany, N.Y.: State University of New York Press, 1990), pp. 203–14. He also contributes to a splendid example of the genre, *Portraits in Steel*, photographs by Milton Rogovin, interviews by Michael Frisch (Ithaca and London: Cornell University Press, 1993). Both Frisch and Rogovin, and Judith Modell and Charlee Brodsky, 'Envisioning homestead: using photographs in interviewing (Homestead, Pennsylvania)', in McMahan and Rogers, *Interactive Oral History Interviewing*, exemplify the use of photographs as a technique for generating memories and narratives in interviewing.

On multimedia and radio, see Charles Hardy III, 'Aural history and the digital revolution', unpubl. ms., July 1996; on video, Pamela H. Henson and Terri Schorzman, 'Videohistory: focusing on the American past', *Journal of American History* (Sept. 1991): 618–27; on museums, John Kuo Wei Tchen, 'Creating a dialogic museum: the Chinatown History Museum experience', in Ivan Kemp, Christine Mulleer Kreamer and Steven D. Lavine (eds), *Museums and Communities:*

The Politics of Public Culture (Washington D.C.: Smithsonian Institution Press, 1992), pp. 285–326.

35 Paula Rabinowitz, 'Introduction', in *They Must be Represented: The Politics of Documentary* (London: Verso, 1994), p. 12.

36 Not, however, by 'microhistorians' themselves. Although some influential oral history work was published in the Microstorie series of which he was general editor, Carlo Ginzburg omits all mention of oral history from a recent review essay and methodological discussion of microhistory: 'Microstoria: due o tre cose che so di lei', *Quaderni storici* 86(2) (August 1994): 511–39.

37 Theodore Rosengarten, *All God's Dangers: The Life of Nate Shaw* (New York: Knopf, 1974); Ronald Fraser, *Blood of Spain: An Oral History of the Spanish Civil War* (New York: Pantheon, 1979).

38 Cristina Borderías, *Entre Lineas. La compañia telefónica 1924–1980* (Barcelona: Icaria, 1993); Liliana Barela et al., *Barrio y memoria* (Instituto Histórico de la Ciudad de Buenos Aires, 1992); Tamara Harevan, *Amoskeag: Life and Work in an American Factory City* (New York: Pantheon, 1978); Ronald Fraser (ed.), *1968: A Student Generation in Revolt* (New York: Pantheon, 1988).

39 Rosanna Basso, 'Myths in contemporary oral tradition: a children's strike', in Raphael Samuel and Paul Thompson (eds), *The Myths We Live By* (London and New York: Routledge, 1990), pp. 61–9; András Kovács, 'The abduction of Imre Nagy and his group: the "Rashomon" effect', in *International Yearbook of Oral History and Life Stories*, vol. 1: *Memory and Totalitarianism*, ed. Luisa Passerini (Oxford: Oxford University Press, 1992), pp. 117–24. On the other hand, my *Biografia di una città* stretches over 150 years.

40 See for example, Carlos Sebe Bom Mehy, *Canto de morte Kaiowá, Historia oral de vida* (São Paolo: Loyola, 1991); Philippe Joutard, *La legende des Camisards* (Paris: Gallimard, 1977).

41 Raphael Samuel, *East End Underworld: Chapters in the Life of Arthur Harding* (London: Routledge and Kegan Paul, 1981), an individual life story; Bianca Guidetti Serra, *Compagne. Testimonianze di partecipazione politica femminile* (Turin: Einaudi, 1977), a series of interviews with women in the Resistance; Anna Bravo and Daniele Jalla, *La vita offesa dei Lager nazisti nei racconti di duecento sopravvissuti* (Milan: Franco Angeli, 1987), a polyphonic montage of interviews with survivors of the Nazi concentration camps.

42 Mark Baker, *Nam* (London: Abacus, 1982); Wallace Terry, *Bloods: An Oral History of the Vietnam War by Black Veterans* (New York: Ballantine, 1984). See 'As though it were a story: versions of Vietnam', in Portelli, *The Battle of Valle Giulia*, ch. 11.

43 Nuto Revelli, *Il mondo dei vinti. Testimonianze di vita contadina* (Turin: Einaudi, 1977) and *L'anello forte. La donna: storie di vita contadina* (Turin: Einaudi, 1985). The use of 'testimony' and 'lives' in the titles underlines the effect of objectivity; Revelli goes so far as to incorporate his own questions into the informants' answers, so as not to appear to intrude: 'Do I believe they sent a man to the moon?' Revelli uses a very different, dialogic and self-reflexive approach in his recent *Il disperso di Marburg* (Turin: Einaudi, 1994), which focuses on the history of a research and on his own response to the problems it raises.

44 Luisa Passerini, *Torino operaia e il fascismo* (Milan: Feltrinelli, 1984).

45 Maurizio Gribaudi, *Mondo operaio e mito operaio* (Turin: Einaudi, 1987).

46 Contini and Martin, *Verba Manent*, p. 47n.

47 According to Luisa Passerini, the combination of montage and narrative contextualization in this book causes 'a seeming disappearance of the subject, or, rather, an ambiguity as to who is the subject in this game of re-writing and extrapolation – who plays which role in the piling up of quotations' ('Il

programma radiofonico come fonte', in *Storia e soggettività. Le fonti orali la memoria* (Florence: Nuova Italia Scientifica, 1985), pp. 172–3. Ultimately, as the name on the cover indicates, the speaking subject, responsible for the overall statement, is the historian himself. See Portelli, *Biografia di una città*.

48 Luisa Passerini, *Autoritratto di gruppo* (Florence: Giunti, 1988).

49 For another Italian example of transition from oral history to theatre, see Domenico Starnone, 'Scuola, ricerca e teatro. Per riprendere la parola', *I Giorni Cantati* 4 (1983): 52–65.

50 See 'Tryin' to gather a little knowledge: thoughts on the ethics of oral history', in Portelli, *The Battle of Valle Giulia*, ch. 40.

51 Michael Frisch, *A Shared Authority* (especially ch. 13, 'The presentation of urban history in big city museums'); Paul Thompson, *The Voice of the Past: Oral History* (Oxford: Oxford University Press, 1978), ch. 1. One of my best experiences with oral history was the writing and staging, together with my students at the University of Rome, of a play with music based on my oral history interviews in Harlan County, called *Quilt*. The play was presented at schools and at movement and union venues in different parts of Italy several times in 1990–2.

52 Paul Bowles, *Without Stopping: An Autobiography* (1972; repr. London: Peter Owen, 1987), p. 347.

53 Bill Haywood, *Big Bill's Book: The Autobiography of Big Bill Haywood* (1929; repr. New York: International, 1969); Jones, *Autobiography of Mother Jones*; Woody Guthrie, *Bound for Glory* (1943; repr. New York: Dutton, 1970); Jack Conroy, *The Disinherited* (1933; repr. New York: Hill and Wang, 1963). An immediately visible difference is that Haywood or Jones say very little about their private lives and their childhoods, while these form the bulk of Conroy's and Guthrie's books. Of course, what is presented as a factual autobiography may contain less actual truth than what is presented as a novel. What counts, however, is the quality of the 'pact' stipulated between the writer and the reader; see Philippe Lejeune, *Le pacte autobiographique* (Paris: Seuil, 1975); title essay translated in P. Lejeune, *On Autobiography*, ed. P. J. Eakin, trans. K. Leary (Minneapolis: University of Minnesota Press, 1989), pp. 3–30.

54 John. G. Neihardt (ed.), *Black Elk Speaks* (1932; repr. Lincoln: University of Nebraska Press, 1979), pp. 5, 66.

55 Interview with Dante Bartolini, b. 1910, Castel di Lago (Terni), 4 April 1972.

56 Dennis Tedlock, 'Learning to listen: oral history as poetry', in *The Spoken Word and the Work of Interpretation*, pp. 107–23. I had transcribed it in this fashion also in the manuscript of *Biografia di una città*, but my editors wouldn't hear of it, and compelled me to falsify the passage by printing it as prose.

3

SILENCES

The Case of a Psychiatric Hospital

Diana Gittins

There are many silences. For Quakers silence is pregnant with spirit, prayer, possibility. For some religious sects it is a way of life. It is often used as a form of punishment, especially for children, but also sometimes for prisoners. It can be a place of meditation, of rest, of daydreams, but also of nightmares. For most of us silence in the company of others is embarrassing, a void that we must rush to try and fill. For analysts it is a key to their analysands. In myriad ways it is a gap: literary works never published, historical manuscripts burned, narratives forgotten, denied or ignored. In autobiographies and life stories silences may be a sign either of deliberate exclusion or of lost memory.

Memories can be lost for a number of reasons, and their retrieval is rarely straightforward, arguably more a process of re-structuring than remembering: 'there is no "work of memory" without a corresponding "work of forgetting". So often forgetting indicates suffering.'[1] Fear, pain, shame are undoubtedly major forces in the repression of memory and can be seen as integral to the creation and development of an unconscious in the individual. Much is forgotten because it is seen as irrelevant, and of course the way in which 'irrelevant' is defined is itself full of significance: 'What people do not remember, and what they think is historically insignificant, can nevertheless be a pointer to their community's social practices, but as with recall, the connections are not direct and simple.'[2] Yet events, feelings, images are also deliberately forgotten, or at least kept silent, as part of a refusal to comply, to answer difficult questions, to reveal secrets, or to betray confidences. Silences are thus created consciously, unconsciously, and at a number of levels, not just within individuals but among the collective generally. Silences are, in the widest sense, political.

Silence and power work hand in hand. In documentary records what appears on the agenda or in the variables chosen for analysis often represents only the acceptable, anodyne face of that issue. More controversial aspects tend to be cloaked in silence, discussed outside official hours, outside official meetings; decisions and agreements that 'matter' thus often go unrecorded. Power, as Foucault pointed out, is most effective when invisible. Silent. The power allegedly wielded by a secret society such as the Freemasons, based extensively on silence, would appear to be, at least at certain times and in certain areas, very large indeed.[3] The Mafia is another case in point. Problems can arise for those in powerful positions if such secret encounters and decisions *are* recorded, as Richard Nixon learned. 'The political value of what is forgotten reminds us of the deep connection between memory and freedom.'[4]

Silence is not only a noun. It is also a verb. To silence, to censor: not just individuals but whole groups over time have been left largely unacknowledged, unseen, unheard because a dominant group, or the discourse of a dominant group, defines individuals or groups as 'irrelevant' or unworthy of being remembered. Women,[5] servants, children, ethnic minorities, the elderly, the mentally disordered, those with different sexual preferences and identities: all of these groups at one time or another have been regarded as irrelevant, silenced out of official, public history. Such exclusions are best seen, however, as a continuous process whereby the struggle to be heard is ongoing, as is the power to silence.

Not just social groups, but also historical eras can become cloaked in silence. Luisa Passerini drew attention to the silencing of memories about fascist Italy,[6] and Anna Collard 'has described how the members of a Greek village did not talk much in a historical way about their experiences 35 years earlier, though these were evidently central, given the desperate sequences of the Greek national and civil wars from 1940 to 1950'.[7] *Who* silences *whom* and *why* are thus crucial questions in understanding power relations in any given culture at a given time. Generally speaking, it is fair to assume that reasons for silencing certain groups include fear, feeling that the difference of other(s) from one's self or group is in some way dangerous or threatening.

Silences at all levels, individual and collective, relate to issues and aspects deemed unacceptable, unattractive and/or dangerous to those who impose the silence for whatever reasons. Reasons, of course, change and vary; they can be resisted and they can be redefined. As Portelli comments, some actions 'considered legitimate and even normal are today viewed as unacceptable and are literally cast out of the tradition. In these cases, the most precious information may lie in what the informants hide (and in the fact that they hide it), rather than in what they say.'[8]

To try to understand an individual, a group, a culture by referring only to what is said, recorded and explicit is to deal with the side deemed acceptable, the side which the individual ego or the ruling group would like to be remembered, noticed, left for posterity. Clearly we all have less acceptable aspects to our selves, our collectives, our cultures, all of which are crucial in understanding wider patterns of conflict, contradiction and change. Few would deny that war, oppression, racism and sexism are as much a part of our world as are charity, art, kindness and love. To understand any aspect of a culture, therefore, it is important to consider, as far as possible, all aspects, including those deemed unacceptable.

How actually to do this when the unacceptable is silent is a more difficult issue. Life histories and documents, quantitative and qualitative sources are all full of silences. Direct questions are not always fruitful in interviewing respondents and, of course, as E. P. Thompson said, 'you can't interview tombstones.' There are silences that will always remain silent. Yet there are many silences that can be explored and filled in. As Freud pointed out with reference to the unconscious, repression is constantly being betrayed through jokes and slips of the tongue, and a more oblique, circuitous approach can sometimes result in the discovery that what once seemed so silent can, at times, speak out.

> Tell all the Truth but tell it slant –
> Success in Circuit lies . . .
>
> Emily Dickinson[9]

I am currently researching the history of a psychiatric hospital that was built early in this century and is due to close in 1997. Many histories of psychiatric hospitals – often written by psychiatrists who had themselves worked in the institution – adopt a linear, progressive approach in accounting for changes that occurred. They tend to be oriented to the narration of a chronology of mental health policies, 'innovations' in treatments, and achievements of senior staff. They are often silent about patients themselves except as recipients of treatments or statistics that waxed or waned as the institution expanded and contracted. Almost nothing is said about cruelty or violence to patients by staff, between staff, or between patients. Nothing is said about suicides, deaths caused by misadministration of treatments, or experimental research on patients.[10] Although this research entails scrutiny of surviving documentary sources, I am giving priority to the accounts and narratives of the various groups who lived and worked in the hospital. So far I have carried out some sixty in-depth interviews with patients, ex-patients, nurses, psychiatrists and administrative, maintenance and domestic staff.

At its peak in 1936 the hospital contained nearly 2,300 patients. Like other psychiatric hospitals of the time it was located outside the town and was surrounded with high fences; inside, railings and ha-has enclosed courtyards adjacent to the wards. One ex-patient, who was certified in the early 1950s, described his early days in the hospital:

> I was put into a bed. I was – could walk – and I didn't feel all that ill. . . .
> They didn't say what it was. I didn't feel ill. I had no idea what was
> wrong with me. And they put me into a bed and I was in there for a
> week, without getting out of bed, only to the toilet. And I was under
> lock and key, lock and key, not to go out of the grounds at all, not even
> outside for a long long time. . . . I still to this day here, I have no idea
> why I was put in. . . . And I was put in against my will. . . . I was pushed

around. . . . Ward 3 was just like a prison. Under lock and key. . . . And we were bathed by somebody and shaved by somebody. And even in Ward 3 I had to have ECT against my will. . . . After about six months on Ward 3 we were allowed out in the garden. The gardens were surrounded by a fairly high wrought-iron fence, right the way round, so you couldn't get out. Oh, it was terrible. . . . When I was first admitted the staff nurse said, 'You're at the Queen's Pleasure,' whatever he meant by that.

The hospital was largely self sufficient with some 300 acres of land, two working farms that provided vegetables, milk and meat for the hospital, its own electricity supply, fire service, blacksmith, kitchens, bakery and range of craftsmen. The overwhelming majority of staff lived within the estate or on its periphery and it was organized in a tight and rigidly disciplined hierarchy. It was not unlike a feudal estate. Its location symbolically singled it out – and by implication also madness generally and the mad in particular – as Other, 'out there', a kind of collective unconscious or lunatic fringe where all that was undesirable to the 'normal' community was locked safely away. *Shut up.*

Madness is a recurring and endemic fear in most human beings, if only unconsciously. The fear of losing control, losing the capacity for rational thought, losing one's social status in the community and of ceasing in some fundamental way to be considered part of 'normal' society is undoubtedly a common fear in our culture, and certainly has been in the past. What is considered normal, however, varies not only culturally and historically, but also between different social groups; what is 'mad' for the poor man at his gate is often deemed 'eccentric' for the rich man in his castle. Little wonder, then, that psychiatric hospitals have been places feared and viewed with suspicion, used as a source of threats to children: 'Behave yourself or you'll be going on the Number 5 Bus' was the common threat in this area. Even less wonder that if a person became mentally disordered and was put into a psychiatric hospital, their family tried to silence the fact. Many people were apparently 'dumped' by their families, literally locked in silence to protect their family's reputation from such once shameful misdemeanours as pre-marital pregnancy or rape, or to enable a husband who was tired of his wife, and wanted to get rid of her, to replace her with a new lover.[11]

So fear of madness has focused for a long time on psychiatric hospitals: the bin, the nuthouse, the loopy house; the two apparently converged. *Shut up.* Arguably the whole institution, at least until 1960, was about silence. Madness itself was a silence and something to be silenced. So were psychiatric hospitals. Those who worked – and often lived – in them were faced with an often suspicious outside world that could equate them, given half a chance, with their irrational charges on whom their lives and jobs depended. One male nurse who was offered work there in the 1930s, and who badly needed the income and security it (unusually) provided a working-class man at that time, had to confront his mother's fears: she pleaded for him to reject the offer in case he 'caught the mania'. Madness and the mad were feared as contagious, polluting, Other, both by the outside world and by those who worked in the hospital.[12] Their status in the outside world depended on the silence and silencing of any activities, events or behaviours that would draw attention to their precarious position of liminality, perched on the threshold as they were between outside and inside, rational and irrational, sanity and madness.

Within the overall silence of the hospital itself, other silences proliferate like subtexts. Staff who are still employed in the hospital seem terrified of saying anything negative about the place whatsoever. Many, understandably, are frightened of what will happen to their jobs when the hospital finally closes. Others refuse to be interviewed at all. I know there is a fair degree of hostility to the project, and some see me as a pawn of senior management, although I am employed by a university. Many members of staff have grown up in and around the hospital community. Many are third-generation employees who, in earlier times, worked side by side with members of both their own immediate family and wider kin. It is ironic, tragic, for this group of people that in the name of 'community care' what has for them always *been* a community, and indeed a very close and tight-knit one, is being destroyed.

Consequently they will say little against it generally. Many of them are angry. Virtually all of them are sad. There is thus a loud political silence in interviews with many people from this group about anything except 'the good old days'. Their subjectivity, their whole identity, their sense of kinship and community are intertwined with this hospital that is being closed down. They have a vested interest in being silent about all except the positive aspects of it; they stress the leisure occasions such as sports days, dances, the times when Dr So-and-So had a few jars too many and did the hokey-kokey in the staff social club, or when somebody put a pair of women's knickers on top of the lightning conductor and the fire brigade had to come to take them down. What little is said about patients refers to them like children, their names generally prefaced by 'Little' – Little Jack, Little Jane and so on.

One man, for example, who began working as a male nurse in the 1930s, gave a four-hour interview that contained a plethora of detailed narratives about nursing education, nursing practice, ward routine and structure and various events and changes in the hospital during the time he worked there. Much of his account contained remarkable detail and was often highly amusing. Except for one brief reference to doctors sometimes giving extra doses of ECT to patients 'for luck', however, he never mentioned any instances of violence or cruelty. Of course, this could be taken as evidence that this was an exceptional hospital where violence never occurred. Or it could be interpreted that while there was probably violence/cruelty going on, this man never chanced to witness, experience or inflict it. Or it could be seen as a sign that he knew full well it was endemic, but was not willing to share that information with the interviewer; it was not part of the narrative he wanted to give either about the hospital or about that aspect of himself. Or it might also be the case, as Portelli argues, that

> today's narrator is not the same person as took part in the distant events which he or she is now relating. . . . There may have been changes in personal subjective consciousness as well as in social standing and economic condition, which may induce modifications, affecting at least the judgement of events and the 'colouring' of the story.[13]

In the end I had only the informant's word for it, or, more precisely, his silence.

In a study of this sort, however, narratives soon begin to overlap and in the end a kind of palimpsest develops where one person's silence is elucidated by another person's narrative, and *that* person's silence partially filled by someone else's. There is never a complete picture: 'the whole of anything can never be told, we can only take what groups together' (Henry James), but a collection of voices begins to give a clearer melody, a patchwork of images begins to offer at least a partial outline of the greater quilt.

Serendipity or synchronicity: two days after transcribing the interview with the male nurse above, I interviewed a man who had begun work as a male nurse in the early 1950s. He told me how he had been beaten up by another, more senior nurse from the 'old guard'. As a student nurse, this younger man had been instructed to dispense medication to the patients in a ward where the older man was charge nurse. The latter, while the student nurse was giving out the tablets, ordered the patients to sit down for dinner. 'Hang on a minute. I haven't finished giving them their medication,' the young man protested. Next thing he knew he lay flat on the floor. He had been knocked out by the older nurse mentioned above. Here is a longer extract of the younger nurse's account:

> I went right straight across to the Chief Male Nurse, and nothing ever came of it. In actual fact, I was the one that was criticized at the time – and I was very unhappy about that, but that was just something that happened. It was hushed up and kept very quiet, you know, and I think it was even the fact that the person himself had been here for some time, therefore the old clique. . . . My name was never put forward for any awards or anything after that occasion. . . . I'm sure a lot of things could have been – you know – covered up, because it has to be remembered that we were young people, we'd come into this establishment in the mid-fifties and the first sort of generation of people were retiring then, the second generation had taken over from them . . . and a lot of the habits or, if you like institutionalization, of the staff carried on . . . a lot of us objected to this situation and it would be very easy for the old clique to hide things – because it was a *hole* at the time . . .

51

I remember – I was not quite seventeen – and the Deputy Chief Male Nurse's first words to me, he said to me, 'if you get any trouble with 'em, knock 'em to the floor and lift their head up that high and put it down smartly.' I'd only been here a week! . . . I think it was a society here that didn't want any – without being critical of it, because we enjoyed our time here – but I think it was a society that *needed* to keep things quiet. There was no doubt about it. It didn't like *anything* that occurred that would be detrimental to the name of the hospital or for the name of the staff or for the name of the administration there.

This man left at the end of the 1950s. He had no vested interest in keeping silent about such controversial issues, it did not affect his sense of self-worth to relate them. But those, such as the older nurse, whose very subjectivity and identity were entwined with the hospital, could not admit, or perhaps could not remember, incidents such as those which put him and the hospital in a bad light. The divergent accounts also told me a great deal about power relations in the hospital at the time and how a combination of reward and intimidation among various levels of the nursing staff ensured their continued position and status, despite the overall power of the Medical Superintendent. Loyalty to senior nursing staff and the keeping of silences almost always meant eventual rewards and promotion. Transgression of the existing traditions and pecking order could mean exclusion from the group and the promotion system, whereby the Chief Male Nurse recommended nurses for promotion to the Medical Superintendent.

The older nurse, however, was not adverse to providing negative information on those he blamed for changes to the above system and to the hospital in general. Dr Barton was one whom he particularly seemed to blame for what he saw as destructive changes to the hospital. Dr Barton came as Medical Superintendent in 1960, at a time when new legislation abolished the process of certification and sought to transform mental hospitals from custodial to therapeutic institutions. He instigated many changes in the hospital structure, routine and treatment of patients very quickly. Some staff referred to the process as 'turning everything upside down'; a woman patient, however, who has lived in institutions for over sixty-five years, and in this hospital for nearly forty, said:

That was Dr Barton who got this hospital open. I can remember him! He used to *talk* to me! I liked Dr Barton. That was him that opened this hospital. Took the railings down. He used to come round the wards and *speak to the patients*. Reopened the hospital.

The fences and railings were taken down. Locked wards were opened. Long-term chronic patients, many of whom had spent years more or less confined to bed, were encouraged to get up, get out, and everyone who could work

52

was given work, whenever possible, whether outside the hospital or within it in the new industrial units set up by Barton. He promoted outsiders on to the nursing staff at senior level. He initiated extensive education and re-education programmes aimed at reducing the stigmatization of mental patients and mental hospitals; he courted the media and groups in the wider community. For many, especially patients, he was a hero; for some, especially older staff, he was a man who destroyed the very fabric of the community they had grown up in and believed to be stable, secure and *theirs*.

The older nurse was shocked by the rapid changes Barton brought about. Although he was clearly impressed with much that he did, he saw the result as anarchy, chaos:

> Barton was clever. He used to come in, take his coat off, put it back of the chair – could always see him sitting in his shirt-sleeves. Leave the door open. None of this make-an-appointment-with-the-Chief-Male-Nurse to go and see him. Anybody could walk in. *Patients* used to walk in and tell him. And that's how he got to know what was going on in certain wards, you see. That's why you had to more or less be careful . . .

> When Barton was then beginning to become unpopular – with the management committee and with the – cause he was doing a lot, he was doing a lot of things. But the thing is, there was a time when a lot of patients were going out and hanging themself. . . . There was 49 – and they got so bad – it was 49 went – committed suicide. They went missing. Found a fortnight after by people perhaps going to work on the farm and things like that. They were going up the railway, jumping in front of the trains. Dear, dear me. And that looks so bad on our part. . . . This was a matter of two or three months. 1963.

Forty-nine suicides seemed like a lot. I checked the Medical Superintendent's reports for 1960–9 and found a total of fourteen – successful – suicides for the *decade*. There was only one in 1963, though it was a particularly disturbing one that involved a woman voluntary patient who while on leave killed both herself and her child. Undoubtedly this upset many people. But I found no trace of the kind of number the nurse insisted on. Was this a case of a silence, a cover-up on the part of the administration, a case of suicides somehow being laundered, presented as some other form of death? Or was the nurse exaggerating excessively? He mentioned people going to work on the farm, but the farms had been sold by the end of the 1950s, and I had found other fairly marked inaccuracies in the rest of his narrative. It is certainly possible, however, that because substantial numbers were discharged from the hospital, some of these may have taken their lives once outside the hospital; the nurse may have recognized their names in media accounts of their deaths. On the other hand, it could be there was an increase in *attempted* suicides, which were never recorded in the Medical

Superintendent's reports. I checked the records for the previous ten years and found that between 1950 and 1959 there had been seven successful suicides. The figures did indicate a doubling in the suicide rate in the 1960s. Later I interviewed Dr Barton and asked him about this:

Was there any marked change in suicidal trends after you went there?
I don't think there was. And I wouldn't have thought there was because we were admitting perhaps twice as many patients. I don't have the figures – we do have them somewhere – but if you're admitting twice as many patients[14] . . . if you were admitting a thousand a year and you take up to two thousand it means the turnover of patients is much faster and the – you have a much larger number of suicides. Keeping them in isn't going to stop it, because they suicide in hospital . . . but it can be made by a wily statistician – you know, figures can't lie, but liars can figure. It may look as if the hospital is getting more suicides because it's dealing with a much greater population.

In a sense both had valid points to make, both were right. Perhaps both contain some silences on the issue; dialoguing between them, however, is a useful way of shedding light on a difficult issue. What may ultimately be of greatest interest is not so much the precise information on suicides, but the fact that this nurse, and there were undoubtedly many of his generation who would have shared his views, regarded the sort of policies Barton was implementing as dangerous and foolhardy and contrary to all their well-ingrained ideas about the way mental patients should be treated. What he saw as a soaring suicide rate was *symbolically* important, if not statistically valid. Moreover, he seems to acknowledge that central to Barton's new policies and administration was a breaking of old patterns of silence and silencing.

Cross-referencing sources is a time-honoured technique. What I also discovered, however, is how apparent silences are not always silences at all, *once you learn to decode them*. Looking through the management committee minutes for the 1950s I did not see anything I took as unusual, for instance, in the appointment of a neuro-surgeon in 1949 and the subsequent performance of a number of leucotomies from then until 1956. In most British psychiatric hospitals at this time leucotomies were flavour of the month. After 1956 I found no further records of leucotomies performed. This, too, seemed to correspond to wider national trends, although it could also indicate that the operations were no longer being *recorded*. In the Medical Superintendent's reports to the management committee I took little notice of an entry for 17 December 1958: 'On 1st December I received from the Senior Administrative Medical Officer of the Regional Hospital Board a letter concerning neurosurgical treatment and cranial operations, and indicating a decision which I understand has been conveyed to the Hospital Secretary.' I would not have regarded this as of any particular significance had not Dr Barton annotated that entry to this effect:

Dr Sherwood had operated on a number of patients, implanting an indwelling catheter leading to the third intracranial ventricle. The exterior end of the catheter was sealed by a rubber catheter through which Sherwood had been injecting neurotropic drugs. He reported these experiments and results in medical journals. It was a non-ethical thing to do . . .

I re-examined the committee minutes and Medical Superintendent's reports. In the former I discovered that from Sherwood's appointment in April 1949 reports focus on his *leucotomy* operations: between 1949 and 1955 he carried out 267 leucotomies.[15] Intertwined with these reports, however, is mention of Sherwood's – unspecified – research work and requests for funding, especially for an electroencephalograph, which he had installed in 1953. The sentence that follows the reported number of leucotomies performed in 1953 states: 'Intraventricular injections, 82 in all, were given to 10 patients.' In 1954, 222 were given (there is no record of how many patients received them); in 1955 there were 76 intraventricular injections, and in 1956, 224. Had I not been tipped off by Dr Barton, I think I would have assumed these 'injections' were simply part of the leucotomy operations. I reconsidered some early interviews with nurses to see if others discussed this. Another male nurse who started work in the late 1940s said:

> Leucotomies. Yes. Oh yes. It was the worst job you could ever have. I used to work in the operating theatre with a Dr Sherwood, and you'd got to hold this sucker, and you'd got to hold it that close to the brain, and you weren't allowed to touch it while he was doing . . . oh, and you were only there a few minutes, but by God, you'd gotta hold it still. So, they used to do leucotomies *and undercuts and all various things.* (My emphasis)

If I had not been looking specifically for this information, I doubt that I would have attributed much, if any, significance to 'undercuts and all various things', but now this seemed to manifest a coded awareness of not just the leucotomies, but the intraventricular injections, although it was clearly *associated* with the leucotomies and Sherwood's work generally. This also seems to be how the accounts of the management committee viewed them. A similar association was found in this account by the older nurse who began work in the 1930s:

> As time went on, we had all this build-the-patients-up-a-bit and then a couple of different doctors came with different ideas altogether. They come from America, you know. One was Mr – he had a German name – but we used to call him Mr Sherwood. He was a surgeon – and he started off the leucotomies. Well, we used to have certain patients for that, you know, some used to have it both sides and some of them one

in the centre, you know. . . . Well he come here and – I don't like to say this, but – you've never seen – that didn't do the trick it was supposed to do. . . . Well, the thing was you saw more failures – than you did cures, you see. . . . It was a crying shame really – because their personality changed. It did change the personality, but not necessarily for the better. Cause some of them were bad enough as it was – and they got worse. See? And then you had to be careful when they were feeding because then they stuck the table out – just like an animal! They used to pick it up in their hands! . . .

Leucotomy – that was shocking. Cause you know my cousin's wife when she went into the hospital the doctors wanted to give her that and he wouldn't let them do it. . . . He wouldn't sign the paper. . . . 'Don't you touch her!' he said, 'I've seen too many failures – I'd rather take her home and nurse her.' So he did. . . . The Medical Superintendent played hell! . . . What a bloody temper! He said, 'I had a good mind to pull him off his seat and duff him up. . . . And then he got on to me and I told him, I says you haven't seen *anything* in this hospital yet! . . . You come up to Ward 11', he said, 'you got no – you ask my cousin, he's in charge there, you ask him and he'll *show* you some!' And I could. I could have took him round and shown him *animals*! And yet they were – blokes who'd been just a bit run down or overworked and – you know, for ten or twelve years and all that sort of thing – worked on farms. *But they had to experiment on someone!*

The notion of 'experiments' is obviously understood, whether or not this nurse or other staff related it just to leucotomies or to the intraventricular injections. In an interview with Dr Barton, I asked him for further information about Dr Sherwood – although Barton was not appointed as Medical Superintendent until two years after Sherwood had left:

I met him at the Royal Society of Medicine when he gave a very interesting paper on the work he'd been doing. And before one blasts Sherwood – he shouldn't have done it and it was wrong – one must remember that ————, who's very well thought of, was putting needles into the livers of new-born babies without their mothers' permission to get hepatic samples. . . . Jenner had no right to give this dairymaid smallpox and infected – well, to see if she were immune from it, because he thought the cowpox – it worked, fortunately, but I think that sort of experimentation is dreadful, and Sherwood was doing this. Admittedly he chose very deteriorated patients, but he would drill a small – it's not very difficult to do – hole, and then insert a cannula, which is a non-reactive metal, down into the mid-ventricle, and then at the top there'd be a little screw with a rubber pad, you know, a piece of rubber, a rubber diaphragm, and he would inject into that various substances to see the reactions. And this came out and there was a huge scandal and the *News of the World* had it and so forth, and this had made the Regional Boards and the ministers and the Ministry of Health and all that very worried about experimentation ... he was trying to show that there was absorption of these active chemicals through the third ventricle into the cerebro-spinal fluid, and that it was this that changed mood.

I searched for the story in the *News of the World*, but could not find it. I think Barton may have cited the wrong newspaper. What I did find, however, was the following note in the *Lancet*: 'On December 17, 1955 questions were raised in Parliament about leucotomies "alleging that in an unnamed hospital in England experiments were being carried out for sheer experimental purposes on these patients" by a Dr Sherwood.' This had come to the notice of certain people and MPs as a result of reports in the press; I have yet to find these. I also found a report from the Board of Control in May 1957 which clearly showed that, despite questions raised in Parliament, Sherwood did continue his work: 'Some investigation is taking place with regard to the treatment of catatonic schizophrenia by intra ventricular injections of Cholinesterase and synthetic endocrines with encouraging results.' When I interviewed the Hospital Secretary, who started work a year before Sherwood left, he had no recollection of any press reports (which would have been prior to his coming) but gave information that nobody else had so far mentioned:

Do you remember Dr Sherwood?
I do. What are you going to ask me about him?
Well, I've heard quite a bit about him. I know he was doing research on patients, for instance.
Cutting brains open, yes.
Do you remember, at the time, was anybody on the staff uneasy about what he was doing?
Eventually Dr Duncan (the Medical Superintendent). You see, eventually, you see, he'd encouraged his coming. ... He'd encouraged his coming because a friend of his at the London Hospital had recommended him, was a doctor. ... He was a German, of course, his name was Schoenberg, as you probably know, and he experimented on these patients, and eventually one died, and the coroner was very critical, and Duncan decided that was the end. ... As far as I know, it got no publicity, not from this end.
What was he like as a person?
A charmer. I should think in his forties. ... I don't know that he was popular with his medical colleagues so much, but some, I think, regarded him as an innovator. But I think there was suspicion from the chief doctors on the Board, the Hospital Board, you know, Regional Board, got worried about him.

57

It was kept quiet locally?
Well, yes. Mental hospitals on the whole were a bit isolated, you know, except all the local people that worked there – and there were a lot, of course. But – you see, they were doing leucotomies in places all over the country, so – it was reckoned that he – he was experimenting – but this patient who died caused a lot of trouble [sic!]. I can't remember who was the coroner. But that's what happened, and so Duncan asked the Board to – cancel his contract . . .

Nobody so far had mentioned the death. I can find no record of it in the Medical Superintendent's reports for that time. Though the nursing staff obviously knew some form of experimentation was going on, they seemed to confuse the leucotomies with the intraventricular injections; perhaps this was deliberately encouraged. Neither of them had mentioned a death associated with the experiments, though there are deaths recorded to do with the leucotomies. I thought the student nurse who had given me the account of being beaten up might have a clearer recollection, or be prepared to be more open about the issue:

Leucotomies were the vogue at the time. But of course these faded out when the – what we used to call the chemical leucotomies came in, the Largactils and things like this which were better because they were adjustable. Cause once you'd been Attila the Hun with the leucotome you couldn't put it right afterwards. I know it sounds a bit crude, but that is roughly how they were doing it. . . . Sherwood was a chap with a beard. He had a beard and he would come in wafting – an all very powerful man. I knew what he did was to put these cannulas, intraventricular cannulas in – here – and that was quite a few patients – I couldn't hazard a guess at the numbers really – there wasn't *vast* numbers. I can remember one. . . . I can remember going down with him when he was just injected through this cannula. Cause Sherwood had to be there. He cut up a bit violent in the ward with other patients and was just escorted down and injected. I don't know *what* was injected what mixtures he was using. . . . He came back on a trolley and we left him there. Later he was a bit subdued, but it didn't make any difference to him after, he just carried on. . .

I knew that there was some thought around – that this – may not be an acceptable form of treatment. So. Personally I can remember on the odd occasions I went down with patients – I don't remember them being asked if it was all right with them! . . . I mean it was somewhat taken for granted that they would have this treatment. Nowadays, even today, staff tend to forget the consent form sheet should be signed here and filled in beforehand and explained. But I don't remember seeing any consent forms in hospital around in those days. . . . I don't think permission was asked, frankly. . . . Sherwood suddenly departed

and nobody ever took up the work afterwards. I don't think he ever
came back and took his cannulas out! I think some poor chaps and
ladies were going round and had got these cannulas still in. I don't
know . . .
Somebody said there was a death.
Probably. But it would be quite possible in a society or establishment
of this size for that sort of thing to happen. I would imagine that
things could have easily been kept quiet.

This nurse again seems to be able to admit much more about what was really
going on than the other two, both of whom stayed at the hospital until their
retirement. He really had very precise knowledge about the technique and
indeed the ethical dimension to its practice. What he *didn't* know about, and
what nobody else has mentioned, is that there had been a death.

The Hospital Secretary was in a powerful position and controlled information between the Medical Superintendent, the management committee, various subcommittees, the regional boards and the wider community. It would
seem that he was able to silence crucial information quite effectively at this
level. Had he not admitted to this death years later, I think there would have
been a total silence as to exactly why Sherwood left and under what circumstances. Even Barton did not have this information and assumed Sherwood's
departure had been a result of the media scandal, which in his memory had
presumably elided with the *earlier* scandal and the question in Parliament in
1955. Dr Duncan, of course, must have known. The Medical Superintendent
had virtually total *de jure* authority over the hospital, yet this was ultimately
dependent on the management committee, who were appointed by the
regional board. The Hospital Secretary admitted to me that he was able to
exert some influence over whom the regional board appointed to the
management committee, and that tension existed between the committee
and the Medical Superintendent:

My first day . . . was amusing. There was a Chairman . . . and he came to
see me in the morning and he said, 'Now look' – he'd just been to some
conference, some chairman/management committee and he'd picked
up all the bright ideas – and 'Look,' he said, 'we've appointed you as
secretary *to the committee*. You're not secretary to Dr Duncan.' I said,
'Oh.' As I said, my predecessor was a dear old man who didn't, never
opened his mouth, you know. 'And', he said, 'you're responsible to us
and we want to see some changes'. . . . So he said, 'Now be careful of
Dr Duncan,' he said, 'and don't get under his influence, and don't just
be his yes-man. We want you to be our independent officer.' So I said,
'Thank you. Thank you.' That afternoon, Dr Duncan came in and he
said, 'Well, how are you getting on?' And he said, 'Can I give you a word
of advice?' He says, 'I saw the Chairman in this place. Don't trust him,'
he said, 'he's a most untrustworthy man.'

Just as both the Chief Male Nurse and the charge nurse were able to enforce silence on those below them, so too was the Hospital Secretary. In a position between the management committee and the Medical Superintendent, his power would seem to have been considerable.

To speak
To speak of sorrow
works upon it
      moves it from its
crouched place barring
the way to and from the soul's hall —

Out in the light it
shows clear, whether
shrunken or known as
a giant wrath —
      discrete
at least, where before

its great shadow joined
the walls and roof and seemed
to uphold the hall like a beam.

          Denise Levertov[16]

One of the wards that has shut its door to patients is full of rows of cardboard boxes. The boxes are regimented like soldiers, silent as graves, rows and rows of them, in the dusty and deserted ward. *Shut up.* They contain patients' case-notes. Thousands of them. The silence is deafening. Many of them now are dead. Some have been rehabilitated into the community. Some, no doubt, are still living in cardboard boxes, but cardboard boxes under bridges and in shop doorways.

Patient Number 21122[17] was admitted in 1943 at the age of twenty-three. She was certified; the certificate said, 'She lies in bed gazing vacantly before her. She would not answer simple questions or carry out simple commands. She has on previous occasions in the past fortnight displayed generalised rigidity. On occasions she has had lucid moments when she volunteers the information "The Mother of God has put her in a trance."' The physician's report says she is sparsely nourished and her abdomen is not relaxed. Each year a medical report reiterates 'she is in a state of catatonic stupor. She is mute.' Monthly reports repeat 'no change', 'little change', 'mute'. She was diagnosed as catatonic schizophrenic.

A social worker spoke to her father and found the living room in their cottage clean, but 'rather muddled and airless with rather a lot of flies'. The father told the social worker his daughter was a happy baby, quite normal, a splendid scholar, but she left school at fourteen to look after her father and three brothers after her mother died. Apparently she did not pick up with any boys on the street, was religious, and was always in good health. One summer evening after supper she suddenly 'turned funny' and did not know anyone. She went stiff and mute and the father could not think of anything in particular that precipitated the attack.

In 1950 she had a bilateral frontal leucotomy. Later she was put on Largactil. Still there was little change noted. She remained mute. In 1970 she developed frequent vomiting over four months and the neurologist concluded this was due to scar tissue from the leucotomy (I wonder if she had been one of Sherwood's guinea pigs for intraventricular injections). Nobody had visited her since 1945. She died in the early 1980s. A short time after her death a brother came and explained that she had been raped prior to admission. I do not know by whom. After she was certified the family pretended she had never existed.

Silences are everywhere. They are woven into the very fabric of the hospital. Silence has long shadowed madness, and though the shadow may at times grow shorter, even disappear momentarily, it still can grow again. Silences, when it is possible to explore some of them retrospectively, can reveal an enormous amount about the more hidden but often central, aspects of an institution's (and indeed an individual's) history, as has been at least partly possible with Dr Sherwood. Tracing silences and clues, like a sleuth, begins to reveal interesting patterns of power and control. Cross-referencing, dialoguing between written sources and respondents can be illuminating, exciting, moving. The tragedy is that so many silences can never be accessed, and in cases such as the woman cited above, the words and the explanation that could have saved so much come too late. The knowledge that such things happened, of course, is itself important, providing it, too, is not relegated to silence.

NOTES

1 Luisa Passerini, 'Memory', *History Workshop Journal*, no. 15 (Spring 1983), p. 196.
2 Elizabeth Tonkin, *Narrating our Pasts: The Social Construction of Oral History* (Cambridge: Cambridge University Press, 1992), p. 124.
3 Michel Foucault, *Discipline and Punish* (Harmondsworth: Penguin, 1975); Stephen Knight, *The Brotherhood* (HarperCollins, 1983).
4 Passerini, 'Memory'.
5 Women writers have been particularly vulnerable to silencing, as Tillie Olsen pointed out in *Silences* (London: Virago, 1980).
6 Passerini, 'Memory'.
7 Tonkin, *Narrating our Pasts*, p. 116.
8 Alessandro Portelli, 'The peculiarities of oral history', *History Workshop Journal*, no. 12 (Autumn 1981).
9 From poem 1129 in *The Complete Poems of Emily Dickinson*, ed. T. H. Johnson (London: Faber, 1970).
10 This certainly does not apply to works such as those by Digby on the York Retreat

or Mackenzie on Ticehurst, see Anne Digby, *Madness, Morality and Medicine: A Study of the York Retreat 1796–1914* (Cambridge: Cambridge University Press, 1985); Charlotte Mackenzie, *Psychiatry for the Rich: A History of Ticehurst Private Asylum, 1792–1917* (London: Routledge, 1992).

11 See, for instance, Andrew Scull, *Museums of Madness* (London: Allen Lane, 1979). Various respondents, including the Medical Superintendent, have indicated that this often happened and that certification of an 'unwanted' spouse or relative was very easy to obtain. One man who worked as an electrician said that wives of Freemasons were often 'dumped' in the private ward. The Medical Superintendent until 1959 was high up in the Masonic order.

12 Jodelet found in her study that these fears continued quite markedly when patients were rehabilitated in the 'community', living as lodgers in other people's homes, see Denise Jodelet, *Madness and Social Representation* (Brighton: Harvester Wheatsheaf, 1991).

13 Portelli, 'The peculiarities of oral history', p. 103.

14 Central to Barton's policy at the time was to rehabilitate as many patients as possible into the wider community while admitting larger numbers for short-term stays in hospital.

15 It is interesting to note that there was a marked imbalance in the sex ratio of those he operated on. In 1949 all 52 leucotomies were on women. In 1950 he carried out leucotomies on 3 men and 42 women (3 of whom died). In 1951, 6 men and 34 women. Although there was a greater ratio of women to men in the hospital overall, it was nothing like this (it generally stood at slightly less than a third more of women). For leucotomies between 1950 and 1952 the ratio of women to men was 128:9.

16 From *Denise Levertov: Selected Poems* (Newcastle-upon-Tyne: Bloodaxe, 1986).

17 This is not her real identifying number.

4

A BRAZILIAN WORKER'S AUTOBIOGRAPHY IN AN UNEXPECTED FORM

Interweaving the Interview and the Novel

José Sérgio Leite Lopes and Rosilene Alvim

During our fieldwork twenty years ago in Paulista, a textile company town in the Brazilian North East, Adauto Machado, a worker in the factory, gave us, one year after we had a long interview with him, a remarkable auto-biographical text, in the form of a novel.[1] It is a written testimony of the experience of survival amidst social change. This document, written by hand in about fifty pages of a large school notebook, with the title 'The miserable ones', was in fact one of the few documents written by the workers themselves which we were able to collect.[2]

In his article 'Le Témoignage' Michel Pollak, analysing the experience of women in concentration camps in Nazi Germany, shows the strategic value of oral history interviews, among other possible sources of information. These interviews can give access for example to the viewpoints of those women who were imprisoned for non-political reasons, or to the camp's daily routine. The written autobiographical accounts, such as novels or written testimonies, were by contrast all biased towards the experiences of those who were familiar with writing through a long schooling, usually leading on to a period at university. Moreover, these writings were usually by authors who had strong political or ethnic motivations, and who therefore attracted publishers. To overcome this textual and editorial filtering which tied his theme to its more political and already visible dimensions, Pollak skipped over the relatively numerous written testimonies, and instead emphasized in-depth interviewing and the stimulation of oral testimonies in order to gain access to the other sectors of the population who had also suffered the concentration camp experience.[3] But although written accounts of the experiences of uneducated manual workers are unusual, where they exist they can bring up other dimensions of daily life, described in the language of those workers who chose to venture into the realm of written expression. Thus, though it is certainly necessary to emphasize interviewing and the making of oral histories, given the almost absolute dominance of oral communication among Brazilian working classes, we should not neglect those few autobiographical accounts which workers have written. Adauto Machado's initiative, surprising us with a written text inspired and occasioned by our research with his own social group, gave us the rare opportunity to follow closely the context and the making of this unusual form of written communication.[4]

* * *

A few words about the structure of the text. Adauto was in no way a naive writer. What were the sources of his art? He drew little, it would seem, from classic literature, and had not even heard of the famous novel by Victor Hugo which shared the same title as his own. It seems more possible that he gained something from his participation in the theatre activities of the Young Catholic Workers' League in his youth in the 1950s. But it is clear that his main debt, including the use of dialogue, comes from the oral culture of the North East. Here the form of verbal duelling is common in ordinary oral storytelling, and the *cordel* booklet provided, as we shall see, a link between oral and written genres.

Adauto's narrative certainly uses some skilful rhetorical tools. On the one hand, he presents three versions of the same story – as seen by three characters, whose relationships the reader discovers in the course of the text – a story that gets richer as the text goes on. On the other hand, he makes general comments, either through inversions of official history, or through fables in which the characters of his story have an exemplary role. Besides that, his narrative is very entertaining, presenting the story through little riddles and surprises. The title of the first part is 'The anonymous heroes', and here the author writes about 'active heroes' and 'passive heroes'. The former are the official heroes, the models of which are the military heroes, 'those that you always know about, such as a man that has killed the greatest number of human beings in some war, a national hero'.[5] The latter, on the contrary, are 'those which you never know about, people that you probably never heard of, and you know why? Because there is no publicity for their heroic feats.' The terms he uses are very general, but they are appropriate to describe the characters he is going to introduce. So when he speaks of the 'passive heroes' – 'I am speaking of common men, men that die little by little all along their lives, losing a little bit of life each day so others can have better conditions for living' – he is speaking of the character José Farias, the same character that also personifies the other image used by Adauto in the second part of his account: 'The minimum wage man and the north-eastern donkey'.

In this second part, Adauto brings up images which are usual in the oral tradition of north-eastern *cordel* literature, a literary genre with which he was especially familiar. The north-eastern Brazilian *cordel* booklets are a continuing form of literature which go back to a secular European tradition – particularly Spanish and Portuguese – of ballads and chapbooks. Eric Hobsbawm has discussed the use of *cordel* among Andalusian peasants who were linked to the anarchist movement at the beginning of this century in his classic *Primitive Rebels*. The English equivalent was the broadsheet, a single sheet rather than a booklet; and both typically combined the text with dramatic woodcuts. But its particular Brazilian characteristics were closely linked to its principal means of performance, which was not through silent reading but generally by reading out aloud to groups of peasants and labourers in the Brazilian North East during the last century. The audiences reached could thus be very large, for some of the booklets sold more than a hundred thousand copies each. This Brazilian 'invention of tradition' offers an interesting record both of major historical events and also of ordinary daily life. They are mostly written in poetic form, many of them using a duel between two opposing forces – men, animals, saints – as the means of telling the story.[6]

Adauto himself was also sometimes a writer of *cordel*. At about the same time that he wrote his autobiographical novel he wrote a *cordel* booklet for the Catholic Workers' Action (ACO) movement in Recife in 1977. Although not himself an activist, he was persuaded by militants he knew to write a booklet on the theme of inflation and the high cost of living for Brazilian working people, to be used in the organization's popular education programmes. Its title was 'A briga de Ze do Brejo e Pedro Velho por causa da Pechincha' (The fight between Joe Fields and Old Peter because of haggling). It portrays a verbal duel between a peasant who is sceptical about the exhortations from the economic authorities encouraging people to haggle and bargain and so keep down inflation, and a man who drowns his continuous delusions about the results of haggling in drunkenness.

Adauto is thus drawing on a familiar kind of imagery when in his autobiographical novel he describes the donkey as part of the peasant's family in the *sertão*.[7] The donkey is presented as an extreme case of exploitation: having spent all his life doing the hardest work, the donkey is killed when it gets old, so that men can eat its flesh. It is the idea of sacrifice itself that permits comparison.

Besides the image of the donkey, Adauto uses two other images to describe 'the minimum wage man'. The first one has to do with sand: 'The minimum wage man is a hero, I say, and I give him all my respect. Because in fact he is a man who has no right to live, a man who has no right to send his kids to school, has not the right to eat, nor dress; his life is like a pile of sand that the wind blows and disappears as if by magic.'

The other image is that of a bottle for intravenous drip connected to a sick person in the hospital: 'An intravenous drip that drains the bottle slowly, drop by drop, until all its contents are gone; and when the bottle is empty, it is thrown into the rubbish bin, while at the same time the sick person has become a lot stronger.'

The idea of unselfish giving and emptying oneself on behalf of others takes full shape, but also acquires a more desperate tone, when the author shows the reproduction of the condition of the 'minimum wage man' through his children, because of their exclusion from school. In this point, Adauto reproduces a typical feature of workers' written autobiographical accounts throughout the world – the focus on the importance of school and the value of learning in adverse conditions.[8]

If on the one hand the title of the second part of the text is a comparative allusion to the burden carried by the *anonymous hero* typical of his narrative – 'the minimum wage man and the north-eastern donkey' – on the other hand, the title of the third part keeps the fable mood so as to reiterate the theme of sacrifice. 'The lion's hunt', this third heading in the text, is an allusion to the subordinate and oppressive situation of the minimum wage worker. Even though this worker is not directly represented by the lion's prey, his situation is compared to the action of the little animal that waits for the moment when the lion is full and forgoes the remnants from the chase so he can have access to the 'leftovers of the lion's meal' (*sobejo do leão*): 'That is precisely the name of the minimum wage, the leftovers of the lion's meal.'[9] It is by the end of this part of the text, when he likens the image of the animal eaten by the lion and the donkey eaten by men, that the author comes back to the discussion about the minimum wage man's destiny, with a bit of irony: 'We think that the north-eastern donkey and the minimum wage man have a lot in common, with only a small difference: they still don't eat men when they get old and tired. But who can tell the future? Brazil moves ahead!'

* * *

These general reflections take a concrete form in the character José Farias – 'a man that, from the day he was born, was always a victim, victim of the circumstances; victim of poverty, and then victim of society itself'. At this point, in the title of the fourth part, 'José Farias', Adauto starts presenting the plot of his novel to us. This character was born in 1934 in the municipality of Nazaré da Mata, whose economy was in the grip of the large sugar cane plantations. Adauto emphasizes that José Farias, the son of poor worker-peasants, had very little milk to drink when he was a child, and started working when he was seven years old, when his father made him a small hoe so he could start helping with the family's toil. When he was fifteen, José was the oldest of eight brothers and sisters, and was his father's main helper in his activities as small farmer and market seller in the town of Carpina, where the family was now living. Besides helping the father in the family's agricultural work and doing occasional jobs as a wage worker, he also sold fruits and vegetables in the streets. Notwithstanding the large size of the family, moving into the new town made life a little better, and to demonstrate this the author emphasizes that José was able to attend a night school, where he was striving to finish the second grade. But then his father died in a road accident while going by bus to Recife to sell some farm products in a free market. From that moment on, José and his mother had to take on themselves all the burden of assuring the family's survival.

At this moment of the account, the author describes an interview of his own with José Farias – which reminds us that it was our interviews which instigated him to produce the text: 'At this moment, we are just getting to Sr José Farias's house, in the city of Olinda, where we expect to continue our talk, which was interrupted a few days ago.' At this point, José Farias describes, in the first person singular, how he worked as a rural wage worker to help his mother and brothers. His mother worked at sewing and got some help from Catholic nuns to keep the children in school. It was the self-exploitation of both José and his mother that made possible, in one way or another, the schooling of the other children, even though these also had to help in the survival efforts of the family, using all of their free time to sell home-made cakes and candies in the streets. The text shows both the sacrifice of the son who became the household's main support and the sacrifice of the widow, and finally shows the result of all this – the schooling of all the children except the oldest son.

After my father died, I felt that everyone depended on me; I was only fifteen, but I was the oldest one, so I put my hoe on my shoulders and went to work the *ticuca*. What is a *ticuca*? It is an amount of land that the man measured and we had to weed it, he had a stick and he measured twelve times that stick's length in a square, and that was a *ticuca*. I was paid fifteen *mil réis* for each *ticuca*.[10] I started to work at seven [in the morning], and many times it was already night when I stopped, and each day when I finished working I got some money. I couldn't go home without that money, because back home all the kids were waiting for me so they could eat. But I felt good inside me, I felt very happy when I went back home bringing with me corn flour, manioc flour and pieces of *jambiras* [a kind of dried salted beef]. My brothers and sisters were very happy when I got home, sometimes I only got in at eight o'clock at night and then my mother would still go and make that tasty *cuscuz* for dinner.

But soon my mother began to sew; she bought a sewing machine on an instalment plan. The machine had to be powered by hand, because it didn't have the pedals that make it possible to move it with the feet. My mother started working at the machine at five in the morning, and sometimes she kept on going until ten at night. Thanks to that, we were able to eat a little better and my younger brothers and sisters were able to go to school, they all learned writing, even the one that attended school for the least time was able to finish junior high school; the only one that doesn't know how to read is me, I can hardly write my name.

In 1955, six years after his father's death, his mother decided to move with the whole family to Paulista, a textile company town, where she had a sister. This is a typical trajectory of many 'widow's families' that moved to this company town, making use of the working capacity of those children who were old enough to work in the factory. In the 1930s and 1940s the factory used to send out recruiting agents to search for large peasant families who might see in the jobs they offered a solution for their hardships – and the extreme cases were the 'widow's families' like José's. But in 1955 the factory was not expanding any more, the turnover rate of the labour force was very high, and dismissals were more numerous than admissions. José ended up engaged in less stable jobs outside the factory, expecting that his brothers would little by little be admitted to work in the factory. At the age of twenty-one, and as the main support of his family, he was ready to accept any job opportunity that happened to show up, and for a male worker it was mainly the heavy (*pesados*) jobs which were at hand.

In 1957 his mother received a marriage proposal from a company employee who worked in the housing sector of the company town, a widower twenty-two years older than herself. The household's level of subsistence rose with the help of this man; but on the other hand, José's role as a substitute for his father was diminished, and he felt that as a loss. In fact, destiny had made José a substitute for his father, first as a peasant, then as an unqualified manual worker, diverted into a position which was more typical of men a generation older than himself in the company town – the position of a peasant, illiterate, male head of family, working in the company's heaviest and least stable jobs. With his mother's marriage, the symbolic value of his self-exploitation in unstable jobs, for the benefit of the household's subsistence, was greatly reduced. Two years after his mother's marriage José, who was then already employed as a worker in the factory, also got married.

During the early years of his marriage, José was relatively well-off, for his wage corresponded approximately to the minimum wage, but with the birth of children it became inadequate. In the 1960s the factory dismissed hundreds of workers, and José, as an unqualified worker (*servente*) was fired. He then started working on many odd jobs in Recife, but in 1970 he had an accident which left him in the situation of an invalid and forced an early retirement. At that time he had seven children, and began trying to complement his very small pension – less than a minimum wage – with occasional light jobs (*trabalhos leves*). His older children helped him in these jobs and so they in turn ended up not going to school at all.

José's history is told in the first person by Adauto, as if he were transcribing the words of a person being interviewed. He ends the part of his novel devoted to José Farias by yielding the floor to his character-as-interviewee:

'My children were never in school, the oldest girl is going to be eighteen and she still doesn't know how to write her name . . . I was born amidst misery, I have lived and I still live amidst misery, so naturally I am a miserable man.' The increasingly emotional mood of the account, where both the *informant* and the *interviewer* start crying after these last words, reaches its climax when the author at last reveals that José is his brother, and that the text is dedicated to him.

*　　*　　*

After an interlude, with the title 'Hunger is a universal plague', where Adauto offers some general thoughts about social injustice, about the concentration of landed property in the hands of a few, and about the lack of attention of the government to the peasants, small farmers and rural workers, he presents his second character: 'The woman who didn't surrender'. Once again the account takes the form of an interview carried out by the author, narrated in the first person. Dona Antônia was born in a sugar plantation (*engenho*), called Engenho Boa Fé, seen retrospectively as an isolated place. Her father was a *morador* (tenant) quite well situated in the plantation's hierarchy:

> We lived completely apart from the world. When a stranger happened to show up, me and my brothers ran and hid ourselves . . . In our house we had no comforts, but everyone always had a full stomach. When I was seven, I went to school and learned to read and write. From ten years of age, I used to work with a hoe like an adult. My father loved me very much. I often weeded the land with him and I finished my part before he did. Then I laughed and teased him, and he got bashful, but after that he would carry me on his shoulders. It was an innocent happiness. We didn't know anything better.

When she was twenty years old, she lived with her family in a hamlet in the municipality of Nazaré, where they had moved to when they left the *engenho*. There she married a man who had worked in large cities but never in the countryside. In 1947 they moved to the town of Carpina, a regional centre north of Recife, where she had a brother. At this time, the work of her husband and of her oldest son resulted in a slightly better level of livelihood, which made it possible for the other children to go to school.

However, when she was thirty-six years old, she lost her husband in a road accident. From then on she had to make a living from her oldest son's work and her own work sewing and washing clothes for other people. By then she had eight children whose ages ranged between fifteen and less than one year. Every day, when the children came home from school (except for the oldest one, who was sacrificing himself by working full-time), they were sent to the streets right away, to sell the produce of their mother's domestic work: manioc cakes, coconut cakes, maize cakes and so on. At this point of the text, we can already guess that the woman is the author's mother, but in this version the story brings up more details about this survival-oriented asceticism, made more rigorous in the case of this 'widow's family'. At one time, the oldest son got sick, and Antônia managed to get a job as a cook in the town's dispensary, which was directed by Catholic nuns. Her son recovered his health in this dispensary, but the nuns then helped her to put three of her other children, two girls and a boy, into a boarding school in Recife.

As the mother tells the story, this was then followed by the flight of the boy from the boarding school to which he had been sent, his disappearance, and then by her trip to Recife to look for him, her pleading with the juvenile court judge, the use of newspaper and radio appeals in attempts to find the boy, three days of unsuccessful searches, and finally his reappearance in Carpina of his own accord, ten days later.

In 1955 Antônia took her family to the large company town of Paulista, where she had a sister. One of her sons, the eldest, started working for the company, while two of the younger girls were put in the boarding school together with their other sister, at the same moment when the older sister was taken back home from the boarding school to help in the household's daily chores. The story shows her making successive strategic moves with her children. When she got married to a sixty-nine-year-old widower, one of the company's employees, she wanted to have a place for all of her daughters at last: for three of them were still in the boarding school, and Antônia wanted to see them all together with her oldest daughter, at home. Of her sons, only the eldest was with her; the second oldest, after a long time living in the city, came back very ill, and subsequently died; another one was conscripted for military service; and a third was living with relatives, in Carpina. With her marriage they would be able to be together with her again, and that made Antônia happy. But after three years of marriage, however, her husband's alcoholism showed itself strongly, and she had to struggle for five years before he finally gave up drinking. 'I have been married for twenty years now,' says Antônia in front of her aged husband, her seven children and twenty-eight grandchildren – so the author tells us, resuming his narrative and offering this new surprise to his readers: that the 'interviews' with his mother ended up in a complete family meeting.

* * *

The last part of the novel, 'Machado', is written as if Adauto were now interviewing himself: for, as one might guess, the time has now come for the author himself to be made into one of the characters of the novel. As in the accounts of the two preceding characters, in which the interview was the form chosen to present the characters' words, the author now yields the floor to himself as a character, speaking in the first person, but this time without explaining how the meeting between the interviewer and the interviewee took place. The account begins when Machado was eight years old, when his father had just died. 'At that time I was a boy who liked to eat earth. I was anaemic, and one of the things I soon learned was to lie. It was a form of personal defence.' Afterwards, he had the opportunity to study in the nun's dispensary and complete his basic studies.

It is not by accident that he describes in full detail the episode of his flight from the boarding school in Recife to which he had been sent by the nuns, at his mother's request: for it illustrates his adroitness. Taken from Carpina to the boarding school by one of the nuns, the first impressions little Machado has about the boarding school, as he sees hundreds of children at recess time, are pretty discouraging:

> There were about a hundred kids, all of them very thin, as if they hadn't seen any food for a long time. As soon as I got there, they ate my toothpaste. I was very surprised: I had never seen anyone eat tooth-paste. So I reasoned that hunger there must be worse than at home, and I thought that if it was so, then I would be lost.

After a few days, and having learned that any attempt at dialogue with the boarding school managers was impossible, Machado plans his flight, based on the principle (related to his own capacity to lie and dissimulate) that 'the cunning man's success is in proportion to his stupid looks.' He got information from the other boys and from the boarding school's employees about the school's location in Recife, for he was entirely ignorant about the city's geography. He also asked some of the boys if they had ever tried to escape, and what the consequences were. Then the author gladly takes several pages of his account to convey to the readers many details of his escape from the boarding school during the night; about how he took a bus to downtown Recife, got some information about the train routes, and took a train to a suburb where he knew that a friend of his mother lived; about how this friend of his mother helped him, and how he got back to his family's town by bus; and about his sudden presentation of himself to his desolate mother (whom he had seen through the window as he furtively approached his house), in such way as to escape any punishment. The narrative works in this case as an exemplary story of his initiation as an independent, shrewd and crafty man (*malandro*).

As to his arrival at the town of Paulista, in his novel Adauto does not explain, as he did in the interviews and informal conversations we had with him, that he started working at the factory when he was fourteen, as an apprentice. But in his text he emphasizes that he was able to attend high school for two years after his mother had married the widower who was an employee of the company. After completing his period of military conscription, Machado stayed on with the army for a few years, quite happy with the opportunity to show his courage in patrols and also with his work breaking in horses and donkeys.

After his marriage to a young girl who belonged to a workers' family from Paulista, and the birth of their first son, he left the army because of the insufficient salary. 'I broke in many donkeys, now I had to break myself in.' He started working in many factories, but he never stayed in any one for too long: a characteristic response of young workers, who are uneasy with accepting all the managerial authoritarianism that comes with factory discipline. Afterwards he worked for three years in a big mill in Recife, which was more in line with a married man's situation. But with the industrial crisis of 1964–5, he was dismissed in 1965. At that time he had three children and lived with his family in the house of his parents-in-law in Paulista. After six months without a job, he starts thinking of emigrating to São Paulo, but his wife and her family are against it. Firmly rooted in Paulista, this family shows the strong identity and 'group charisma'[11] that distinguishes such a workers' group, well established in that textile company town for several generations.

The last part of the novel describes Adauto's second flight, that is, his emigration to São Paulo. A former factory supervisor who had decided to go to São Paulo offered to pay his bus fare to São Paulo. Machado lied to his family saying he had a job offer in a nearby town. During the trip to São Paulo he got into debt because of his food expenses, which were greater than he had expected because the bus broke down. This led to a strong disagreement between him and his friend, so he ended up losing access to the network he was counting on when he reached São Paulo. When he got there, he didn't know where to go, and a policeman took him to the immigrants' shelter, where he was protected from the city's cold winter (its climate is subtropical, but it is at medium-high altitude). There he met a man who offered him work on some rented lands in the state of Paraná, further south. Such meetings in the immigrants' shelter are typical of the adventure narratives of workers throughout the world. A group of men were threatening a girl who was alone in the shelter, and Adauto defended her and even got involved in a fight on her behalf. The girl's brother had gone out to buy cigarettes, and when he came back, he helped to put an end to the fight and was very thankful to Adauto. He invited Adauto to come with them and work in agriculture in southern Brazil. Our author went and stayed there for a few months. He then wrote to his wife's family in Pernambuco, and since the harm from his fleeing to the south was already done, they sent him the address of a relative in São Paulo who could help him get a job.

Finally, having established himself in São Paulo with his wife and children, he worked in many companies and acquired professional skills such as those of a mechanic, carpenter and electrician. But during one winter, one of his daughters died because of lung disease and poor medical services. He ended up having a fight with his boss in the company, who refused to advance him some money to pay for the funeral expenses. This episode makes Adauto think over his life in São Paulo, so he decides to go back to Recife, now with four children (two having been born in São Paulo, including the child who was born and had died in that city).

While Adauto was in São Paulo an industrial centre was established right in Paulista, which is located in greater Recife, and many branches of companies from southern Brazil had just opened new factories. Machado was just the kind of worker they were looking for in these new factories, which were in need of qualified workers. The fact that he had work experience in São Paulo was very important for them. So he went back to the house of his parents-in-law in Paulista and started a new career as a maintenance mechanic in a textile plant just established in town.

It was at this moment that we carried out our series of interviews with him. We were acquainted with him through a friendship network of long-term workers whose relationships went back to their much earlier common participation in the local Young Catholic Workers' League activities in Paulista.[12] However, Adauto mentioned nothing about these activities in his written account, and hardly anything in his interviews. Maybe this was an unconscious way of emphasizing his individual merits in his adventures and, rather than this earlier occupational group, his own ascending trajectory towards a group of more qualified, apparently more stable workers. In this way he is able to end his account at the moment he goes from São Paulo back to Recife, showing his pride in the experience he acquired as a worker. After having paid homage to 'the miserable ones' – his older brother, his mother, and to a certain point even himself – he concludes, confident in his upwardly mobile (until that moment) trajectory as a qualified worker: 'I had no savings, my wealth was on my own shoulders, with those experiences and professions that wouldn't let me go hungry anywhere in the world.'

*   *   *

The unusual characteristics of this written autobiographical narrative can be compared with those of other autobiographies by workers. In fact in Brazil, because of the relatively low level of schooling and literacy, and the restricted spread of habits like writing and silent reading among the working classes, this kind of autobiography is rare. The best-known earlier author in the genre is Carolina Maria de Jesus, a São Paulo slum-dweller who published five books about her life, beginning in 1960. With the resurgence of trade unionism in the late 1970s at the end of the period of military dictatorship more workers' autobiographies began to be published, including some others by north-easterners.[13] It would require detailed comparisons with the English, German, French and Mexican cases to clarify the social and cultural conditions which are needed to stimulate the practice of autobiographical writing by workers.[14]

Adauto Machado's account has several characteristics in common with other Brazilian working-class written autobiographies. The interweaving of oral and written styles of language is a typical feature. Another is the emphasis on the efforts at self-instruction by the author himself and by other persons near to him. This focus on self-instruction efforts appears in the description of the differences between Adauto and his brother José Farias, and also in the description of his mother's early access to writing; it is also emphasized when he describes his mother's efforts to ensure the schooling of her children, and stressed through the mention of the years of supplementary schooling obtained by the main character, who is the author himself. Other traits also typical of this genre are the descriptions of family relationships; the narration of travels and adventures; the stories of adroitness, craftiness, cleverness and courage; the descriptions of encounters with other cultural experiences; and of his desire for individuality in relation to his own social group – as, for example, in his escapes.

Again as in other texts of this genre, the role of religion appears, in the image of the dispensary nuns; and also the need to record threatened social origins, here in the rural areas; the experience of survival and of overcoming hardships related to poverty and migration; and finally the focus on the improvement of living conditions, in spite of all difficulties.[15]

After the moment when his account was completed, Adauto Machado and his fellow workers had to confront yet other difficulties, with the industrial crisis of 1983 and the growth of unemployment in the region's industries. Dismissed from the factory together with many other workers, he had to rearrange his life in order to start informal marketing activities, such as bringing in men's clothes from small towns in the region's hinterland, where there was hand-made, low-cost production, and selling them at the factory gates and in working people's neighbourhoods in the city.

But this is suddenly a different kind of history. It could have allowed Adauto to write an account of this new period in his own life and that of most of the working-class group of which he is part. But if on the one hand this is indeed the world of the present, with its new and unknown challenges, on the other hand Adauto Machado remains still the bearer of the social history of his origins, which he has been able to evaluate, in an effort at self analysis, through creating his written text. The up-to-date character of this text, which ends at the moment of his promising return from São Paulo to Recife bringing with him all his working experience, is thus maintained as a testimony of a period when industrial labour was a more dominant general social perspective and indeed, in some cases, did offer upwardly mobile trajectories. By ending the narrative just before this new period of relatively unstable factory labour after 1983, 'The miserable ones' maintains its value with its focus on the experience of transformation from peasant life to a booming urban and industrial labour life, which was then not yet shaken by the industrial employment difficulties which were to follow in the 1980s and 1990s.

As an autobiographical text itself based on a form of anthropological research using fieldwork, deep interviews and the collection of life histories,[16] the work of Adauto Machado oscillates between testimony and observation, between involvement and withdrawing. Thus, even though he is his own third character in 'The miserable ones', sometimes he positions himself as someone who has overcome that condition and can now be an observer. At the beginning of his text, when he describes the 'anonymous heroes', his own participation as a character is temporarily excluded: 'We are now going to meet *two* anonymous heroes, and through our acquaintance with them we shall be able to give them some of the respect, some of the understanding, some of the affection, which they [his brother and mother] really deserve.'

It is not by chance that the episode of the escape from boarding school when he was a child assumes such significance in the story, appearing in his mother's version, in his own version, and in a way reappearing when he was already an adult, in his flight to São Paulo. The author seems to counterpose his brother's complete sacrifice, and his mother's sacrifice – which will only be compensated at the end of her life – to his own initial sacrifice, which since his childhood he overcomes through cleverness, adroitness and craftiness.

The author thus seems to incarnate something similar to the spirit of characters of *cordel* literature and popular tales such as Pedro Malazartes, with which he would long have been familiar.[17] Pedro Malazartes is a rural worker who perfectly embodies Adauto's saying, 'the cunning man's success is in portion to his stupid looks.' In fact the initial situation of the complex tale of Pedro – which has many variations in its various oral and written forms – has similarities with Adauto's own origins, particularly in the weakness of his parents and his relationship with his eldest brother.

The Pedro Malazartes tale goes something like this. An old couple have two boys, João and Pedro. As they are poor, the boys have to look for work when they are very young. Pedro is described as 'astute, vagrant and artful', attributes that justify his name Malazartes ('bad arts'). The eldest brother, João, goes to work on a *fazenda*, a large farm or plantation. Its owner is 'rich and cunning'. He establishes contracts that are impossible for the workers to fulfil, and so he does not pay them. The contracts are that, first, the employee cannot refuse any type of work, and second, that neither the employer nor the employee can show their anger. If one of these conditions is not fulfilled, the worker – or the boss – loses a piece of his flesh from between his neck and the bottom of his back. This happens to João; after a year of work, he returns home without money and with no skin on his back. Pedro becomes furious, and seeks revenge for his brother. At this point, his adventures begin.

Pedro asks for work from the same farm-owner, and he accepts the same kind of contract. The farmer orders Pedro to work in a cornfield, sending a dog along with him. He is only allowed to stop work when the dog comes back. After half a day's work, Pedro realizes that the dog does not even move, and recognizes that it is a trap. He hits the dog with a stick, and the dog goes home. Pedro can now leave. The farmer becomes angry, but according to the contract he cannot show it. The second day the farmer orders Pedro to *limpar* (to weed or clean) the manioc field. Pedro uproots all the manioc leaving everything 'perfectly clean'. He asks the farmer if he is satisfied, and the farmer, in order not to appear angry and so lose the contract, says 'yes'.

The next day, Pedro's task is to bring in an ox-cart filled with wood that has no knots in it. So Malazartes cuts the entire banana plantation, explaining that banana trees have no knots. Again the farmer does not show his anger. However, after two or three more similar incidents in which he now loses part of his animal stocks, he decides to kill Pedro. He claims that there is a thief hiding near the corral and the two men take up arms, in shifts, to guard the corral. The farmer hopes to kill Pedro and then claim that by accident he mistook him for the thief. The first night, the farmer is guarding the corral and Pedro is supposed to replace him when the first cock crows. But when he hears the cock, Pedro wakes the farmer's wife and tells her that her husband wants her to go to the corral. When she arrives she is shot dead by her husband. Pedro accuses the farmer of being a murderer. The farmer offers to pay Pedro a lot of money to go away. Pedro accepts, and returns home rich.

If it is interesting to understand how Adauto emphasizes some themes in his life story, it is also revealing to consider those which he apparently preferred to ignore. Certainly he did not include in his narrative some facts about which he did talk to us in conversations after our initial interviews – conversations which we wrote down in our field notebooks. These related to his work as an apprentice in the textile factory at Paulista. Thus, although he told us about an episode which shows his daring attitude, when he reacted to his overseer's harshness and was consequently fired, Adauto strangely enough didn't emphasize that episode – which fits with the defence of his honour – either in the interviews or in his text. Maybe the Paulista textile factory is too strongly associated in his mind, on the one hand, with his stepfather's protection, which released him from the need to continue working in the factory and to continue the disputes between the young workers and the overseers; and on the other, in a later moment, with his parents-in-law, his wife's family. These relationships represent a dependency on the family which does not conform to the standard of independence, shrewdness and adroitness which he would like to express in his narrative.

He also omits to describe his recent experience as a specialized worker in the region's factories, the courses which the factory provided in a professional school, his relations with his colleagues and with his subordinates, and his observations about the working milieu. We were able to learn about this recent history through the interviews and because of the interest of both the researchers and Machado as interviewee. But it seems to be too recent and uninteresting a history for it to be included in the plot of the novel about 'the miserable ones' and the overcoming of poverty through labour in the fields, social and spatial migrations – from the rural area to the cities, from the North East to the South and back again – but above all by means of cleverness.

Similarly, his participation in the local Young Catholic Workers' League, especially in theatrical activities, which may have been one of the seeds of his literary interests, was mentioned by those who were his contemporaries in that Catholic association, but not by Adauto himself. It is again as if they did not have any significance for the account of his Pedro-like struggle for survival, in which his success is due to his cleverness more than to the collective activities in which he also participated.

It is equally important to notice, however, that while Adauto's auto-biographical text omits to mention some facts and dimensions which are or were important in his life, and which we know about through interviews and informal conversations, there are other dimensions which were unmentioned in our encounters with Adauto but are strongly described and emphasized in his novel. While his written reflection was inspired by our previous inter-views, he chose to focus on some issues which the interview situation did not help to bring out. By comparing 'The miserable ones' to Adauto's oral testi-monies, we can see how the start of the interview focused on questions related to factory work, so that the interviews end up dealing only with the period starting with his conscription for military service. The richness of content and the fluency of these interviews left little time for asking more questions about the period previous to his arrival at the company town, which was the social and spatial unit central to our research. The interviews covered Adauto's initial period of work in Recife, then his trip to São Paulo and his working experience in the South, and finally his more recent experi-ence as a qualified worker in Recife and Paulista, after the return from São Paulo. Adauto's initiative in writing his autobiographical novel gave us a rich description of his childhood and youth, through a work of socio-analysis which included himself and his more significant relatives: his mother and his older brother, who was his father's substitute.

One might think that Adauto's reason for writing lies in a socially con-structed propensity to work reflexively on one's past experience and social origins. Through Adauto's literary work, the complex social determinations of his relation with the social history of the family from which he came are outlined. The need to explain and understand the social logic of peasant and rural worker life – with its manifold strategies in the context of a small town – based on an experience as industrial worker and migrant to the large cities, the compulsive efforts to explain his differences from his older brother, emphasizing his own position as a younger brother, too weak for agricultural work – and, later on, for heavy industrial or urban work – that made possible his longer schooling: all these singularities that make him move away, or want to move away, from the social group from which he came impel him to search for lonely reflection facing the notebooks, and to find in written language a means of working symbolically on the past.[18]

Adauto Machado's autobiography is thus of threefold interest. First, it conveys unique information about the life of a worker and how he interprets it in relation to his own self-identity. Second, it allows us to look at the socially constructed context which enables a worker to reflect in a written literary form on his own past experiences and social origins, and to distinguish some of the written and oral genres on which such a worker-writer could draw, in this case ranging from modern anthropological fieldwork interviews to the longstanding traditions of oral storytelling and the *cordel* booklets of the Brazilian North East. Lastly, it offers a model which could also be a liberating instrument for self-knowledge for other working-class individuals, even when, as is still the case in Brazil, they belong to social classes which have historically deep-rooted and severe difficulties with both schooling and writing.

NOTES

1 The fieldwork was carried out in the town of Paulista, which is today part of greater Recife. Our first stay in the area was in 1976, and our first interview took place then. The manuscript was given to us in 1977, during our second trip to the area. Many stays followed in the 1980s. This fieldwork contributed to two monographs about the same workers' group: an ethnography and history of workers' family life, Rosilene Alvim, *Constituição da família e trabalho industrial* (Family formation and industrial work), (Rio de Janeiro: Museu Nacional, 1985); and a study of the making of the specific mode of domination in a textile workers' village, J. Sérgio Leite Lopes, *A tecelagem do conflito de classes na cidade das chaminés* (The weaving of class conflict in chimney city) (São Paulo/Brasília, 1988). See also Rosilene Alvim and J. Sérgio Leite Lopes, 'Familles ouvrières, familles d'ouvrières', *Actes de la recherche en sciences sociales* 84 (1990): 78–84; and 'L'Usine et la véranda: théâtralisation de la domination industrielle', *Études rurales* 131–2 (1993): 39–56.

2 Among these few documents there were the minutes of workers' union meetings and assemblies, other union documents, and documents from the local branches of JOC (Juventude Operária Católica, the Young Catholic Workers' League) and ACO (Ação Católica Operária, Catholic Workers' Action). We also obtained a book of chronicles and remembrances of local life, self-published by an author who was a municipal clerk married to a former company worker (see note 13).

3 Michel Pollak, 'Le Témoignage', *Actes de la recherche en sciences sociales* 62–3 (June 1986); and from the same author, *L'Expérience concentrationnaire* (Paris, 1990).

4 The relation between written evidence stimulated by research initiatives that involve the making of interviews, on the one hand, and oral evidence, on the other, is discussed by Paul Thompson in his editor's introduction to *Our Common History: The Transformation of Europe* (London, 1982), pp. 14–15. He also mentions adult teaching experiences in England that stimulated the writing of autobiographies through the practice of oral history, as in the case of the collection of booklets from London called *Our Lives*: see Paul Thompson, *Voice of the Past: Oral History* (Oxford, 1988), p. 172.

5 He includes in this category even 'subversive' heroes, such as Tiradentes, who were taken up later on as national heroes.

6 For more information on Brazilian *cordel* literature, see A. A. Arantes, *O Trabalho e a Fala: estudo antropológico sobre os folhetos de cordel* (São Paulo/Campinas, 1982) (from his PhD dissertation 'Sociological aspects of *folhetos* literature in Northeast Brazil', Cambridge, 1978); and Candace Slater, *A vida no Barbante: a literatura de cordel no Brasil* (Rio de Janeiro, 1984). For brief discussions in English, see Eric J. Hobsbawm, *Primitive Rebels: Studies in Archaic Forms of Social Movement in the Nineteenth and Twentieth Centuries* (Manchester, 1959); and William Rowe and Vivian Schelling, *Memory and Modernity: Popular Culture in Latin America* (London, 1991).

7 *Sertão* is the name given to the Brazilian north-eastern region's hinterland, distinguished by its semi-arid climate and its cattle-raising and sharecropping economy.

8 For the English case, see the collection of workers' autobiographies edited by John Burnett, David Vincent and David Mayall, *The Autobiography of the Working Class: An Annotated, Critical Bibliography* (3 vols, Brighton, 1984).

9 It is interesting to notice that this 'miserable' image of 'the minimum wage man' in this novelesque text has a relation with French sociological discussions about the image of working-class culture as a *repoussoir*, a French word that means something that is repulsive, or also something deteriorated, falsified, something that comes as a worsened imitation of the dominant classes by the working classes. This image can be found in Pierre Bourdieu's text about the 'taste of necessity', defined as a relation of deprivation, see *La Distinction* (Paris, 1979), p. 200; the discussion about this image can be found in C. Grignon and J. C. Passeron, *Le Savant et le Populaire: miserabilisme et populisme en sociologie et en littérature* (Paris, 1989), pp. 115–51; and in Pierre Bourdieu, 'Les usages du peuple', in *Choses dites* (Paris, 1987), pp. 178–84.

10 According to the Brazilian dictionary *Novo Dicionário Aurélio*, *ticuca*, a regional expression from Pernambuco state, has to do with the practice of weeding: 'A round pile of weeds made after hoeing.' In the more relational and less substantialist meaning that our author employs, it is a measure of the amount of work involved in weeding, or hoeing, which is used to calculate the wages by production unit or by task to be paid to the worker.

11 See Norbert Elias and J. L. Scotson, *The Established and the Outsiders: A Sociological Enquiry into Community Problems* (London, 1994), Introduction.

12 About the significance of the Young Catholic Workers' League from the 1930s to the 1960s, in the making of a social network and in the formation of workers' leaders, see Rosilene Alvim and J. Sérgio Leite Lopes, 'Reconversions politiques d'une militance religieuse: la génération jociste dans une cité ouvrière textile du *Nordeste* brésilien', *Biographie et société* 13 jointly with *Pratiques sociales et travail en milieu urbain* 11 (December 1989): 33–54.

13 During the 1970s, and especially with the resurgence of the workers' unions in the late 1970s, many workers' autobiographies were published. One of the first was of the worker Manoel do Ó, called *100 anos de suor e sangue* (Hundred years of sweat and blood) (Petrópolis, 1971), 139 pages, with a foreword by Alceu Amoroso Lima, a Catholic intellectual of wide renown, which was written by a team of ACO educators in Recife on the basis of the oral accounts of this worker on the occasion of his hundredth birthday. This same Catholic publishing house produced two books by Abdias José dos Santos, a worker and union militant from the shipyards of Rio and Niterói, who was also Catholic and of north-eastern origin: *O biscateiro* (Petropolis, 1977), 66 pages, and *O dia-a-dia do operário na indústria* (The daily life of the worker in the factory) (Petropolis, 1978), 130 pages. The worker-priest Ignácio Hernandez wrote about his experiences in the metal-working

industry in the state of Minas Gerais in *Memória operária: cidade industrial – Contagem – Belo Horizonte 1968/1978* (Worker's memory: industrial city – Contagem – Belo Horizonte) (Belo Horizonte, 1979), 160 pages, foreword by Edgar Mata Machado, a Catholic intellectual from Minas Gerais. The writer Roniwalter Jatobá, an ex-worker in the automobile industries in São Paulo, wrote *Crônicas da vida operária* (Chronicles from a worker's life) (São Paulo, 1978), 60 pages, foreword by Fernando de Moraes, a journalist and well-known writer. The slum-dweller Manoel Gomes wrote *As lutas do povo do Borel* (The struggles of the people from Borel) (Rio de Janeiro, 1980), 73 pages, with a foreword by Luis Carlos Prestes, leader of the Brazilian Communist Party. Before this period, with the gradual redemocratization at the end of the military rule, when this kind of publication became more frequent, there are very few autobiographical books written by workers. The most famous earlier example of this genre in Brazil is the book by Carolina Maria de Jesus, a slum-dweller in São Paulo, *Quarto de despejo: diário de uma favelada* (Back room: diary of a slum dweller) (São Paulo, 1960, 4th edn 1995), 174 pages, foreword by Audálio Dantas, the journalist who discovered and edited the manuscripts; there are also translations into other languages. This same author later published four more books. In my research on sugar mill workers in the Brazilian North East (José Sérgio Leite Lopes, *O Vapor do Diabo: o trabalho dos operários do açúcar* (The Devil's Steam: the labour of sugar workers) (Rio de Janeiro, 1976), I found a book by the former sugar mill worker José Martins, *Gente de Usina* (People from the mill) (Recife, 1954); he is a self-taught worker who writes chronicles and picturesque episodes of life in the sugar mills.

14 See Thompson, *Voice of the Past*; Burnett, Vincent and Mayall, *The Autobiography of the Working Class*; Patrick Joyce, *Visions of the People: Industrial England and the Question of Class, 1848–1914* (Cambridge, 1991), chs 8, 11, 12; Hugh Beynon and T. Austin, *Masters and Servants: Class and Patronage in the Making of Labour Organization* (London, 1994), ch. 12; Georges Duveau, *La pensée ouvrière sur l'éducation pendant la seconde république et le second empire* (Paris, 1948); Roger Chartier, 'Revisitando um conceito historiográfico', *Estudos históricos* 16 (1995): 179–92; Werner Plum, *Relatos de operários sobre os primórdios do mundo moderno do trabalho* (Bonn, 1979); Amigos del Museo Nacional de Culturas Populares, *Relatos Obreros Mexicanos* (2 vols, Coyoacán: Museo Nacional de Culturas Populares, 1984): selected texts from a contest of workers' accounts promoted nationally by this museum.

15 See the introduction to workers' autobiographies edited by Burnett, Vincent and Mayall, *Autobiography of the Working Class*.

16 See the comments by Paul Thompson about the different literary genres associated with autobiographies and interviews, in *Voice of the Past*, pp. 243–7.

17 The 'classic' version of the Pedro Malazartes tale is related by the folklorist Câmara Cascudo in his book *Contos tradicionais do Brasil* (Rio de Janeiro, 1967). An anthropological analysis of Pedro Malazartes was made by Roberto Da Matta, 'Pedro Malazartes e os paradoxos da malandragem', in *Carnavais, malandros e heróis: para uma sociologia do dilema brasileiro* (Rio de Janeiro, 1979).

18 This relation between autobiographical texts and even an autobiographical novel and reflection about social origins and relationship to the family one came from also appears clearly among French elementary school teachers of rural origin at the beginning of the century, see the analysis made by Francine Muel-Dreyfus in *Le métier de l'éducateur* (Paris, 1983), ch. 2: 'Trajectoire sociale et roman des origines', about stimulated autobiographical texts and autobiographical novels which were annexed to 4,000 answers to a questionnaire sent by mail in the 1960s to 20,000 elementary school teachers by the historian Jacques Ozouf. See also Jacques Ozouf, *Nous les maîtres d'école; autobiographies d'instituteurs de la Belle Époque* (Paris, 1973) and Jacques Ozouf and Mona Ozouf, *La république des instituteurs* (Paris, 1992).

5

FAMILY FABLES

Chris Mann

I have been using life stories in my present research with young British women. I needed a methodology that would not just seek facts and events, but that would look for the ways in which such narrated facts and events suggest a woman's relationship to the society she lives in, and her current construction of self. This is an approach developed by Chanfrault-Duchet who wished to find ways to access and then analyse material about women's lives, throwing light on how they, more or less consciously, interpret their status in society.[1] Following Chanfrault-Duchet, I view life stories as a cluster of genres in which it is not only the temporal and causal organization of facts and events within a narrative that are significant but also the value judgements that make sense of these experiences. I do not discuss the analysis of such material here. Instead, I concentrate on the process of the collection of life stories. I draw on material from an empirical research project to demonstrate that the context within which life stories are collected may shape different presentations of self; may reveal different, even contradictory, life experiences; may affect the choice of the evaluative terms used to make sense of these experiences; and may even act as a catalyst that initiates the reassessment of a lived life.

My aim was to work with girls on the threshold of adulthood at a time of great social change. As Britain approaches the second millennium young people are growing up in a society where there is a plurality of norms which are recognized as legitimate. In particular, complicated shifts in many family and household structures are affecting social behavioural norms and render concepts of marriage, and social and sexual standards, particularly confusing for young people. This was to be an exercise in contemporary history, tracking the social nature of the self, experienced by some girls, in a Western culture where children are likely to experience a range of beliefs about the nature of the family, and even a variety of family settings, as they pass through childhood. The sensitive nature of the research led to a decision to collect versions of life stories in a programme of increasing intimacy. The girls, aged seventeen to eighteen, were in the final two years of advanced schooling, and many were preparing to move out of the home and into the

81

world. At this educationally crucial and emotionally delicately poised time in their lives, they volunteered to meet me regularly, in small groups, at their schools, to discuss aspects of their lives and family history. Towards the end of the group sessions they wrote an autobiography. Up to nine months later volunteers from the groups took part in individual life history interviews.

This research sought the life stories of its informants. That is, it sought to uncover how they organized, and justified, their life experience within a social setting. It may seem that girls would be insufficiently mature to describe, interpret and set within an evaluative framework their own lives and the dynamics of the family. Certainly young female lives are frequently marginalized or 'voiced over' by more powerful others. One young woman summed up the significance of being a girl asked to tell a life story: 'There's so much to say that I've never been *allowed* or asked to say before, that it's hard to say what the truth is' (my italics). In fact many girls were able to 'explain' their lives with sophistication and great emotional insight. I would suggest that girls, by virtue of being in a position of little power within the family, have in fact a very clear view of the world they inhabit. Perhaps, as psychologist J. B. Miller suggested, 'subordinates . . . know much more about the dominants than vice versa. They have to. They become highly attuned to the dominants, able to predict their reactions of pleasure and displeasure.'[2] The girls' depth of understanding is the more impressive as their lives are not 'remembered in tranquillity' in the calm waters of late maturity but described in the full flood of experience, riding the rapids of tumultuous feelings.

The volatility of youth may well have affected the life story process. No doubt the adolescent struggle for identity has contributed to the multiplicity of ways in which girls organize their life experience; perhaps older informants would have settled upon and 'polished' a consistent storyline to a greater extent. However, as Basso has argued,[3] some conceptual frameworks, or myths, may be intense but transitory, their vitality connected to the collective expectations of a group at a crucial moment in time. She connects such transient myths with imaginative shared projections into a tantalizing future. For instance, as I shall describe, girls drew on their mutual interaction at this pivotal time in their lives to experiment with new ideas centred around the position of women in society. Collecting life stories from young people seeking an identity may allow historians to examine social norms in the making, as the process of 'myth-making' can come under scrutiny.

* * *

At this point, the significance of the mode of story collection must be considered. A life story does not only consist of life experience up to the moment of telling the story: it is also formed by the moment at which the story is told. My research process drew into sharp relief the well-acknowledged differences between narratives elicited by different methods.

It became clear that adolescent girls use language in different ways, for different purposes, in different contexts. For instance, a family 'story' might be presented to a group of peers; it might appear in written work conducted in privacy and in a mood of quiet reflection; or it might develop in the immediacy of the conversational stimulus of an interview. As these stories about families appeared in different forms, the syntax, content, terminology and emphasis varied. Even more crucially, the value judgements that were used to make sense of facts and events – those very judgements that offer hope of understanding a young woman's sense of self and her status in society – were not necessarily consistent between accounts. Time and place, mood and context, and above all interview relationships affected the narrative. The researcher, and other people in the perceived or actual audience, entered into a resonant relationship with the storyteller, forming the chrysalis from which the story unfolded. It is clear that to understand this cluster of genres we have to ask about these relationships. We have to ask not only who is telling the story but who is listening. For 'the ways we tell our stories – the kind of stories we tell – are brought into being within particular power relations and are elicited by different audiences.'[4] Equally, when we examine a life story we must recognize that the 'manner of its telling' is 'as important as what is told'.[5]

I shall now describe the three methods I used in more detail, beginning with the group discussions. I used a life story methodology, in a group setting, to examine girls' representations of family and self as presented within the subculture of adolescence. Group discussions allowed the girls to spark off ideas, and to reflect on experiences, in a dynamic manner, while I held a facilitating role. Specifically the discussions were to explore the collective identities of the group as 'girls', and to identify their shared experience within the family as daughters, sisters, nieces, grandchildren and so on. Dynamics within the group affected the resulting narratives. Life stories express a sense of self but they are also a very important means by which individuals communicate this sense of self and negotiate it with others. In some situations stories are used primarily to claim group membership and to demonstrate a proper understanding of, and allegiance to, the social and moral identity of the group. This search for group identity may suppress alternative understandings of events. As I was to discover, oral life histories in a group context are in fact performances to an audience, involving both presentation of self to the group, and presentation of the group to outsiders.

Mixed groups, or groups of men, frequently need to establish power relations before focused discussions can start. In contrast the girls' first impulse was to seek acceptance in the newly formed group. Their early narratives, characterized by current slang and shared verbal mannerisms, were used as a means to coalesce the group as a unit, touching only glancingly on personal family experience. Once the group had bonded, many of the uniform conversational mannerisms fashionable with these adolescents fell away, although the stronger syntactical patterns of class and locality remained. These linguistic characteristics were much more pronounced in the spontaneous, and often theatrical, stories told to the group than either in the more formal, written life story or the private interview with me. Once they were at ease within the group the girls' narratives became more individual. The storyteller might seek to impress the group with a dramatic performance in which she projects herself as a heroine, or anti-heroine, in the home. The setting of the scene, the pace of delivery, such techniques as humour, exaggeration, acted dialogue, delayed climax and so on, displayed a self-aware narrator consciously 'telling a story' to the giggles and exclamations of a responsive audience:

> It was on a college night and I wanted to go out until early in the morning. Me and dad had a big row and he forbade me to go out and he said, 'You're not going out. I don't care where you go at the weekend and what time you come in but you've got to be home at that time in the week' – which was about twelve or something like that. And so we have this *big row*. And my friend (and she drives us) phones up and I was crying my eyes out and she says, 'What's the matter? What's the matter? I'll see you later.' And I say 'No, I can't come out', and so she came [laughter]. She came round. My bedroom is at the top at the front and she came and she beeped the horn and I changed in my room and I opened the window and I left it ajar so I could get back in [laughter]. I went through to the lounge and they were all sitting round, and also my aunt and uncle were round to try and speak to me [laughter]! I RAN and got in her car and said 'Quick! Go!' [laughter].

A virtuoso performance that dramatizes such flamboyant acts of independence or rebellion might provoke admiration, debunking humour, or mark the beginning of a matching stream of anecdotes.

Other girls sought to draw on the solidarity of the group to share more personal family stories with others who would understand. Frequently an initial nervousness would settle into an intent, rhythmic, almost hypnotic narrative in which the storyteller might apparently lose all sense of self and place and be heard in absorbed silence. Occasionally the narrator would realize that her story had run away with her and use techniques of deflection, for example, apparent loss of memory, or disclaimers of earlier comments, if she felt that she had over-exposed herself. This level of storytelling often touched deep chords, and girls shared experiences of confusion and hurt, frequently the aftermath of family change following divorce or bereavement, in a highly supportive atmosphere.

The collective understanding of the group was also used as a secure base from which to explore, or to consolidate, experience and to experiment with ideas. A girl might call on the group to bear witness to her testimony about others. Idealized portraits of family members, particularly mothers, were offered to the group with protective pride, and generally received without challenge, although alternative versions of 'the ideal' would surface later. In contrast, valued but less emotionally intense relationships, such as those with grandmothers, seemed to allow girls to experiment publicly with evolving value judgements, especially those relating to the status of women within the family and wider society.

Josie: Basically my nan's a slave to my granddad. And she absolutely adores men. She thinks, you know, you should provide them with everything they want. And I'm thinking 'No way!' Like when she comes to our house she gets my dad some toast 'do you want it cutting in half?' 'Yes' 'Do you want it cutting in quarters?' 'Yes'. She really thinks that we are here to slave – to be slaves for men. Like no way! [laughter]
Sarah: [changing tone] But, like – my nan's really brave. 'Cos my grandfather had a really bad stroke and couldn't do anything for years. And all that time she didn't put him in a home. She never went on holiday or anything. She just looked after him. Like my mother kept telling her, and my father as well, everyone kept telling her 'Put him in a home. Live your life.' But she kept saying 'No', and going on about her wedding vows and everything. And she just stayed with it. She never complained which was weird. It makes her sound a bit of a martyr but she made me respect her.
Christine: It's like my nan. My granddad died when my mum was sixteen and my nan had to go out to work. She worked real hard and didn't have a lot of money. But she didn't make my mum stay at home or get a job or whatever. She let her go to college.
Claire: [picking up on the developing group sense of pride in grand-motherly behaviour] My granny went to university – she finished her degree just at the beginning of the Second World War. I think that's really brilliant. She didn't have much of a career 'cos she had a family. My granddad was going off to fight so she got married and then she had children so she was like – a part-time teacher. And I'm not sure if I want to go to university and she's like 'You should go. Do. You'll regret it if you don't.'

Girls also draw on contemporary public theorizing about the family to con-textualize and explain troubling aspects of their own experience as young people. In this spirit of analysis others would feel free to offer alternative ideas and discussion would follow. In the following dialogue, rural working-class girls struggle to come to terms with the concept of a 'normal' family background.

Jane: I knew a girl went off the rails a bit because she had a bad home life.
When you say a bad home life do you mean unhappy or deprived in some sort of way?

Jane: Just weird. A weird household. I know at times it *could* be unhappy but like it didn't conform to what was seen to be normal. It didn't conform to normality. It was a one-parent family [small laugh]. I'm not saying anything about one-parent families [laugh]. But – like – it was very poor – erm – quite a few kids. The mum was always seen as like, 'get as much as you can', type of thing.

Yvonne: When I was at primary school there were a couple of kids there who came from a very poor family. Lived in a council flat and wore sort of second-hand clothes and things. People used to go, 'They smell, they smell, don't go near them. They've got nits, they've got fleas.'

Jess: I knew a girl like that but she was – really nice [small laugh]. And it was basically because her parents had never taught her basic personal hygiene. It was nothing to do with her whatsoever – it really went back to her parents – she'd never been taught anything.

Have any of you felt unfairly judged in that kind of way?

Mandy: Yeah. It happened to me at my primary school. We weren't really *poor* but we weren't well-off – we're like poorer than everyone else 'cos it's just me and my mum – and she was on social security at the time. I got really bullied. But it's rubbish what people say about single parents . . .

As argued earlier, such oral evidence can reveal how new conceptual frameworks are negotiated at a time of social flux. Public and private myths may be developed, or discarded, as a result of sharing a range of linking experiences.

Girls also found ways to discuss volatile family dynamics within a public forum. Some girls drew on family history, 'My mum left school at fifteen but my dad worked and then got an Open University degree. So I've got big clashes. Dad says,"Go to university" and Mum says, "you don't want to do that – go out and see the world!" Aaah! [laughter].' Other girls drew on fate, 'all Dad's side of the family really complain and argue all the time – they just can't help it – it's in the blood', or even astrology:

Me and my dad – We're both Aries. My mum keeps going on about how two Aries in the house together doesn't work out. And she's like – she's a water sign – she's different basically. 'Cos me and Dad both get fired up about things and start saying things we don't mean – leading to something out of our control. We just carry on and on and on until my mum says 'Stop doing that. It's really silly!'

It seemed that overarching explanatory frameworks allowed girls to diffuse the potentially raw experience of some private relationships, distancing the narrative from the self by introducing themes of general interest to the group as a whole.

On other occasions the group sought to present experiences in the family 'at our age' to me, the outsider. Their shared terminology would be re-emphasized, and murmured agreement, adjustment of tone and echo stories would reinforce the group 'position'. This united front would often be characterized by a teasing, high-spirited atmosphere where the admonishing tones of parents are mimicked, their body language mimed and the spoken vocabulary, and unspoken attitudes, of the family as 'oppressor' paraded and mocked. The following is a rapid group response when I questioned a term of approbation that one of the girls had just described as commonly used in her home:

> *Can any of you explain what a 'good nice girl' is actually like?*
> Someone who doesn't start arguments.
> She's really passive.
> Does her work. Schoolwork.
> Does her homework. *Before* she watches television!
> Puts others before herself.
> Does the dishes without being asked!
> Doesn't get into trouble. Doesn't go out and come home late – drunk!
> Responsible.
> Social 'enough' – but not *too* sociable!
> Sensible. Someone you wouldn't be embarrassed to be with.
> Presentable to parent's friends – and clients.
> No green hair. No drugs.
> My family are always arguing. And if you're passive you're a good girl
> because you're not taking sides in this.

The individual aspects of life stories clearly have a fractured quality in a group context. One girl may begin a narrative which is then co-opted and transformed by the interjections of others. However, although frequently interrupted, such stories are an invaluable means of observing the life perspective an individual may choose to present within a specific societal setting. The stories girls presented to the group provided public representations of the dynamics of family life, and public explanations of how these family issues had affected feelings and behaviour in the past and the present. By giving clues as to what is considered publicly acceptable, these stories throw light on which value judgements the girls view as being held in common, or at least recognized, by other adolescents within a particular society. This is not to suggest that the presentation of life events in a manner acceptable to the group is personally inauthentic. Overlapping membership of different life groupings creates personal identity rather as overlapping colours create white light. Each member of the groups I worked with was female, adolescent, academically successful, and part of a family unit. Most girls touched on these joint experiences. Even when they gave voice to aspects of their individual experience, they evaluated it within a group frame of reference. In consequence, general themes were consistent across the different groups.

In particular these were issues of independence versus security; the construction of femininity in the family; conflict in the family; and coping with family transitions.

*   *   *

I suggested that the girls wrote an autobiography at a time when this group work had allowed hidden, complex or previously unacknowledged factors in their lives to rise to the surface. Sometimes these areas were freely discussed by the group. At other times a girl might raise some part of her experience hesitantly, or with embarrassment, signalling that she had no wish to take the matter further in the group. The autobiographies were to allow girls to explore such issues in privacy. The group dynamic had fostered thematic discussions around the shared experience of being young and female in families. The autobiographies allowed the girls to place 'self' at centre-stage. The written texts were the product of hard work. The girls had chosen the manner in which they wished to be seen as constructing their lives in this form, and many of them prevailed upon me to allow them to continue their narrative in their own time. They approached the autobiography as a 'proper' story; a finished, created object that would exist in the world. Many girls must have written rough drafts as the handwriting in the booklets I provided was often immaculate. Faced by the challenge of constructing this personal statement, they made immediate choices about style and approach. Some chose a literary mode, consciously writing a 'fiction'. They worked at eye-catching first sentences:

> I was the first child and grandchild in the entire family so it was automatically me who was to get to go through everything first!

> I was five when the nightmares of school were first revealed to me.

> The most significant happening that changed every aspect of my life was when I moved house.

From the start such narratives would bound along, using a range of literary techniques to keep pace and passion in the narrative, until the denouement of the moral at 'The End'. Other girls, aware that I wanted them to explain as well as remember, approached the life story more as an essay, often adopting formal, sometimes stilted or convoluted language, and attempting to make sense of events in a dignified manner: 'In most respects I have always enjoyed school, so this must have resulted in a "HEAD START" in my approach to school work, and I suppose also my social outlook – leisure activities, friends.'

It was rare that these narratives could sustain their gravity to the end. After a few paragraphs a more conversational tone would break through as the girls became absorbed in the fascination of their lives. A few girls used the opportunity to pour out their aching hearts in a stream of consciousness: haunted by 'nightmares in the past', feeling that they existed 'trodden in the dust', and looking forward to 'blackness'. These narratives only seemed to be checked by running out of paper, although one girl had already filled a pile of extra sheets pinned to the booklet. One girl stapled together the edges of her work so it would not be seen by any eyes other than my own. Several scripts were tear-stained where particular events had been described.

Written personal histories do not fragment narratives as dialogue does, so this writing process allowed the girls to begin an interpretation of their lives uninterrupted by the actual presence of others. They alluded, in ways they saw as relevant, to their own life context: class, race, religious framework, family size and position, and so on. They also set key family events, and their own experiences of loss, bitter disappointment, eating disorders, depression, even attempted suicide, within strong narrative storylines. Many of these issues had not surfaced in group work. Contentious areas like race, class and religion had been skirted round or ignored. Family 'secrets', the 'shame' of alcoholism, unwanted pregnancies or violence, had stayed secret in the group. Most secret of all were the girls' own deep insecurities, or alternatively their pride and ambition. These issues, which might have destabilized the group, or left the girl too exposed within it, were often woven into the written narrative. In effect the narrative was allowing girls to say the unsayable, to give space to their 'muted' voices; voices that had been silenced even within a supportive group of female peers. For instance, one girl who had been in an otherwise all-white group began, 'I think the main motivation for me to do well is the fact that I'm black.' In the groups the unspoken constructions of femininity sometimes made it impossible for girls to admit to self-satisfaction. One girl could write, 'I was popular, pretty and clever,' but added, 'you won't ever catch me saying that to anyone!' Other unsayables were emotional: the isolating, 'I don't really talk about this very much because I don't think there is anyone who would really understand'; and the not yet confronted, 'I found this difficult to write – there is so much more I could tell you.'

All these stories were constructed around a vision of self, contextualized in past and present, and moving towards the future. Family legacies and ancestor myths often provide a setting for narratives that concentrate on change.[6] However, there seemed to be specific characteristics to the aspects of change addressed in these adolescent life stories. While the stories revealed many different personal experiences and viewpoints, the majority of scripts shared a basic storyline: these were histories of family (and peer) acceptance and non-acceptance; stories of the loss or gain of personal self-esteem. Most scripts, in a major or minor key, described a situation where personal confidence was threatened or lost, followed by a description of the strategies that were used to strengthen or regain it. In these stories, strategies for ensuring acceptance, or surviving rejection, and issues of changing or 'proving' oneself were persistently raised. It was within this context that traditional literary themes were adopted. Paul Thompson and others have identified such areas as 'the journey from darkness into light', the 'feather in the hand of fate', the event 'that changed everything' or the 'person who persevered'.[7] Many girls seemed to utilize these conventions in order to make sense of their adolescent experiences. In addition, there were stories of survival, stories of 'the rebel' and stories of despair, 'sometimes I think it will all swamp over me and I will drown.'

The family was incorporated as an element in the key theme of the emerging self, as can be seen in these examples:

> I had an exaggerated fear of people leaving me because as far as I could understand all the people I loved had left me. [This girl felt judged harshly for behaving rebelliously at school after the break-up of her parents' marriage]

> I am, according to family tradition, meant to settle down, have kids, and live supported by my husband. I don't believe I would have the guts to break this cycle if not supported by my father. [This girl was realizing gradually that traditional family patterns need not impose a stereo-typical woman's role]

> She is like a mum, dad and the sister/brother I haven't got all rolled into one person. [This girl described winning through in a single-parent family with the love and support of her mother]

Other girls described the ways they saw family experiences as affecting their subsequent behaviour, for instance searching to avoid painful family circum-stances by seeking substitutes such as 'father-figures', 'God', 'loving groups of people'; looking continually for an emotional 'home' as a result of fre-quently moving in childhood; recognizing you are detached from everyday life to 'protect' yourself because you have the responsibility for bringing up your siblings while living with a depressed and alcoholic father, and so on.

This was private written work but, although there were no interjections from others, it was still part of a relational context. The girls were writing for themselves and for the other – the reader. In the first instance this was to be me, and it was clear that many girls were addressing me directly, as their concluding comments often showed:

> There is so much more I could tell you but it would take forever.

> I hope this didn't drag on too much and it was useful.

> I hope that doesn't sound big-headed as I've never told anyone about it before.

However, I had also stressed to the girls that their stories might appear anonymously in publications where they might prove of help to other girls growing up, and their families. Apparently with this audience in mind, most girls sought to entertain, reassure, instruct or inspire the reader. Most narratives concluded with a personal statement that summed up the distilled experience of the narrative and some exhorted the reader to make some change in their own lives. 'Strive for what you want – life's too short to be a sheep!' These distinct characteristics draw attention to a key element within the genre of life story – that is the significance of motivational factors to the form of the story told.

* * *

The individual interview gave me an opportunity to clarify the terms that a girl might have used to talk about her life in either the group context or her written narrative, and a chance to explore further the family dynamics that the girl herself had signalled were significant. It was my agenda that the interviews would concentrate on the complexity of family relationships, set within the girl's experience of family life in the past and the present. There is a sense that these stories were felt by the girls to be the most private, the least available for sharing with anyone, as the simplest narrative themes would frequently come up against the hidden areas of power relations and/or sexuality within the family.[8] The three quotations below describe events in reconstituted families, but all family situations presented possibilities for complex relational processes that forced the young women to confront these difficult areas.

Jane's mother has recently remarried and Jane describes her reaction to her mother's revived sexuality:

Like you go in the living room, or something, and they're being like huggy and stuff, and you just go [ironically] 'Great' – and you just don't want to see it. They're very open about their relationship and what they get up to. It's really irritating 'cos I don't want to know, if you know what I mean. I think it's good that they're not *shy* about it but I'd rather not hear the ins and outs of everything! [laughs] Like her saying 'Oh, last night – '
'Oh, thanks, mum, great.'
'Oh, you're such a *prude*.'
And I'm going, 'No, I'm not. I'm just not interested in your love life thank you!' It's not that I think they *shouldn't* be up to that at their age, it's just that they're my *parents*, you know – like, 'Shut up about it!'

Connie suggests herself that she has used denial to protect herself from confronting her relationship with her stepbrother:

My stepbrother was a bit of a psycho when he was younger and he

91

used to beat me up and stuff and try to – [voice fades out] – I dunno – he was a bit violent really. On one occasion – this was the worst one – it's like I had a lock on my door. And he bashed the door in and I went, 'Aaah', and ran off to my mum's work. It was really bad. I was so scared. He used to like – slap me around. I dunno. I suppose I've blacked it now. Can't actually remember apart from particular occasions like that one.

Rachel came to terms with her father's treatment of her younger stepbrother:

Dad gave Peter hell. I think it was because he wasn't his son. 'Cos, like, Peter had a speech problem when he was younger and, like, he couldn't say stuff like, 'Can I get down from the table please?' – in that order. And Dad, he used to sit Peter at the table for hours, because he couldn't say, 'Could I get down?' He used to make him sit there, and shout at him, saying, 'You're gonna sit there until you say it!' And it made Peter even worse.

It was a privilege to be told stories of such a private nature, and, gratifyingly, many girls also affirmed that it was a relief to have an opportunity to air them in a confidential setting. 'It was good to talk about it. I hardly ever do – Mum's had it up to here. I tried to tell my best friend but she didn't seem really interested so I thought – "OK – let it go –".' However life stories elicited through interview methods are perhaps affected by the 'audience' even more acutely than either autobiographies or group work. Here, more than ever, the context of the story is a vital element – and a key part of the context is a profile of the interview process. It is not only power issues like age, gender and ethnicity that are relevant, although, of course, they are; it is also the agenda that the interviewer pursues, and the means that are used to pursue that agenda within the relational dynamic of the interview.

Gilligan suggests that there is a particular positive resonance that takes place in interviews between girls and older women, as the latter recognize 'strategies of resistance' from their own experience.[9] Certainly I was aware that the girls I met on their own were 'presenting' differently from when they were in the group. I had seen them together, loud and raucous, joking and preening, arguing and teasing. Now they were alone and on their best behaviour. The body language was different, particularly at the beginning of the interview. Some girls were cautious, contained, adopting a formal interview posture with hands neatly in the lap. Others were nervous, fiddling with rings and transposing words. One girl sat stiffly, face expressionless. The majority leaned towards me expectantly. It was clear that many were unsure of the conventions of being interviewed and wanted to do it 'right', while others, for their own reasons, were indeed 'resisting'. I realized that the girls were aware that I already knew a great deal about their families and themselves – perhaps more than was comfortable.

It was clear that the manner in which the oral life stories were told depended on the girls' assessment of appropriate language both with an adult and in an 'important' interview (one girl apologized for using the word 'fuck' even in reported speech); the boundaries they set on their confidences (the girl with the rigid face spoke in enigmatic phrases that did not invite elaboration); and, above all, their emotional state of mind. Some girls appeared to me confident, expansive, reflective – in control of their personal boundaries but generous with their confidences. Others, while still aware and articulate, were bound up in palpable sadness, their voices sometimes barely raised above a whisper. These personal characteristics were often different from the persona projected in the group. Quieter girls might blossom and chatter, clever girls might feel able to display all their ability, boisterous girls might admit to deep insecurity, and so on. One girl whose group stories had been mumbled and incoherent said, 'Because of my family I've no confidence. I can't shine anywhere. I hear people talk nonsense – like sometimes at school – and I know it's nonsense but I don't dare interrupt or contradict.'

The relaxed, confident girls seized the opportunity to shape memories and experiences of their family into a coherent whole that would contextualize even unhappy events. They embroidered the main theme with telling anecdotes that illustrated their points, and often acted like part of a Greek chorus commenting on the drama they were unfolding. Sarah ran through her mother's marital history with a blithe air, punctuating her narrative with expansive hand gestures and Gallic shrugs:

Mum says that she's made mistakes. She's always married for the wrong reasons I think [wrinkles her nose]. I mean she didn't get on with my Nana – my Nana's not very affectionate at all. She got married to get away from Nana and granddad. 'Cos he was a violent man my grand-dad was. And her first husband, was like a little boy [tone of amused contempt]. He couldn't keep his hands to himself [mimes a male pawing a woman] – he was always dawdling around. I mean they went to Germany to live and he'd disappear for days on end and then come back and tell her about the women he'd been with and stuff like that. And it got so much for her after a while that she came back and met my dad – and that was to get away from being on her own. Which was the wrong reason – she wanted security [shakes her head severely]. And then she left Dad, because he was violent. She went with James – he was a snob. He thought he was – more than what he was – he was too involved with himself. He was never violent – but he was strict – we did what we were told. Very obnoxious man. I didn't like him at all [flaps her hand in a dismissive gesture]. And Mum found out he was having an affair. And she couldn't stand that thought, so she got out. I think now she's got so accustomed to being on her own that she's got – not selfish – but it would be hard for her to live with another man, because – you have demands when you live with a man – and right now she has no demands.

The stories of unhappy girls were often characterized by pauses, sighs, anecdotes that trailed off into silence, or the doubtful 'I don't know'. Jenny's father has been getting progressively worse from a muscular disease. She talks about this quietly, in a voice bleached of life and colour, except for sudden flashes of bitterness when she mentions his behaviour.

I think, talking to my mum now, there's always been tensions between her and Dad, sort of thing – Mum always feels really guilty if we get involved but Dad tends to sort of involve us if he can, sort of thing. He'll involve anyone [said bitterly]! Like, last night, Mum and Dad were arguing as he was getting into bed – 'cos she has to help him get into bed – and like – um – if he calls and she doesn't come, then sometimes he'll shout for me – not expecting me to come, but just to use it against her. – Dad doesn't try to spare our feelings too much [rising tone of bitterness], but Mum just goes round looking unhappy [voice sinks even lower]. Sometimes when I'm around nice people who I like I feel sad [pause]. It's quite embarrassing [pause]. So I have to be really quiet [long pause] 'cos they're going to realize I'm sad [laughs sadly].

Other girls show a manic energy, talking in staccato phrases with urgent emphasis, but leaving a sense that the story is a smoke-screen. As Gilligan argued, 'We know that women, in particular, often speak in indirect discourse, in voices deeply encoded, deliberately or unwittingly opaque.'[10] Viewing life stories as a genre in which it is important to consider the value judgements that make sense of experience, lack of clarity can be frustrating. It is a particular quandary for women, working with women and using an interview approach for life story purposes, to find an ethical position from which to approach a 'deliberately or unwittingly opaque' area of narrative. Some of the most dramatic moments in these interviews took place when a young woman noticed that I had registered a discrepancy in her story, a glossing over of some half-explored area, and was heard finally to make the decision to open out: 'Well, to tell you the truth . . .'

But it is disingenuous of me to say simply that the girl 'noticed' my reaction. In any interview the initiator's interests can consciously or unconsciously deflect the delicate nature of narrative. This may be by the use of body language – an artfully raised eyebrow, an encouraging nod or an expression of boredom can change the story in its tracks – or it may be by other means. In the dialogue below it seems to me, in retrospect, that I chose to follow a conversational area I was interested in by engaging emotionally with the young woman, rather than picking up on her hint that she might find it easier to let the subject drop:

> *So you're saying that things were difficult at home even before your dad left?*
> Yeah – it's been a long time really, but these past couple of years have been like really, really awful. [sighs] Oh, it's too much to explain in just one session, you know – it's only an hour, so –
> *Yeah – you look so tired –*
> Yeah
> *Mm*
> [Very quietly] Yeah, I've not been very happy.
> *Is this painful for you? Do you not really want to continue?*
> Oh, I don't mind. I don't mind. I'm not really bothered. Not many people know so it's not like I talk about it loads.
> *Well, it's how you cope, you know, that I would like to hear about –*

As well as allowing the interviewer to direct the agenda of the interview in subtle, or not so subtle, ways, the dialogic process can also begin to rewrite history. As speaker and listener work towards understanding each other, they make small compensatory linguistic moves as they collaborate in helping the conversation to move forward. Within the conversation itself they negotiate the reality that is the life story of the speaker and the understanding of the listener. In the exchange below I have, in effect, organized Gemma's experience in a way she might not have thought to do herself.

> *It seems to me that what you're saying, what you're describing, is that you spend a lot of time in your room, occasionally talking to people on the phone, doing your homework and not going out – and it comes across to me as quite . . . lonely. But maybe it isn't?*
> It is.
> *It is?*
> I'm lonely – and so isolated. It's really bad.

The temptation is for an interviewer to feel that a particularly rewarding in-depth session with an informant has gone 'deeper', got closer, uncovered 'more' of that person's life story. In fact that feeling may arise largely from the interviewer's own involvement and investment in the process. The final narrative is partly a 'reality' the interview process has constructed, and the stamp of the interviewer is firmly upon it.

*   *   *

As in oral history, this research was concerned with actively seeking out the lives of a non-dominant group, but to address this aim it encouraged both written and oral techniques. Both these approaches provide narratives about which more can be told than the content of the text. Indeed, I would argue that, at the stage of analysis, as much as possible must be told about the circumstances in which the story came into being. If one of the aims of life story analysis is to elucidate a personal view of self, enmeshed in, and making sense of, a life context, then all clues must be seized upon. The dynamics of a conversational exchange registered in qualities of voice and mutually understood body language can only be hinted at in a transcription, but omitting to grapple with these difficulties is to lose the sense of the non-verbal 'presences' of the text. A silence that is someone choking on a memory is not the silence of absence of talk. In different ways an autobiographical 'original' may also give clues beyond the text. This is an object one step removed from its appropriation by a second party. Everything speaks of the author: the quality of paper, the colour of ink, the pressure of print upon the page, handwriting that cascades or sits cramped in a corner, and so on. But there may be more. Precious extra detail might be available. To know that a life was described sideways, in tiny writing, with a pencil stub, in the borders of one of the few treasured books left in a besieged ghetto, grounds our understanding.

But above all, to a greater or lesser degree, both written and oral methods assume, are responsive to and often collaborate with the presence, contribution or perspective of a perceived audience. Once it is acknowledged that no method of eliciting life stories can produce a 'pure' product, the character of this cluster of genres must be clear. It is a process in which participants offer an organization of life events, and value judgements about these events, in a manner that depends upon a specific relational context and a particular personal motivation, at a given moment in time. It is the responsibility of those who may wish to take these personal stories into the public sphere to define that context to the best of their ability. This may mean including their own questions and comments whenever they present material from an interview or it may mean giving a detailed description of the different ways in which the atmosphere in which the life story was told was emotionally and intellectually charged. The life story is a powerful genre in any of its guises. If it is reaching an audience through the medium of another person, it is in the professional as well as ethical interest of that person to situate the text. Otherwise it weakens the power of the very story they wish to incorporate.

My initial response to the stories of the girls I worked with was that it was the material from the individual interviews that took me closer to their sense of self and their awareness of their status in society. Inspecting my research more closely I see that I flattered myself. I assumed that the most reality could be found in the very stories I had contributed to most. Now I can turn to the different versions of life accounting each girl has experimented with and see that they offer equal insights into multiple identities. For instance, group discussions were dynamic and unpredictable, taking unexpected turns, exposing unforeseen opinions, absorbing the range and complexity of each individual's testament. Comments made in the group might hang unnoticed in the air, be co-opted or evaluated by others, or might change the content and tone of the discussion. Such volatile interaction between peers, particularly in adolescence, seems to have the potential to confirm, threaten or transform the emerging contemporaneous self. Thus a girl might describe and evaluate her life experience in ways that shift between evolving individual and group identities, her experiences and perceptions becoming part of a potentially catalytic process bringing about personal and social change in herself and the group.

Although the act of writing a private written history might also be personally transformative, the narrative itself allowed each girl to temporarily 'freeze' her experience within an evaluative frame of her choice without the stimulus of challenge or interruption. Perhaps for adolescents, above all, it is true that 'to get ahead you need a good theory and theories most often begin inside.'[11] The autobiographical writings demonstrated that, given time for reflection, girls found a variety of ways to explain their current construction of self in relation to relationships with family, friends and society at large. Clear differences could be drawn between girls who explained their lives in terms of emotional dynamics and those who adopted a more pragmatic rationale. It seemed that individual approaches might focus on issues of intention, reason or cause, a girl presumably choosing whichever form of personal and structural evaluation offered her the best possible theory for making sense of her past and planning her future. These were not choices offered in the individual interview. My questions tracked, above all, the emotional underpinning of girls' lives. In some ways this focus gave depth of understanding, yet, by neglecting other modes by which girls might interpret their lives, my agenda also silenced some girls' voices.

I shall finish with these small excepts from the narratives of one girl. She is like all of us. She has many lives and many ways to describe and justify them, as these accounts alluding to her family confirm.

[Group session]

I've got this *absolute* – anyone who knows me well knows – I have this absolute fascination for weddings [general laughter]. I *don't* know why. I really don't know why. Just whenever I hear of anyone else getting married – I'm just like 'What was her dress like? Did she have a big wedding?' 'Cos I've just like got this thing I'm going to get married and just going to have the *biggest* of everything. I don't know why. It just seems such a special day. And Mum's like, you know, 'I wouldn't be happy seeing you getting married until you were like twenty-three, twenty-four, at *least*' [shakes finger imperatively to general laughter] 'Cos I think that's when she got married to Dad – maybe a little bit older . . .

[Autobiography]

I am a very confident person and have many aims in life that I am sure to fulfil. I hope to be very successful in life and achieve all of my dreams and with the encouragement and support from my family, I know that I can accomplish anything that I want to . . .

[Personal interview]

These past couple of years have been like really, really awful – I've not been very happy. Mum has just literally had so much that nobody, but nobody, would – unless they're a fly on the wall permanently – know exactly what she's had to put up with. Because these last few years Dad – he's an exceptionally clever man. Really, really clever man he is. He's had his own business. He's just been in the top of the rank all the time. And he's just come *right* down to being unemployed, to being alcoholic. Having an *affair* – with someone. And he just feels absolutely nobody now. So – he had a very big argument which ended up in a fight between him and Mum which was really really . . . Walked into the town. Slept in the railway station and took the first train that came the next day.

NOTES

I should like to thank Madeleine Arnot and Carol Gilligan for their invaluable advice and support. This research is funded by the Economic and Social Research Council, UK.

1 See Marie-Françoise Chanfrault-Duchet, 'Narrative structures, social models, and symbolic representation in the life story', in Sherna Berger Gluck and Daphne Patai (eds), *Women's Words: The Feminist Practice of Oral History* (London: Routledge, 1991), pp. 77–92.
2 Jean Baker Miller, *Towards a New Psychology of Women* (London: Penguin, 1976), p. 11.
3 Rosanna Basso, 'Myths in contemporary oral transmission: a children's strike', in Raphael Samuel and Paul Thompson (eds), *The Myths We Live By* (London: Routledge, 1990), pp. 61–9.
4 Sue Middleton, *Educating Feminists* (New York: Teachers College Press, 1993), p. 69.
5 Samuel and Thompson, *The Myths We Live By*, p. 2.
6 See Elizabeth Tonkin, *Narrating our Pasts: The Social Construction of Oral History* (Cambridge: Cambridge University Press, 1992).
7 Samuel and Thompson, *The Myths We Live By*, p. 10.
8 Chris Mann, 'Girls' own story: the search for a sexual identity in times of family change', in Lisa Adkins, Janet Holland, Vicki Merchant and Geoff Weeks (eds), *Sex, Sensibility and the Gendered Body* (Basingstoke: Macmillan, 1996), pp. 78–96.
9 Lyn Mikel Brown and Carol Gilligan, *Meeting at the Crossroads: Women's Psychology and Girls' Development* (Cambridge, Mass.: Harvard University Press, 1992), p. 24.
10 Ibid.
11 Jerome Bruner and Susan Weisser, 'The invention of self', in David Olsen (ed.), *Literacy and Orality* (Cambridge: Cambridge University Press, 1991), p. 147.

6

ANECDOTE AS NARRATIVE RESOURCE IN WORKING-CLASS LIFE STORIES

Parody, Dramatization and Sequence

T. G. Ashplant

Over the last fifteen years, some of the most valuable work in oral history has been concerned with analysing the *forms* of the life histories which respondents produce. Increasing attention both to the structures of such narratives and to the genres on which they draw has proved a fruitful source for understanding the ways in which people make sense of their lives. This has not so much displaced concern with the accuracy of life stories (so prominent a theme in oral history work in the 1970s), as resituated it in a new and richer context. Hesitations and silences, on the one hand, and factual inaccuracies such as transpositions in time and place, on the other, are all now seen as potentially revealing both about the historical events being recounted, and about the current understanding of the speaker.[1] During the same period, there has been an extraordinary efflorescence of work in literary studies on the previously almost disregarded genre of autobiography. Oral historians and others interested in life history narratives can learn much from this work.[2]

Most recently, a social anthropologist working as an oral historian, Elizabeth Tonkin, has added her voice to the argument that the historical value of a life story narrative rests not only (or even especially) in the discrete facts which it may yield, but also in the interpretation of lived experience which it (like any such narrative) necessarily embodies.[3] In *Narrating our Pasts* (1992), drawing especially on her work among the Jlao of Liberia (West Africa), she argues that oral narratives can be as complex as those which are written. I want to highlight two points in particular from her dense and wide-ranging account. First, Tonkin argues the need to break down a rigid differentiation between supposedly oral (or preliterate) and literate cultures, stressing the continuing centrality of oral communication even within highly literate societies.[4] Second, she draws attention to the importance of understanding 'genre' (including the cues which introduce it, and the codes which govern the speaker's use of and the audience's response to it) in interpreting oral narratives.

> The different conventions of discourse through which speakers tell history and listeners understand them can be called genres. A genre signals that a certain kind of interpretation is called for. ... Genres provide a 'horizon of expectation' to a knowledgeable audience that cannot be derived from the semantic content of a discourse alone. Since genres are the level of discourse through which interpretation is organised, any analyst seeking to understand a verbal message must learn the genre. Oracy has its genres just as literacy does . . .[5]

In this article I want to explore how literary analysis of textual structure and a focus on genre can help to reveal political and personal meanings within one well-known work of British oral history, Angela Hewins's *The Dillen* (1981).[6] George Hewins was born in 1879 in Stratford-upon-Avon, a typical market town distinguished only by its nascent Shakespeare industry. The illegitimate son of a woman in service, he was brought up by his great-aunt Cal Cook. Her extreme shrewdness in her management of her shop and lodging-house meant that as a child George enjoyed some small margin of working-class comfort. But the abrupt termination of his apprenticeship when he found himself at the age of twenty forced to marry his pregnant girlfriend, the impossibility of finding secure or decently paid employment as a building worker, and the birth of eight children over the next fifteen years condemned him and his family to a place among the poorest in Edwardian Britain. Always a survivor, George came through these hard times and – worst of all – through two years service in the trenches during the First World War which culminated in his being severely wounded. After nearly two years' convalescence, he returned home damaged both as a worker (his leg had been ripped open), and as a man (his genitals had been mutilated). He continued to live in Stratford, dying at the age of ninety-eight in 1977.

When he was in his mid-nineties, at George's suggestion, his granddaughter-in-law Angela began to record some of the songs he sang so freely. In the course of these recordings, he revealed himself to be a consummate storyteller as well as a singer.[7] Both of these (essentially oral) roles were ones he had occupied all his adult life; they contributed to defining his identity within his own community.[8] In childhood, he and other boys were to be found absorbed by the music-hall entertainment at the local theatre, and then putting on their own show to earn halfpennies. He eagerly learned songs and stories from army veterans staying at Cal's lodging-house, with whose marginal way of life outside the family he identified.[9] In adult life, he took on the role of a regular neighbourhood singer, the source at first simply of free beer, but later of valuable extra income in his years of disablement after the war.[10] As well as being a singer, he also played the part of a storyteller within his community.[11] It should be noted that Tonkin's main focus was on those who played the role of 'oral historian' within the West African communities she studied. George may have taken on this role of historian only towards the end of his life, when prompted to do so by Angela Hewins's intervention. Nevertheless, I would suggest that his consequent narrative was shaped by, and hence can best be read in the light of, his earlier performances (through song and storytelling) in the role of community 'commentator'.

The concept of genre as defined by Tonkin can, I believe, be fruitfully applied to an understanding of the life story narrative which George Hewins produced. That narrative draws on a wide range of genres. It incorporates pre-industrial 'folk' elements, present in the still strongly rural world of plebeian Stratford c.1900. Angela Hewins, in her commentaries on *The Dillen*, has noted the appearance of traditional English songs such as 'The green bushes', and stressed the presence of elements of fairy tale and legend (including witches and ghosts).[12] However, alongside these are more contemporary elements, in particular musical and dramatic items, characteristic of late Victorian/Edwardian urban life. Many of its songs are shared with music-hall, which was a dominant form of popular culture in Britain during Hewins's childhood and early adult life, and which by that date had become a market-oriented form of entertainment with the capacity for mass dissemination of its products.[13] The fundamental and by far the most common unit of Hewins's narrative structure, as it no doubt was of his speech, is the anecdote.[14] Simon Dentith, identifying anecdote as a 'characteristic organising form' of working-class autobiography, has commented that it is 'a way of mediating between rawer, more unformulated experience and more general or formulated truths; it does so by turning such truths into narrative and character.'[15] The range of genres present in the text help to shape different categories of anecdote which it deploys.

My analysis will develop three main points. First, I will define one specific category of anecdote and suggest that a comparative study of Hewins's deployment of this category helps to locate the political stance of the narrative, to place it within a broader pattern of working-class speech and writing. Second, I will examine the shaping of other components of the narrative by genres derived from the institution of the music-hall, and suggest that these genres provided a shared resource between narrator and audience. Third, I will explore ways in which the narrative's framing, juxtaposition and sequencing of anecdotes serve to generate a level of meaning which goes beyond both the semantic content of the separate stories themselves, and any explicit comment by the narrator. To focus this discussion, I will concentrate principally on one passage of the text which relates what happened to George on his return, badly wounded, from the war in 1918; and on two individual anecdotes within it.

* * *

Hewins's skill in his role as storyteller is evident in the stories he tells. What characterizes the typical anecdote in his narrative is its pithiness, its densely (re)constructed dialogue and its humour.[16] This humour is by turns deflating (when turned against figures of authority) and self protective, muffling (when used to depict the stress and suffering of working-class experience). The first anecdote I want to look at occurs early in this sequence when, injured and unemployed, he has gone begging.[17]

> 'Wait there', said one bloke. I thought I was in luck.
> He gave me a book: *The Complete Works of William Shakespeare*. A *book!* Someone had writ inside: 'It is hoped that this will always keep you in mind of the true greatness and glory of the cause for which you have fought and suffered.'

Authorial comment is kept to a minimum here; just the contrasting phrases 'I thought I was in luck' when the man goes to fetch something, and 'A *book!*' when he returns. The main weight of the anecdote comes through in the direct quotation of the inscription: 'It is hoped' – the impersonal passive voice of self-concealing authority; 'always keep you in mind' – literature as disciplining force; 'true greatness and glory' – as opposed to the mud and blood of the trenches.

This brief fragment exemplifies one form of anecdote to be found throughout the narrative. In this kind of anecdote, Hewins offers a complex deployment of upper-class registers (such as those of instruction or exhortation). Either authority figures – such as parliamentary candidates or army officials – are allowed to condemn themselves out of their own mouths (as here), a form of quasi-parody by carefully chosen quotation; or their language (for example, that of a magistrate or a school chaplain) is directly parodied by the narrator.[18] Sometimes, a further anecdote reinforces the message, but direct authorial comment is usually kept to a minimum.[19] This use of parody within the retrospective narrative of his life story derives directly from his behaviour during his working life. He recalls one occasion when, doing building work at a chapel, he 'got up in the pulpit. "I'm just goin to give you a few words from the Bible!" I said. I puffed myself out, cleared my throat like the Vicar – the others was falling about with laughing . . .'[20]

The implicit politics of Hewins's humour can be illuminated by means of comparison. The first point of comparison is with a published working-class life story from two generations earlier, John James Bezer's *The Autobiography of One of the Chartist Rebels of 1848* (1851).[21] In his analysis of this text, Alf Louvre notes: 'Bezer's fondness for indulging in parody. . . . Recurrently throughout, he adopts the personae of moralists and preachers, recreating the ethos of their attitudes and the cadence of their speech with telling accuracy – only, of course, to debunk them.' He comments that such bitter satire, which serves 'to demystify the representatives of the dominant morality by revealing the gap between their rhetoric and their political practice', in the context of 'Bezer's own insistent materialism', is characteristic of other proletarian classics such as the novel *The Ragged-Trousered Philanthropists* (1914) by Hewins's close contemporary, the working-class socialist Robert Tressell.[22] Hewins's narrative shares certain features with both Bezer's and Tressell's texts: in particular, its materialist emphasis on the exigencies of gaining one's daily bread and its readiness to undermine through linguistic parody (as George and his community evaded through law-breaking action) the claims of authority.[23] This similarity of representation is rooted in similarities of circumstance: Hewins and Bezer both grew up in the midst of financial hardship, while Hewins's living and working conditions as a building worker in Stratford bear a marked comparison with those depicted by Tressell in his fictional Mugsborough (based on the town of Hastings).[24]

Yet there are also important differences. Louvre argues that:

> what is striking in Bezer is the space given over to the *narrator* as against the protagonist. Continually, the interest shifts from what *happened* and what it *felt like* (the arena of the protagonist), to how best to describe it and what he (the narrator) and we (his imagined and sometimes dramatised audience) should think about it *now* (the arena of the narrator).[25]

This is not true of Hewins's narrative. Although there are important moments in the text where Hewins the narrator comments on the conditions experienced by, and the responses to them of, Hewins the protagonist, these moments are not crucial in determining narrative form.[26] Partly, this is a matter of intent; Hewins's recalling of his past is not intended as a direct political intervention, in the way that both Bezer's autobiography and Tressell's novel clearly were. More broadly, it is a matter of underlying political stance. Louvre claims, of the two poems that frame Bezer's autobiography, that they

> insist on going *beyond* the experiential: the future, the dream, liberty are counterposed to and considered more significant than *past* event and suffering. Material conditions are . . . enormously important for Bezer, but their depiction is always accompanied by an interrogation, a resilience, by resistance and a strenuous idealism.[27]

Similarly, it can be argued that Tressell's depiction of the conditions of the workers of Mugsborough is always subordinate to his aim of demystifying what upholds those conditions, and pointing to the possibility of changing them, via a Marxist politics.[28] Hewins, too, does not dwell on the harshness of the past (though it is starkly revealed). His narrative, too, shows resilience, but it is rather the resilience of survival which he both records and celebrates – the ability to withstand and outwit those harsh conditions, and to continue where possible to take pleasure. That outwitting demanded the ability to see through those in power, that pleasure could be enhanced by their mocking.[29]

*   *   *

The second anecdote I want to analyse shows George, still searching for work or assistance, receiving a letter from the army.[30] At first he assumes it is from the medical board, about his disablement pension (this leads to a nested flashback of him and a friend having previously got the better of the board); but instead it turns out to be from the recruiting office, demanding that he report to them. Two soldiers turn up at the house to fetch him and there follows a confrontation in dialogue between the soldiers and his wife Emma, standing at the door with her arms folded. Foiled in their attempt to take the crippled George, they find out he has a son and namesake, and offer to take the youngster instead.

This rather longer scene typifies another form of anecdote found throughout the narrative. Here the settings and dialogue owe much to the conventions of the comic music-hall turn. As with many of the songs contained in the text, the narration of the scene contains what Tonkin terms 'cues', which prompt the audience to recognize the genre and respond within its 'horizon of expectation'. Emma is the dominant female, controlling the men with her forceful presence. The scene ends with what may be termed a dramatic, serio-comic curtain-line, as George, spotted by Emma sneaking away, announces that he is going out, not (as she might expect/fear) for a drink, but to fetch 'a *Magistrate*'. In retelling this anecdote, then, Hewins uses the conventions of music-hall to *dramatize* the confrontation between himself and the military authorities. The foolishness of officialdom is shown through their attempt to re-recruit a cripple, while working-class solidarity and resourcefulness are depicted through Emma's resistance (and the allusion to his friend's earlier manoeuvre). The comic sketch format both brings the incident alive and primes the audience to respond with both mocking and sympathetic laughter.

This scene which closes George's army career echoes, in its mode of dramatization, his presentation of its opening four years earlier.[31] There he used the technique of the false climax. Knowing that as a member of the Volunteers he had agreed to serve in the event of war, he spent the autumn of 1914 awaiting his call-up papers. Two successive false alarms threaten his (and the listener's) equanimity, before the fateful letter finally appears. They are carefully graded so as to convey George's sense of impending disaster, contrasted with his workmates' and family's complacent assumption that, as a thirty-five-year-old father of seven, 'they won't take you!' Here again, music-hall humour offers a frame within which to engage the listener's interest, while leaving room for a darker, more painful subtext. With these dramatized anecdotes, Hewins appropriated popular cultural forms to present critical vignettes of a class-divided society.

In his study of (predominantly) high literature of the First World War, *The Great War and Modern Memory* (1975), Paul Fussell argues that Robert Graves's famous memoir *Goodbye to All That* (1929) is best understood as 'a satire, built out of anecdotes heavily influenced by the techniques of stage comedy'.[32] He goes on to analyse the components of what he describes as 'the form of the short theatrical anecdote or sketch which [Graves] will proceed to impose upon the ... matter offered by the war'.[33] Central to this is the use of dialogue, in exchanges having the immediacy of a *Punch* cartoon with its two-line caption. These scenes draw on the techniques of farce, including astonishing coincidences, climactic multiple endings, bizarre characters, melodrama.[34] I would suggest that many of Hewins's anecdotes can be understood in a similar way, but with their template lying in the working-class popular cultural form of music-hall rather than the middle-class one of farce.[35] My emphasis here is on the music-hall *form*, which can be used for a variety of purposes. Some of these anecdotes which he retells about other people are clearly fictional.[36] But in telling of his own experiences, he can use this form either simply to lend point and wit to an already tragicomic episode (as with the recruiting office incident), or in a more complex way to represent what is troubled or conflictual (as in the account of his call-up).[37] In these two cases, a professional writer from the upper middle class and a storyteller from the lower working class each draw on related popular cultural forms as narrative resources. For both, dramatization serves to undermine in retrospect an abusive authority. Within these dramatized episodes, both Graves and Hewins contrast the truth-telling power of demotic speech against the falsity and sometimes deadly deceit of the written word.[38]

*   *   *

The wider meaning of the life story, however, is conveyed not by the individual anecdotes, but by their weaving together. Within the broader narrative, elements of music-hall form comprise one important strand, generating meaning through their interaction with anecdotes (or songs) from other generic forms. It is in the juxtaposition of anecdotes, the links and elisions between them, the cross-references which they establish in the reader's mind that Hewins's story – the way he renders his life intelligible, and with it that of his fellows in Stratford – is told.[39] In order to explore how such a narrative works, I have chosen to analyse one relatively self-contained sequence within the life story, which recounts his return home from the First World War.[40] This passage possesses its own coherence as a particular segment of the life story (since all the anecdotes are tied to the period and the events immediately after his return), while it also serves as a climax, a drawing together of themes present throughout the text. I shall concentrate here largely on a close reading of the language and structure of this particular sequence. However, its full meaning derives also from its complex implicit cross-references to other passages in the text: those involving individual characters who appear in this sequence, as well as those concerning George's occupation, the army, the church and the Shakespeare industry.[41] Placing the passage in this fuller context will reveal how the technique of interwoven and cross-referenced anecdotes enables Hewins to speak the unspeakable.

The sequence contains sixteen anecdotes which can be divided into nine narrative elements (some comprising more than one anecdote): his mother's burial; his family's wartime casualties; help (or lack of it) from the middle class; the army's attempt to recall him; his consequent rejection of his awards; his position among the old men, defending their masculinity; his inability to return to his old trade; the impact of rationing; and finally his rejection of the war. At one level, this sequence of anecdotes simply records what happened to George on his return home after his injury and convalescence, as he attempted to reintegrate himself into working-class Stratford. But beneath the surface shift from one anecdote to another lies a series of themes, some running through the whole life story, others created or newly inflected by the events of the war. They include the constant pressures of poverty; the impossibility of communication across lines of class; the necessity of practical working-class cooperation, both within and outside the family; and the intertwining of masculinity and the capacity to work in constructing identity. These themes become partly visible through an intermediate level – the clustering of the narrative elements, and the transitions between them. This analysis is schematically represented in the table on p. 107.[42]

The first cluster of anecdotes explores the role of the family unit in coping with poverty, illness and death. Throughout the sequence, one marital partner (the one most immediately affected by an incident) is positioned as expressing emotion, while the other displays the harsh practicality needed for survival. The sequence opens with George back home, injured but safe; the sun is shining. However, the scene is quickly overshadowed by the discovery that his mother, who died while he was at the front, has been buried, not alongside her husband as she planned, but in a common grave with strangers from the workhouse, including a tramp. The stigma of a pauper burial was still a powerful one; George wants to have her reinterred, but cannot afford to. Money can only be spent on the living; as a friend points out, the hard-headed Emma is right, it will do the children more good. George simultaneously recognizes this necessity and cries for his sense of loss and powerlessness.[43] George and Emma are then reunited through their shared loss (his mother, her brother), and damage (his war wound, her hernia brought on by war work); their only consolation is that because of his wound she can no longer become pregnant, so they can safely cuddle. In the absence of a welfare state, Emma can get medical help only by paying, or securing a

Analysis of narrative elements, clusters and themes (*The Dillen*, pp. 158–62)

Anecdote	Reference (page/line numbers)	Narrative element	Cluster	Theme(s)
1 Mother's grave	158/1–10	his mother's burial	Family	Poverty
2 Her fate	158/10–19	*ditto*	Family	Poverty, Cooperation
3 Harry's death	158/20–8	family casualties	Family	Poverty
4 Emma's injury	158/29–159/8	*ditto*	Family	Poverty, Cooperation
5 Book presentation	159/9–13	help (or lack of it) from the middle class	Authorities	Poverty, Class
6 Vicar's advice	159/14–18	*ditto*	Authorities	Poverty, Class
7 Capt. Edwards	159/19–27	*ditto*	Authorities	Poverty, Class
8 Recruiting letter	159/28–32 and 41–160/16	army's attempt to recall him	Authorities/War	Cooperation
9 Sgt. Sanders	159/32–40	*ditto*	Authorities/War	Cooperation
10 Confronts magistrate	160/17–25	rejection of his awards	Authorities/War	Class
11 Gives away medal	160/26–30	*ditto*	Authorities/War	Class, Cooperation
12 Among old men	160/31–6	among the old men, defending their masculinity	War	Masculinity
13 Town changed	160/37–161/6	*ditto*	War	Masculinity
14 Army certificate	161/7–15	inability to return to his old trade	War	Poverty, Masculinity
15 Queue for rations	161/16–162/13	impact of rationing	War/Authorities	Poverty
16 Tommy's death	162/13–21	rejection of the war	War	Masculinity

hospital ticket through a local subscriber. The roles are now reversed; Emma is too proud to beg, so George has to prove himself the hard-headed 'son' of Cal Cook, ready to 'see what the pickins is'.

The scene now shifts outside the home; the next cluster of anecdotes exemplify relationships between the working class and those with power. George's first attempts to beg are met with caricatural responses: the inscribed copy of Shakespeare, and an invitation from the vicar to attend church every Sunday for a year in the hope of being designated a 'deservin'' case. As elsewhere in the text, cultural and religious institutions operate an empty or controlling paternalism towards the working class.[44] Then George gets a letter from the bereaved father of Captain Edwards, whose servant he had been earlier in the war. His account reveals how genuine human sympathy (''E thought a lot o' you'; 'I writ back and told him what a nice chap Captain Edwards had been – well, it was true!') is cut across by the cash nexus; George writes in response to the offer of money, and soon tires of doing so.[45] He next receives the letter from the army, which serves to remind him of his first attendance at the medical board. In contrast to these high-minded middle-class 'false friends', Sergeant Sanders had exemplified necessary working-class self-help, fooling the presiding officers so that George obtained a pension increase.[46] Angered and determined to get himself signed off, George seeks out a magistrate, only to find that they, who were once so keen to sign him up, are too busy. Instead, he attends the recruiting office on crutches, makes his protest, and receives an apology. On the way back, he meets another outsider, an Irish girl, by the workhouse; in a gesture of repudiation, he gives her his silver badge for 'SERVICES RENDERED'. However, when George gets home, the role of realist is again reversed; as Emma points out, they cannot afford such gestures, she could have pawned the badge.

The next two anecdotes explore the damage caused by George's injuries to his identity as man and as worker. With his crutches, and later his stick, he is now positioned among the 'old men' (though he is only thirty-nine). They sit in the sun and discuss the recent enfranchisement of women. Yet this nostalgia for 'the days afore the war', and the deploring of petticoat rule ('We got enough o' that at home!') are also George's personal lament for his lost manhood and the threat to his position within his family. Stratford is changed by war as much as he is; both are threatened with emasculation, there are no men to keep the streets tidy, while women are everywhere. By a bitter irony, George is now to be a 'gentleman' (the opposite of a worker) for the rest of his life. He can neither defend a friend against insult, nor work; he is at the bottom of the competitive ladder, no longer able to 'go up with the rest'. His identity is now defined by the terse and misleading phrases of his army character. Though the paper testifies that his conduct has been very good, the euphemistic 'Scars' hides the fact that 'serving with the colours' has destroyed his 'Civil qualification: Bricklayer'.

The last two anecdotes crystallize George's attitude to the war, and finally make it explicit. The shortage of food in 1918 sharpens class tensions; rumours circulate that the rich are well supplied. The women in the ration queues turn on an immediate target, the shopkeeper, wanting him sent to the front. George, though, would not wish what he has been through on anyone. That experience he represents not through his own wounds, but indirectly through his dead friend, Tommy Taylor, sneered at by an acquaintance as a 'nancy boy' they are well rid of. Here, uncovering the meaning of this elegy does demand some cross-reference. When the young George had had to get work in a hurry, in order to marry the already pregnant Emma, he had taken on the gentle, awkward Tommy, with his 'soft white skin like a wench', as his labourer. In 1900, when harsh winter weather had stopped the building trades, they had cleared snow from the streets together. In this otherwise bitter setting, the text opens out into a utopian moment. The two men go skating together; even the usually clumsy Tommy is here at his ease. 'Two of us would catch hold of each other, and skate, dance, on the ice.' They set off along the frozen canal; their speed and freedom of movement giving rise to fantasies of escape. Tommy leads off '"Let's go round the bend, under the next bridge – round the bend! . . . farther an' farther."' George is surprised, 'He never put more'n two words together as a rule'; but he takes up the theme, '"We can skate to *New Zealand*! . . . or Africa!"' Yet in his mind's eye he can still see ahead of them the lock-gates, 'heavy and black they was, shut ice-tight like the doors of a gaol.'[47] In the war, Tommy had served with the Medical Corps. Now, in 1918, George recalls his friends blown to bits beside him in the trenches. Among them was Tommy, 'who wouldn't a hurt a fly', now 'splattered about in a foreign country where they didn't even speak the language – for what?'[48]

This closing cluster of anecdotes is permeated by tensions around gendered identity and sexual difference (George and the old men against petticoat rule, his acquaintance against the nancy boy, the women in the ration queue against the shopkeeper, even George against Tommy's sisters – 'always a stuck up lot'). In defending his friend, workmate and partner Tommy against the dismissive claim that he's better off dead, George – himself now clumsy and in a sense 'like a wench' – is also vindicating his own right to go on living. Hewins's narrative, therefore, can be most richly understood by examining a complex sequence such as this, in which anecdotes from various genres interact to produce meaning, and thereby to defend and maintain an identity fractured by the social crisis of war.[49]

* * *

Far from being formless, then, Hewins's narrative is a complex construction. It displays modes of irony (and the accompanying literary device of quotation/parody) also to be found in more self-consciously political proletarian writing; and its use of music-hall form has parallels with appropriations of popular culture for critical ends within more conventionally literary texts. Both the presence of parodic anecdote across a range of oral, autobiographical and fictional working-class narratives, and the use within this oral narrative of the cues and codes of music-hall form suggest that Tonkin's case for challenging sharp differentiation between oral and literate applies within as well as between cultures. Among the largely literate late Victorian/Edwardian working class in Britain, it would seem, there was a complex culture comprising a range of elements from the (largely oral) rural/folkloric to the (largely written) urban/commercial. By drawing on various genres within this culture, thereby offering their listeners cues to the appropriate codes, individual singer/storytellers such as George Hewins could offer commentaries on everyday events in informal and semi-formal settings such as workplace, street or pub. Working-class autobiographers and novelists drew on the genres of this culture in their writing. But so, too, did and do those who speak their life histories. The patterns of narrative built up over a lifetime of daily discourse, and the genres which inform their different components, will be present too in retrospective recounting of life stories. Such narratives are not formless, but rather eclectic; they draw, in diverse patterns, from oral and literate, rural and urban, folk and commercial, popular and high-cultural sources. Our understanding of such life stories can be enhanced by attention to structure and genre.

NOTES

This chapter originated in a paper given as part of the panel discussion on 'Narrating our pasts: oral history, life stories and genre' at the British Sociological Association annual conference, on the theme of 'Research imaginations', University of Essex, April 1993. I am grateful to Paul Thompson for the invitation to contribute to this panel, and to all those who participated in the discussion, especially Ruth Finnegan, Laura Marcus, Alistair Thomson and Elizabeth Tonkin. I have taught *The Dillen* for several years on an interdisciplinary history-literature programme at Liverpool John Moores University (formerly Liverpool Polytechnic). My understanding of the text, and of ways of reading it, has been greatly helped by several generations of students who have worked on it with me, and I am grateful to them.

1 See, for instance, the analyses of the life history narratives of Italian political militants in A. Portelli, *The Death of Luigi Trastulli and Other Stories* (Albany: State University of New York Press, 1991).
2 Work in literary studies since the mid-1980s has been published particularly in America, often being concerned with autobiographies by women or black Americans. For examples of oral historians responding to such emphases on genre and textual form, see the essays in R. Samuel and P. Thompson (eds), *The Myths We Live By* (London: Routledge, 1990).
3 E. Tonkin, *Narrating our Pasts: The Social Construction of Oral History* (Cambridge: Cambridge University Press, 1992), pp. 6–7.
4 Ibid., p. 14.
5 Ibid., pp. 2–3; cf. p. 5.
6 A. Hewins (ed.), *The Dillen: Memories of a Man of Stratford-upon-Avon* (1981; Oxford: Oxford University Press, 1982). Henceforth, otherwise unattributed page references in the notes are to this source. All italics in quotations from this text are in the original.
7 For the genesis of the recordings, and of the subsequent text, see Hewins, *The Dillen*, p. vii, and A. Hewins, 'The making of a working class autobiography: *The Dillen*', *History Workshop* 14 (Autumn 1982): 138–42. In the latter, she notes that 'he was a storyteller par excellence,' and that 'he was a narrator more than an interviewee' (pp. 138, 139).
8 'Entertainment had been his raison d'être: he could "make folks happy", he said, summing up his life, but he could never make money.' Hewins, 'Making of a working class autobiography', pp. 140–1.
9 Childhood (pp. 25–6, 29–30); veterans (pp. 45–6).
10 After the premature ending of his building apprenticeship when he had to get married in a hurry (p. 58), George did bricklaying and other casual building work

(pp. 59, 77, 79–81, 83–7) whenever possible; but he frequently had to replace or supplement this by whatever work came to hand, including selling sticks (p. 73), snow-clearing (pp. 73–4), burying the workhouse dead (pp. 83–4), pea-picking (pp. 96–9), scavenging for food (pp. 100–2), and working as a postman (pp. 117–18), a caretaker (pp. 119–20) and as an odd-job man and extra at the theatre (pp. 123–6).

11 See, e.g., his swapping stories with the women pea-pickers (pp. 98–9).

12 Hewins, 'Making of a working class autobiography', p. 139; Hewins, *The Dillen*, pp. vii–viii. For folk elements in the text, see C. Hancock, '"Their tales came straight from faery-land": fairytale and folktale in working-class autobiography', conference paper for 'All by myself: the representation of individual identity in autobiographical writings', University of Groningen, Netherlands, Nov. 1996.

13 For the role of songs in the text, see my 'Song, performance and music-hall form: negotiating identities in *The Dillen*' (forthcoming).

14 Angela Hewins, in her 'Afterword' to the text, comments of her role as editor: 'There was no chronological sequence. It was a tale lovingly pieced together afterwards like one of those ubiquitous peg rugs' (p. 178).

15 S. Dentith, 'Contemporary working-class autobiography: politics of form, politics of content', in P. Dodd (ed.), *Modern Selves: Essays on Modern British and American Autobiography* (London: Frank Cass, 1986), pp. 70–1.

16 In the sequence of sixteen anecdotes from pp. 158–62 examined in detail below, the mean length of an anecdote is 9.8 lines of printed text and the median 9 lines (about 130–45 words).

17 Begging (p. 159).

18 For quotation, see speeches by parliamentary candidates (pp. 103–4), army documents (pp. 156, 161, the latter cited in text below). For parody, see magistrate (p. 4), school chaplain (p. 17).

19 For an example of such reinforcement, see the story of the pickpockets in the crowd at the General Election meeting in 1906 (p. 103).

20 Pulpit (pp. 81–2).

21 Reprinted in D. Vincent (ed.), *Testaments of Radicalism: Memoirs of Working-Class Politicians 1790–1885* (London: Europa, 1977), pp. 153–87.

22 A. Louvre, 'Reading Bezer: pun, parody and radical intervention in nineteenth-century working-class autobiography', *Literature and History* 14(1) (Spring 1988): 32. Robert Tressel (b. 1871) died in 1911, leaving the manuscript of his novel unpublished. A considerably abridged edition was published in 1914, the full text not till 1955. Hewins's parodies of magistrate and chaplain, cited in note 18 above, may be compared with *The Ragged-Trousered Philanthropists* (London: Panther, 1969), chs 17, 20, 30, 38, 39.

23 Hewins, *The Dillen*, notes: 'Money, or lack of it, seems at times to dominate George's story' (p. ix).

24 Compare his account of skimping work (p. 49) and of a cheating foreman (pp. 84–6) with Tressell, *Ragged-Trousered Philanthropists*, chs 2, 7, 16, 43.

25 Louvre, 'Reading Bezer', p. 30 (italics in the orginal).

26 For such moments of direct commentary, see his younger self's ignorance of poverty (p. 57), lack of trade unions and workers' rights (p. 58), irrelevance of party politics (p. 103), inadequacies of early state pension (p. 116).

27 Louvre, 'Reading Bezer', p. 30 (italics in the original).

28 For Tressell's politics, see D. Smith, *Socialist Propaganda in the Twentieth-Century British Novel* (London: Macmillan, 1978), ch. 3; P. Miles, 'The Painter's Bible and the British workman: Robert Tressell's literary activism', in J. Hawthorn (ed.), *The British Working-Class Novel in the Twentieth Century* (London: Edward Arnold, 1984),

pp. 1–17. For his representations of the speech of those in power, see R. Williams, *Writing in Society* (London: Verso, 1983), pp. 254–5.

29 Dentith, 'Contemporary working-class autobiography', explores – in relation to slang, anecdote and irony – the claim that 'certain characteristic popular cultural forms already possess an explanatory capacity, and a political charge, which may differ from the extended discursive forms of political and economic theory but which are all the more powerful as mobilizing forces for that' (pp. 69–71). In their discussion of the autobiographical novels of Jack Common (1903–68), Michael Pickering and Kevin Roberts note a similar use of the 'oral and colloquial tones' of working-class speech from north-eastern England (including the local music-hall), and stress its role in assisting class resistance and self-confidence. See their '"Revolutionary materialist with a leg free": the autobiographical novels of Jack Common', in Hawthorn, *British Working-Class Novel*, p. 79.

30 Letter (pp. 159–60).

31 Opening of army career (pp. 130–2).

32 P. Fussell, *The Great War and Modern Memory* (New York and London: Oxford University Press, 1975), p. 207.

33 Ibid., p. 208.

34 Ibid., pp. 209–10.

35 These forms were not entirely separate; Fussell offers music-hall as one source for Graves's scenes, in 'comic encounters between representatives of disparate social classes' (ibid., p. 210); for his full analysis of the literary components of Graves's comic technique, see pp. 207–13.

36 For an example of such a clearly fictional anecdote, see the coach-driver's story of the 'bottomless cab' (pp. 55–6).

37 A further complex example is provided by the culminating anecdote in the narrative of his courtship and marriage – the account of George's wedding night (p. 62), which puts him into the comic tradition of the blushing groom who is not up to the mark. This serves partly to draw the sting from what had precipitated the wedding in the first place – that George and Emma had already had their first night. Use of such a form does not imply that what is told is wholly or even partly invented (any more than does Graves's use of farce).

38 Just as Fussell, *The Great War and Modern Memory*, notes of Graves's memoir 'how rich the book is in fatuous, erroneous, or preposterous written "texts" and documents' (p. 216), so Hewins quotes or refers to official documents in ways which work to subvert their authority. See, in addition to the army letter (p. 160) and reference (p.161) cited in the text: police rules (pp. 11–12), wedding certificate (p. 60), army pass (p. 135).

39 Dentith, 'Contemporary working-class autobiography', argues: 'we also need a sense of the implicit meanings carried by the larger formal organisations of these texts, if we are to get any real understanding of their potential political charge' (p. 71). Tonkin, *Narrating our Pasts*, notes that: 'The successivity of sentences makes discourse because we simultaneously expect their connectivity' (p. 7). She argues, of the Jlao oral histories she heard: 'These narratives put forward moral and other arguments through their order and plotting, in other words, the shape of a narrative is not neutral' (p. 36).

40 The sequence analysed is pp. 158–62.

41 For such cross-references, see work (pp. 58–9, 79–81, 83–7, 116), army (pp. 57–8, 68, 88, 130–2); and notes 44–6 below.

42 The division of this passage into sixteen anecdotes (ranging from five to twenty-two lines of printed text) is to some extent arbitrary; the precise number could be modified by differing definitions. In singling out from the life story narrative

this 'sequence' made up of 'elements' which can be grouped into 'clusters', I am not suggesting any technical meaning for these terms, but simply using them as convenient markers for this particular analysis.

43 Hewins, 'Making of a working class autobiography', records that: 'the only time he wept during our long sessions together . . . was when he recalled how he was unable to get his mother out of a pauper's grave' (p. 140). Similarly, it was in these sessions that he first told anyone that Cal, too, had had a pauper's funeral.

44 For the meanings of Shakespeare (as text, performance and cultural icon) in the text, see T. Hawkes, *That Shakespherian Rag: Essays on a Critical Process* (London: Methuen, 1986), ch. 1: 'Playhouse-workhouse'; for Church of England clergy, see also Arbuthnot (pp. 17–18, 69), Melville (pp. 112–13, 167, 170–1, 173), Hodgson (p. 164).

45 For Capt. Edwards, see also pp. 136, 144, 147, 149, 151.

46 For Sgt Sanders, see also pp. 163–4, 173; for working-class self-help, see e.g. pp. 37–8, 59, 73, 86.

47 Tommy Taylor (pp. 59, 74–5); skating (pp. 75–6). There is an implicit contrast between the ease of movement across this frozen water, and later hindrance from the penetrating rain and cloying mud of the trenches (pp. 141–2, 162). The importance of this passage as a utopian element in the narrative was first suggested to me by my former colleague, Jeff Wallace.

48 Tommy's war service and death (pp. 132, 162).

49 This final point is, I believe, consonant with Tonkin's argument about the relationship between individual persons and social structures (including those of language) in *Narrating our Pasts*, ch. 7: 'Truthfulness, history and identity' (esp. pp. 131–6). My interpretation of the politics of Hewins's narrative draws on Dentith's discussion, 'Contemporary working-class autobiography', pp. 69–77.

7

MY LIFE AS CONSUMER
Narratives from the World of Goods
Orvar Löfgren

That's my technique. I resurrect myself through clothes. In fact it is impossible for me to remember what I did, what happened to me, unless I can remember what I was wearing and every time I discard a sweater or a dress I am discarding a part of my life. I shed identities like a snake, leaving them pale and shrivelled behind me, a trail of them, and if I want any memories at all I have to collect, one by one, those cotton and wool fragments, piece them together, achieving at last a patchwork self.[1]

In narrating their life histories people often use the acquisition of certain consumer goods or memories of cherished possessions to organize their trajectory through time, just like the heroine in Margaret Atwood's short story. They interweave the biography of their personal life with a biography of things.

This tendency for aspects of consumer life to become part of life histories has turned out to be a vital resource in an ongoing research project on consumer culture in twentieth-century Sweden. The focus is on consumption, as everyday routine and an arena for day-dreaming, as well as an ideological battlefield. We have used different kinds of approaches to the topic, from ethnographic observations and media studies to the analysis of a wide range of historical sources,[2] but it soon became evident that the use of oral and written life histories brought out new aspects in an otherwise somewhat over-researched field. This part of the project, called 'My life as consumer', came to focus on the ways people in different periods and social settings of the twentieth century have acquired the skills and competences needed to be consumers – not only during childhood but in all of the different stages of the life cycle and in situations and epochs in which new forms of consumption are emerging.

The use of life histories has a long and strong tradition in the discipline of European ethnology, especially in the Scandinavian countries, with vast collections in the archives linked to university departments or museums. The popularity of this kind of material has also led to an intensified debate about its special characteristics.[3]

In the following I will draw on this ongoing debate among my Swedish colleagues as I discuss some of the advantages and problems of a life history approach in this field. My material consists of two main types: first of all, more open-ended life history interviews, collected for the project; second, the rich life history material stored in the folklife archives at the Department of European Ethnology at the University of Lund and in the Nordic Museum in Stockholm. The collections used consist of responses to a number of questionnaires where people write about certain aspects of their lives as consumers, from the use of mail-order catalogues or memories of holidays to their relationship with cars, television and radio, or the telephone, to name some examples.[4]

I will also draw on a special study, using both oral and written life histories as well as other sources, on the changing rituals of consumption in twentieth-century Christmas celebrations.[5]

*   *   *

'Just imagine when my brother was allowed to go with my mother to the market in Glommersträsk. They rode on a kick-sled for seven kilometres, and when they got there and my brother saw all the glitter, he fainted with joy.' This recollection comes from a 1990 newspaper interview with the Swedish author Sara Lidman, who compares the reaction of her younger brother back in a northern rural setting in the 1930s with the anticipation local housewives felt when opening their first mail-order packages – the intoxicating feeling of at last being admitted to the modern world of goods.

When people narrate their lives as consumers there is often a focus on processes of learning and unlearning certain consumer skills. The interviews often start with the early memories of learning how to construct a list of Christmas wishes, becoming a collector of Barbie dolls or Smurf figures, or negotiating pocket money. These childhood memories often have a certain freshness; they are memories of the first confrontations with novel styles and scenes of consumption. Like Sara Lidman's brother, they often express the exhilarating feeling of entering a new world of abundance and desire. For older generations with a rural background, these memories may deal with the first trip to the market or even more often the advent of the mail-order catalogue. Many recollect the ways in which catalogue reading at the kitchen table became a family ritual, but also how it turned into a favourite pastime for children:

The country was flooded by catalogues from all sorts of places, I don't remember all of them, but they were numerous and had one thing in common. It was good to have them if you wanted to keep the kids quiet. If they got hold of a catalogue, you were left in peace, it was like a good nanny, and they would hang over the catalogue for hours – they were going to buy this and buy that: As soon as they got money!

Others remember how children made their own scrapbooks of consumption dreams by cutting out pictures and arranging scenes.

For later generations of consumers, new entrances to the world of goods opened up. Here, the early memories may deal with the first visit to a department store or a real supermarket.[6] Fantasy worlds were developed with other props. A woman with a working-class background recalls her childhood of the 1950s:

> In my generation we had paper dolls. We never used the ready-made cut-out dresses but made our own. None of us girls came from homes where there was money for a lot of clothes. We got our ideas from the fashion pages of a more middle-class ladies' journal, which we tried out as clothes for our paper dolls. In a way all these fantasies about clothes, creating some kind of image for those paper dolls, helped us to create an image of ourselves as girls or women.

Consumption as a laboratory for experimentation and identity formation comes out even more strongly when people talk about their teenage years. There are memories of the endless hours spent in front of the mirror, trying out styles, clothes and poses in order to find forms of self-expression. Teenage memories also emphasize the degree to which the battle with parents and the attempts to secure adult freedom are enacted within the field of consumption. A girl from a working-class home remembers how, in the early 1950s, she made her first pair of tartan-patterned trousers with big, shiny buttons:

> Mother was furious and said that I would look like a circus horse! She just couldn't understand how I could go out like that and make her feel totally ashamed for the neighbours' sake ... And I started putting on make-up and she came after me and washed it off ... so I just had to go out to the stairs and put on new make-up. You learned how to do dirty tricks like that.

Another dominating theme in teenage consumer life had to do with learning the nuances of social distinction. A middle-class woman in her fifties remembers the importance of moderation: 'You never dressed in too provocative a manner, or else you were classified as belonging to the greasers. You used make-up, but always very discreet – never too shiny ...'

These teenage memories are extremely gendered, as the ethnologists Berit Wigerfeldt and Maja Jacobson have discussed in their studies of fashion, class and youth culture.[7] Boys usually fought their battles with parents in other arenas than those of fashion and style, but there are striking exceptions, as Berit Wigerfeldt's life history material on growing up in the 1940s illustrates:

And I came home with a shirt that was all black. The kind that had never been seen before in Uppsala. I had a grey suit, a jet black shirt, and a red tie. With turn-ups and cufflinks. The guys were like, 'Where did you buy that?' and they stared. 'Where the hell did you get that shirt?' Sure. You grew.

During later stages of life, home-making becomes a central metaphor for narrating family life. Interviews with this focus underline an important generational change. The idea of home improvement as a family project, uniting wife, husband and children, is present today in a manner that would have been unthinkable in 1900 or 1930. In the postwar period home-making became more and more related to identity formation. Home became a place where one actively tried out different sides of the self, an important site of cultural production. A new space for creativity had emerged in working-class everyday life, an opportunity to develop talents and interests among people who had previously lacked the time, money and energy to invest in their own home. During the 1950s and 1960s a new kind of aestheticization of everyday life developed. Families became engaged in questions about scene-setting in the home, choosing colours, forms and furniture, and the men were drawn into the domestic sphere in new ways. The life histories illustrate that this family project called the home is never finished. People are busy redecorating, fixing, planning, day-dreaming, producing new sofa cushions, putting in new floors, ripping out old ones, changing wallpaper, driving to the hardware store, leafing through furniture catalogues, taking the whole family to IKEA, moving things around, and moving the family on. In a way the family is constantly being repaired and renovated. The home builds the family together, creates a common ground of interests as well as conflicts between spouses and generations.

The life histories of consumers give many examples of these creative processes, with a constant dialogue between day-dreaming and fantasies about 'the ideal home' and the attempts to turn at least parts of utopia into reality. The skills of home-making are acquired early on, in play with doll's houses or in the use of one's first teenage room as a laboratory for experiments with styles of decoration (choosing provocative colours and furniture combinations in order to distance oneself from the hopelessly old-fashioned taste of the parents). As a home-builder one then progresses to the proud and solemn moment of moving into a home of one's own and from then one continues a career of dreaming, planning and redecorating.

Narratives of 'my life as consumer' in the sense of home-builder, car-owner or teenage consumer highlight the ways we have over the years acquired consumer skills which later have often been naturalized into habits, reflexes and routines and thus become hard to notice. It is an approach which could be developed much further. The slow naturalization of these skills comes out very noticeably in the life history material on life with media technologies, from the telephone to the television. Pioneer radio listening or television viewing was surrounded by an almost sacred aura. People remember the solemn atmosphere and the intense concentration in early radio listening, or the ways in which you dressed up for television evenings, hushing both grandma and the kids. Both the radio and the television set were given a prominent position in the best room, rather like home altars. Gradually the media became routine, people learning how to listen with half an ear to the radio or how to have the television on as a background screen for conversation, zapping between channels. In the same way there was a distinct stiffness surrounding early telephone experiences, which moved from the ritual exchange of set phrases to an acquisition of the art of improvised chatting. Typical of this gradual mastery of new home technologies is also the capacity to do several things at the same time: read a paper while listening to the radio, or keep up a phone conversation while watching the television news, etc.

* * *

Several genres emerge in the material on 'my life as consumer'. First of all, the interviews underline the ways in which most discussions about consumption tend to have a moral element. Narrating your life can take the form of a moral argument about a 'now' versus a 'then'. For some it becomes important to stress how one learned how to make do with little, and this is often meant as an indirect criticism of the youngsters of today 'who get everything for nothing' and who never learn to resist giving in to desires or think twice about consumption.[8] Such moral lessons can also be condensed into situations or objects, which may also take on rather stable narrative forms. An old caretaker remembers playing football as a teenager:

> Well, you made a ball out of rags or something like that. You didn't buy one, you couldn't buy one, because you couldn't afford it, we had no money for that. You used what you had, and it was all right. There weren't the same demands as they have now. Now they absolutely must have a first-class ball, a real ball, before they can play.

Interestingly enough, this memory of the improvised football as a moral example surfaces in other working-class life histories from the interwar years.[9]

In the Christmas material mentioned earlier, this moral issue also coloured many narratives. One man remembers the disappointments from all the Christmases when he got no presents, and he feels a stab of pain when he sees his grandchildren in a sea of gifts: 'I would have been happy if I had been given a twentieth of all that!'

The working-class memory of threadbare Christmases is a composite one. Bitterness can be mingled with pride: 'We had it tough, but we had to learn to get by – unlike today's spoiled generation.' A message like this can be crystal-lized in a moral detail in the reminiscences: how Daddy made a church out of a piece of white cardboard, or how overjoyed one could be at the sight of a couple of oranges on the dinner table.

On the whole, these life histories suggest an alternative reading of Swedish Christmas celebrations, as a cultural prism which magnifies, or rather concentrates, conflicts, utopias and ideals of family life and consumer wishes which may otherwise lie hidden or forgotten in the humdrum of everyday life. In the Christmas narratives many lessons emerge on the moral economy of the family. Children learn about possible and impossible wishes and desires, are confronted with the rules of gift reciprocity, and so on.[10]

In her study of how Chilean refugees in Sweden have adapted, Beatriz Lindqvist has shown how the arena of consumption appears as an important ideological battlefield between different groups in their life histories. Intel-lectuals often scorned other, working-class, Chileans for being seduced by consumerism, as they tried to work out new life projects in Sweden. Looking back on the early years in Sweden, one of them remembers meeting other Chileans in department stores:

It was embarrassing at times, for I felt as if I was caught in the act. I was really ashamed of all the unnecessary goods I had in my trolley. The worst thing was when someone made a sarcastic remark, such as 'You're already caught in the tentacles of the octopus!' But people didn't often say anything directly like that. No words were needed, because you knew in yourself that you had done wrong. You had the censorship installed in your brain, like a little old man lifting his finger and saying 'Shame on you!'[11]

There is, however, another moral theme which organizes some of the gen-eral narratives of 'my life as consumer'. It is the feeling of having developed into a much more skilful and critical consumer: 'Back in those early days I was so confused. Now I know what I want, I have found my personal style and taste.' In the same way there might be a need to distance oneself from earlier ideals. A woman born in 1960 recalls how as a teenager she longed for a room in pink with laces and frills, just like her working-class playmate had. At home a middle-class aesthetic of restraint and rationality ruled. Every-thing was to be simple, practical and of good quality. Slowly her admiration for the neighbour's pattern of consumption was turned into dissociation. It was the ideal of the parents that triumphed in the long run.

The need to distance oneself from earlier patterns of consumption often involves an element of irony, which illustrates the ways in which earlier habits and styles come to be seen as 'tacky'. What was once most desirable, natural or elegant has been redefined into something hopelessly old-fashioned or comical: 'How could I ever dress like that!' These aspects of the material call for a further exploration of the social and cultural construction of naivety and sophistication during the life cycle.

* * *

The moral lessons of consumption are quite often tied to questions of class. One of the main themes in our project on consumption was the ways in which the language of class has taken on new metaphorical forms in twentieth-century Sweden. During the new affluence of the postwar decades it often disappeared into discourses of consumption and taste: good and bad habits.

In the life histories it is striking how class differences are materialized in certain consumer items or situations. In working-class memories of the 1920s and 1930s, shoes, for example, have a central position. At school the important boundary could be between those who could afford shoes and those who wore clogs. A textile worker born in 1916 remembers meeting middle-class children on the more neutral ground of the public playing field. 'We played together up to their garden entrance, but then we couldn't come along any further with them, because we only had clogs.' 'If they had shoes, they belonged to the nobs,' was another remark. The daughter of a poor agricultural labourer remembers her church confirmation, when all the children had to dress up. But there was no money for shoes, so she had to borrow her brother's: 'Crumpled newspaper was put into them, because we didn't have the same size feet. I can see those shoes before me, whenever I want. I had them after my brother. Walking up to the altar in a boy's shoes.'

For later generations other markers of class are remembered, and class boundaries often become more subtle. A woman remembers how children in her Stockholm suburb of the 1950s were categorized by the thin grey line after their name in the school catalogue, which meant 'no telephone'.

A special narrative genre is found among those travellers between classes who were resocialized into new patterns of consumption as they were introduced into middle-class circles. Memories of this transition can also be crystallized into a situation or an object. A working-class boy who, unlike his friends, took the step up to grammar school in the 1960s brought his moped to the new school only to find out that this cherished symbol of teenage affluence was not the thing to have in the new middle-class setting: 'After a few days at school I sold it. You were supposed to have a plain, quality bike, nothing else.'

The class element is also present in the ways in which some groups, especially middle-class intellectuals, are obsessed with questions of distinction and taste. There is a recurrent need to distance oneself from other consumers, to stress one's role as a critical observer of the consumption habits of 'the others'. Individuality is a central virtue in this as in other parts of modern middle-class cosmology.

*   *   *

In similar ways, memories of progress and modernity are often condensed into certain objects or situations. In the life histories of those born in the 1930s and 1940s, memories of the first confrontations with modern living stand out very clearly. Some of the great moments of family life during the early postwar era are organized around such material improvements. The first bathroom with running hot water, the first ride in the family car or the first family holiday stand out as utopias which had suddenly come within reach.

There are also striking gender differences here. In life histories of many women of this generation it is the memories of the move to the first modern apartment that stand out. In many cases the expression used is 'it was like a dream', or 'just like paradise'. It is remembered as taking a step into the future. A woman recalls this move in the late 1950s, when she was still a child: 'Oh, it was like a dream! Just crazy. Most of all I remember that we got our first bathroom. We never had had one before. My sister and I didn't go out to play during the first months – we were just lying in the tub.' Hot running water, the first fridge, or a modern sofa suite: these are objects around which women organize the family's progress into modernity.[12] The men remember other things.

In his study of working-class life in Göteborg, Gösta Arvastson has stressed the strong male memories of the first pair of overalls – a piece of clothing proudly shown off in front of the neighbours as a signal that one had taken the definitive step towards adulthood and wage-earner status.[13] Another male narrative has to do with car ownership. In retrospect, life can become a drive along an upwardly mobile freeway, where the buying of better or bigger cars marks a family on the move, going somewhere.

For the postwar teenage generation there are other material acquisitions which mark the entry into modern life. Several interviews mention the butterfly or sling chair of the late 1950s as an icon of modern teenage life, with its bold design (plastic-coated steel with a leatherette seat in the bright new colours). It was one piece of furniture that you longed for as a teenager. In Sweden you could order it from the mail-order house 'Modern Living': 'I remember when I went and bought my first furniture. I remember that butterfly chair, of tubular steel and vinyl . . . You can really feel the smell. That's something I feel was very typical of the fifties.' The sling chair fitted nicely with a new kind of body, the loose-limbed American teenage body, and you sat in it in a way that provoked the older generations. As one women put it, 'that chair became a symbol of defiance.'

These memories of the encounter with modern living can, however, also take the form of retrospective disenchantment: a narrative of loss. This is evident in some recollections about the advent of television, which is often used to organize a marked 'before' and 'after'. 'Before' becomes the golden age of togetherness and informal socializing; 'after' is the period of privatized family cocooning and deteriorating social life. For some the acquisition of the first television set thus becomes a watershed event in the life history, as for example in a collection of working-class interviews from the early 1980s, which stress the disappearance of the old togetherness: 'There were six families for each entrance and you had parties together and nice times, playing cards. Now it's arrived, that great monster standing on four legs in the corner – the telly.' Or:

> I miss the old togetherness. There was more friendship then. Now everybody's got their own to think of. And then there is the telly. People say, 'We've got to be at home tonight, there's this or that on the telly.' Coming together was freer and more simple then.

Here it is important to remember that those ageing workers interviewed back in 1980 had encountered the advent of Swedish television (in the late 1950s) during their most active social period. For later generations the television would appear less like a social revolution.

Comparing the Swedish experience with that of other nations illustrates how memories of modernity have both transnational and national elements. An ongoing project by German ethnologists on 'Remembering the modern' at the University of Marburg asks people to react to a set of photographs from the 1960s, depicting novelties from electric razors to washing machines. Again the gender differences in these reactions are very striking, but so also are the ways in which the global world of the modern is nationalized into a rather specific German version.

* * *

The television examples illustrate how certain objects or acquisitions can become organizing props around which significant periods or changes in life are arranged. They may, as Melanie Wallendorf and Eric Arnould have pointed out, 'serve as beacons or guideposts to orient the individual in, and personalize, both space and time'. Wallendorf and Arnould have also pointed to the tendency for older people to make a more elaborate use of cherished objects to organize their life stories.[14]

In such narratives, objects may acquire a life of their own.[15] There are marked projections of our own lives – dreams, frustrations, anxieties – into these biographies of things. The stories are not only told in words, they may often be materialized in the collections of souvenirs or domestic driftwood which pile up on mantelpieces or on sideboards. In her study of Swedish wall decorations, Eva Londos has illustrated how people may arrange their life histories as a collage of photographs and pictures.[16]

Materializing memories of the past through consumer items is also a technique which has become increasingly popular in the world of fiction and media. Certain commodities are used to signal 'that atmosphere of the 1950s', both in novels and in advertisements: 'of course you remember your first butterfly chair.' This technique can be used as a knowing wink to the readers: do you remember our shared childhood, the smell of Band-Aids, the jingles of certain television commercials or the first Hula Hoop? In the media it is also used to produce a nostalgic consumer history for those who did not grow up during that period. The old saying, 'if you remember the sixties, you weren't there', reminds us of the ways in which 'remembering a decade' is a process of institutionalization and fetishization, and it seems that consumer items work very well as nostalgic time machines. In all these genres we find a process of cultural condensation, in which certain objects and situations become part of the folklore of a decade. These are things surely everyone remembers! This constant interaction between personal and mass-mediated memories means a constant reworking of life histories: are these images my holiday memories or just life filtered through an old commercial?

*　　*　　*

With these short examples I have tried to illustrate some of the possibilities and problems which life history material brings to the cultural study of consumption. On the whole, I think the life history approach may bring a better balance to the field of consumption studies, where certain perspectives seem rather over-exploited.[17]

I am arguing for a stronger focus on the ordinary objects and the everyday routines of consumption. Consumer activities demand a constant allocation of scarce resources, as well as of physical and mental energy. The objects we acquire also occupy time and space in our lives, cluttering up our cupboards and daily routines. The life history approach tells us about processes of learning, unlearning or relearning: how children are introduced into the world of goods, how teenagers experiment with consumption as lifestyling, how families struggle to develop the skills of making ends meet. We see what kinds of skills tend to become superfluous in new situations or settings, what competences need constant improvement, what knowledge can be neglected or discarded. People have trained themselves to make a multitude of consumer decisions during a normal workday, decisions about what to buy, to eat, to wear or discard.

The life history approach can thus provide insights into important processes which have often been overlooked in the cultural analysis of consumption. A comparative historical perspective may also help to problematize some of our contemporary notions of what consumption is all about and how you become a consumer, by studying the experiences of men and women of different generations and social groups. Gender differences come

123

out strongly from the material. Men and women tend to tell very different stories about their lives as consumers, emphasizing different arenas, competences and interests. The material also mirrors battles of authority and preferences in family life. Who decides on the priorities of consumption? Who is depicted as the spender, who as the economizer? Even in seemingly trivial remarks there is a hidden moral message. The narratives also tell us about processes of cultural change, about the ways in which the boundaries between necessary consumption or overconsumption have been moved around. How are yesterday's consumption dreams transformed into new possibilities and later turned into trivialities? How does the exclusive become commonplace?

In interpreting all these stories about 'my life as consumer', there is, of course, a risk of being taken in by the central position of commodities. As I have tried to show, one reason for their frequent appearance or structuring power has to do with the ways in which we have learned to use them as narrative coat-hangers or time machines. Things are simply good to remember with. The exhilarating feeling of putting on a brand new shirt, the humiliating memory of walking up to the altar in a boy's shoes with rolled-up newspaper inside – over time such situations may also become more and more institutionalized and elaborated. Many reminiscences of consumer situations have a strong sensual element: the smell of a new car, the first taste of a spoonful of Jell-O, the tactility of a dress, or the swishing sound of the automatic door in the new supermarket. In the elaboration of such memories we are, as I have pointed out, hardly unaffected by the mass-mediated forms of nostalgia.

There are, however, other ways in which the genres of 'my life as consumer' are influenced by the zeitgeist. Many of the narratives I have quoted have been produced during the last decade, when the virtues of self-reflexivity and identity-building have been increasingly advertised. As Birgitta Svensson has pointed out, life histories become a genre for organizing one's life into a coherent and personal history of identity.[18] When people are asked to tell the story of their life as consumers, they may often turn their lives with things into projects of identity-building; but, as I have tried to show, the ways in which we choose to do this vary with our position in the world of goods, for example in relation to gender, generation and class.

NOTES

A first version of this chapter was presented at the ninth International Oral History Conference, Göteborg, 13–16 June 1996, and I gratefully acknowledge the constructive comments I received there.

1 Margaret Atwood, *Dancing Girls and Other Stories* (Toronto: McClelland-Bantam, 1988), p. 106.
2 For a presentation of the project, see Orvar Löfgren, 'Consuming interests', in

Jonathan Friedman (ed.), *Consumption and Identity* (Langhorne: Harwood, 1993), pp. 47–70.

3 For an overview of this debate, see Birgitta Svensson, 'Lifetimes – life history and life story: biographies of modern Swedish intellectuals', *Ethnologia Scandinavica*, 1995: 25–42.

4 For a discussion of the material emanating from the questionnaire about mail-order catalogues, see the discussion in Birgitta Conradsson, 'När postorderagenterna fick oss att skriva efter varor från katalog', in *Fataburen: Nordiska museets årsbok* (Lund, 1975). The life histories on the use of radio and television collected by the Nordic Museum and the folklife archives in Lund are discussed in Orvar Löfgren, 'Medierna i nationsbygget: Hur press, radio och TV gjort Sverige svenskt', in Ulf Hannerz (ed.), *Medier och kulturer* (Stockholm: Carlsson, 1990), pp. 85–120, while the material on 'my life with the car' is presented in Orvar Löfgren, 'Vägen in i bilsamhället', in Sven Gerentz (ed.), *Vägar – dåtid, nutid, framtid* (Stockholm: Vägverket, 1991), pp. 162–71.

5 See Orvar Löfgren, 'The Great Christmas Quarrel and other Swedish traditions', in Daniel Miller (ed.), *Unwrapping Christmas* (Oxford: Oxford University Press, 1993), pp. 217–34.

6 See, for example, the work of another participant in the project, Cecilia Fredriksson, 'Shopping and shoplifting at EPA: the making of a Swedish department store culture', in Colin Campbell and Pasi Falk (eds), *The Sociology of Shopping* (London: Sage, 1996).

7 Berit Wigerfeldt, *Ungdom i nya kläder* (English summary: 'Youth in new garments') (Stockholm: Symposion, 1996) and Maja Jacobson, *Kläder som språk och handling* (English summary: 'Clothes as speech and action') (Stockholm: Carlsson, 1994).

8 Cf. the discussion in Marianne Gullestad, 'The morality of consumption', *Ethnologia Scandinavica*, 1995: 97–107.

9 See Eva-Lis Bjurman, 'En fotboll av hopskrynklade tidningar', *Rig* 63 (1980): 81–3.

10 See Löfgren, 'Consuming interests'.

11 Beatriz Lindqvist, *Drömmar och vardag i exil* (English summary: 'Dreams and reality in exile – cultural strategies of Chilean refugees') (Stockholm: Carlsson, 1991), p. 64.

12 Cf. the discussion in Kerstin Gunnemark, 'Hemmafruar och tonårsflickor berättar om folkhemmets rekvisita', in Håkan Andréasson et al., *Vardag som vetenskap*, Skrifter från Etnologiska föreningen i Västsverige (Göteborg, 1996), pp. 127–50.

13 Gösta Arvastson, *Maskinmänniskan: Arbetets förvandlingar i 1900-talets samhälle* (Göteborg: Korpen, 1988).

14 Melanie Wallendorf and Eric Arnould, 'My favourite things: a cross-cultural inquiry into object attachment, possessiveness and social linkage', *Journal of Consumer Research* 14(4): 531–47.

15 Cf. Igor Kopytoff, 'The cultural biography of things: commoditization as process', in Arjun Appadurai (ed.), *The Social Life of Things: Commodities in Cultural Perspective* (Cambridge: Cambridge University Press, 1986).

16 Eva Londos, *Uppåt väggarna i svenska hem: En studie av etnologiskt bildbruk* (including English summary) (Stockholm: Carlsson, 1993).

17 Cf. the discussion in Orvar Löfgren, 'Scenes from a troubled marriage: Swedish ethnology and material culture studies', *Material Culture* 2(1) (Mar. 1997): 95–113.

18 See Svensson, 'Lifetimes'.

8

DISTANT HOMES, OUR GENRE

Recognizing Chinese Lives as an Anthropologist

Stephan Feuchtwang

Zita Bernabovi died of old age after a simple life. At the age of twelve she had been taken as a maidservant into the house of the wool merchant Pagano Fatinelli in Lucca, where she remained for the rest of her life. She was canonized by Pope Nicholas III soon after her death in 1278. Her festival on 27 April became one of the most popular in the city. She is said to have given food from her master's larder and clothing from his wardrobe to the poor. Her small and shrivelled body can be seen today, preserved in a side chapel of the church of San Frediano in her home city.

Who is Santa Zita and what is she doing here? I invoke her from obscurity to wonder how different the process of canonizing a very ordinary life is from what anthropologists or oral historians do. We encounter ordinary lives, whose subjects often wonder why we bother to seek them out. We put them on to an agenda not their own. Our publications make them known in ways to which they are usually unaccustomed and of which more frequently than not they are unaware. The story of a village, a town or a life can become a classic – a kind of immortality. But the villagers do not achieve it. We recommend it to another public than their own.

Our accounts give the ordinary, like Zita, a place next to the heroic. Zita is not a heroine, but her ordinariness is celebrated in the same way as martyrs and founders. She joins the events of the great. We do not canonize. We take the ordinary even further away. Saints are still native, whereas we discover and remove the lives of others into a greater distance. We do not sanctify. But we do record what might otherwise have been forgotten and promote it into a record of our own kind.

I shall speculate upon our relationship to our subjects. My field is far off: China. It is typecast for ethnographic distance. (How often does 'China' spring to attention when someone reaches for the completely different?) My speculation will use Chinese gods, rather than saints, to reflect on our activities of recording the ordinary. Catholic canonization of saints and Chinese authorization of local cults are standardizations of local myths and their heroines or heroes. Both are mixtures of historicization and myth-making. If ethnography is another genre, another activity, is it another kind of com-memoration, another historicizing intervention? I will not elaborate the reminders which have by now become commonplace, that ethnography is party to relations of power and that local knowledge is affected by the outcomes of large-scale economic processes which make some places, posi-tions and activities central, others remote. My purpose is not to deny nor to regret, but to expose without shame what might indeed be an admirable academic distance and its minor hegemony, and to distinguish it from state and economic power. It is obvious that ethnography and anthropology are made out of relationships in which academic anthropologists, our docu-mentary sources and informants are profoundly engaged. But does that mean that we and they can or should have equal weight and responsibility for the results? The entrance of a more reflexive, fragmented and partial 'I' has certainly changed ethnography, but not the empirical care and responsibilities of enquiry.

Ethnography is derived from three relations into which I will organize my speculations. They are to listen and record; to be heard and recorded; to present the record. *To listen and record* is the journey we make. It appears to be a modest endeavour, but it is also to seek an entry into reality – that which is exquisitely not oneself, just as China is most far from and other than Europe and its Greek Orient (Asia Minor to India). *To be heard and recorded* is from the subject's point of view the first step in an unlooked-for promotion which I have been comparing with canonization, and in which the life of the informant, the statement, the document become part of the materials for a text. It is to be unexpectedly respected, perhaps grateful, but also dependent, perhaps resentful. *To present the record* is a wielding of the authority of another author, and yet to possess it, a reaching for the mortality of another, thereby achieving textual immortality, revealing the other author through the reality boundary of quotation marks and evidence.

The rhetorical devices of realism, scientific authority and the drama of surprise or irony have already been exposed as conventions of ethnography.[1] I am more concerned with some poignant elements of the relationships which produce ethnography and which I think are inescapable. We may produce a monograph which is written from many sources and in many genres, like a collage in which none is more validated than the others. But the collector, the stitcher who produces it and is one of the sources and writes in a particular genre, has a special place among them. It has its own validation, whatever devices of polyphony are used to counter the stitcher's authority and that of the language into which all the genres are translated and framed: the common language of world capitalism or the language of validation itself.[2]

I shall present contrasting enunciations in this article; in that sense it is polyphonic. But I cannot pretend that it represents the agencies of those

127

enunciations. I hope to demonstrate the implausibility of polytextual integration.[3] It is implausible because it cannot escape questions of validity. This looks like dominance, but it is the inescapability of the authority of an evidential discourse, rather than the dominance of a world-language or a world-economy.

* * *

'Anthropology in the late twentieth century is no longer the "discovery" of terra nova or undescribed cultures, but rather a method of informed critique'.[4] Nevertheless, anthropologists do engage in a retrieval which, by its methodology and its presentation, claims the authority which discovery also claims. We are neither philosophers nor dramatists, nor are we novelists. We do not just speculate, we speculate with and through evidence. Nor should we invent dialogue. Ethnography may well share with other genres the narrative conventions of realism, but our references to evidence and our devices to claim professional authority do require critical conventions of their own which are not those of literary or of philosophical criticism. We quote or refer to findings. We research, not for grist to an invention, but to find objects for our pragmatic or speculative undertakings. Our findings are based on and supported by the observations or interviews, texts or documents which we collect. So we go 'out' to listen and record.

The uneasy relation to grand narratives of universal truth with which this century began, has led the social sciences and the writing of history at the end of it into lower case plurals: histories, cultures, subjectivities. Grand narratives are still told, in the aspirations implied by the currency of the words 'progress', 'liberation', 'improvement', 'development' and the like, which we cannot and should not ignore. Indeed, many of our informants have grand-narrative hopes. But we commit ourselves to a *low* perspective on them.

One of the habits of social anthropology and of oral history is to find objects at a distance from transformative events. Their distance is in being subject to them, rather than active in them. Case studies of leaders and heroes of movements which have shattered or made worlds are rare. Usually our objects are subjectivities which are not those identified as prime movers. They are variants upon or exceptions to the leading actors or ideologies to which great events are attributed, though possibly illustrative of social forces which were active in them.

Our agenda remains one of global significance. Events in one place can have spatial ripple effects on a global scale. More personally, not one of the people and none of the social identities and their mixtures with which we deal can be so remote as to have no border-crossing impacts beside our own writings. Through diasporic connections resulting from migration or through the attentions of non-governmental organizations and 'development' schemes, if not through governments, they can come back to our writings by other routes than our own journeys. Furthermore, the same global dimension and a long temporal dimension of historical events and discontinuities remain the comparative dimensions in which we deal. But we habitually deal into that global significance the silences, the omissions, the negatives ('without' history) which give us a slant on the revolutions, events and transformations which make our lives and those of our subjects. We go out to find and bring back these negatives and distances into relations to those events. By this means we offer critiques and at the same time evaluations in which our subjects become participants, but through a professional 'us'.

It has often been remarked that anthropologists have inborn predispositions to bring the outsider inside. We seek to question but also to test what are the great, which is to say the shared or collective, events and subjects of history. To question received wisdom, including our own, we investigate motives, senses of direction, shared orientations and habits of thought not our own. Of course, an anthropology which objectifies the wisdom of others as if it were a consensual and collective fact is not only possible, it is usual. We write regional, if not tribal biographies. It is also not only possible but usual to pretend to translate such a fact without questioning the assumptions of the conventions into which it is rendered. But if it ever was, such complacency is rightly no longer secure. We uneasily elevate our findings in a process of modified identification with them, putting ourselves somewhere between places on the line of translation.

This will not be a psychological analysis, but I do think that a straightforward interpretation of ethnographic enquiry as a process of identification is helpful. The premise of identification is an object, which is to say something incorporated from outside. It may be an attribute, an icon like Zita's key or her virtue of stealing. It may be a quotation or a slogan. More than that, the object is that by which I join others, as in the assumption of shared likes and dislikes or of an unconscious affectation – a way of walking or coughing, or the mannerisms and habits of thought in a language I learn. At the same time, and by the same token, identification is also that by which I am taken out of myself, as in the dream of an ideal world or the love of another. Finally identification is the process by which I distinguish myself, set myself apart, but always by means of the objects which I incorporate and in which I am reflected.

What we choose to study and the means by which we gain rapport to achieve our results of listening and recording must surely involve identification. Seeking another story and incorporating it is a personally and professionally formative work, by which I, like generations of anthropologists before and after me, have gained academic and professional entry to 'social anthropology' and its register. My fieldwork took place in Taiwan while the mainland was engulfed in the momentous events called the Cultural Revolution. I was interested in popular religious practices which had been

129

severely suppressed in the mainland, and which I had personally rejected for myself.

Confrontation with the religious and miraculous is a foreign territory with which I have, by a journey similar to those of a thousand other anthropologists, become familiar. I have made local cults and festivals in rural China my own claim to fame. I undertook a journey of displacement in seeking the roots of others for my subject of study. I listened in another language, leaped into another register which any listening and recording involves. Is it not a displacement and a new, a re-identification? I was fascinated and respectful, treating gods or saints and their festivals as collective poetry, or as histories people tell of themselves. Objective neutrality and the empathetic 'a-ha' of the professional listener is a mere instrument. It is the insinuating edge of a larger procedure. Hearing another is to find what can be construed, and then be reconstructed (in written notes and selected recordings and images). The otherness becomes one's own production.

Outside my professional role as anthropologist I would never have made such close acquaintances with the subjects of my research. But I am an anthropologist; there is enough in its profession to treasure after critical attacks, to own it with a shameless 'we'. We listen in order to represent the other. We not only record; we remember. In our own memories, some are more vivid.

A favourite informant in my formative fieldwork was Chen Jinde. He represented for me the vivid history of the place as a ritual location. The place was a very small town, Mountainstreet, whose main industry was a coal mine. He was a miner, but he had also been a musician and actor and trained younger men in martial arts to perform in local festivals. One of the gods celebrated in the local temple was The Immortal (Xian Gong), a deification of the Taoist adept Lu Dongbin who appears as one of Eight Immortals which figure all over China in its popular arts. The centre of The Immortal's cult from which Mountainstreet's own was an offshoot is on a mountain in the suburb of Taipei city called Mucha. My notes for 10 October 1967 record a conversation in which Chen Jinde linked his own life to The Immortal's.

When he was acting in the town's troupe they were called to perform at the Mucha temple. His lover at the time was an actress in the same troupe. But a young woman in the audience, attracted to him and admiring his acting, asked him to come home after the performance. He refused the invitation, not daring to go because his lover was watching. Even so, he got an inflammation on his arm similar to one which the young woman had on her face. His inflammation died down again when he returned home. It had been the curse of The Immortal, he told me. Lu Dongbin was very *hongliu* (dissolute, but also a pun with 'inflammation' or 'swelling'). He interferes in any sexual affair which takes place on his mountain because he doesn't like a woman to be taken away from him.

In other conversations, Chen Jinde had mentioned how in his travels he had had several affairs, but they were serial. He had never two-timed any of his lovers. The stories demonstrated how he had found it easy to attract sexual interest, but also that he was upright. The Immortal appeared in our conversation, I imagine, as a character with Chen's own attributes writ large. Chen in his turn represents for me a romance of another kind: my entrance into another world of identification.

When we listen and record, we hear another story and we maintain an apparatus of noting and recording which holds the other story at a distance, further away than the memory of the encounter would be held. We check memory against notes and recordings. We test our reconstruction with the records. On the other hand, our records become a treasure for the sense we can make of them. Often a memory retaining a vivid detail, a feeling which was not recorded or noted, is a clue to the way we should select and use our notes and records. Other new material, new utterances by our subjects in other encounters, might damage the treasured construction. Chen Jinde talking to someone else, or reported by someone else among his acquaintances, might spoil my picture of him. When we end the fieldwork we end that possibility, but it is part of our professional role to fear and respect the damage that could have been done by the authors of the stories we reproduce. That is the mark of our professional relationship of listening and recording.

Because of it, we are engaged in a process of constantly arrested identification. Listening and recording is a process of arrested identification.

* * *

Who is listening and recording? Who are we to those we record? They have other models for intermediation, others who register their stories and lives. Those models can be described as distinct genres, like that of canonization.

In 1990 I asked Chinese research colleagues to collect oral histories from the most articulate and knowledgeable informants they could find in each of several villages in mainland China.[5] Providing a history of family as the inclusive subject of the events of their own lives seems to have come naturally to our informants. Their stories start with memories of the earliest ancestor they can remember. The history of the big event enters the family biography like a calendrical date, marking a chronological watershed. One such is 'Liberation (1949)'. 'After Liberation, my father was a deputy director of the cooperative . . .' Or 'until 1979 when the collective economy ceased to exist . . .' And the biography goes on with the family line and the personal connections by which the respondent has furthered his own family's fortune and come to the support of close kin.

Each significant relative for whom the informant has a particular responsibility or by whom he is particularly affected is the subject for a new short narrative. Here is the last narrative in the account of a man of sixty-two whose family during land reform had been categorized 'middle peasant'. Previously he had said that he was liberated sufficiently to have married for love after divorcing his cousin, with whom his parents had arranged a marriage. (They accepted his divorce eventually 'because', as he put it, 'I was totally clear.') Here he tells of his brother's marriage and family. I preserve the idiosyncratic English of the Chinese researcher who translated it (but not the spelling and grammar of English as a second language), because it is an account to a *Chinese* stranger. Note also the Communist Chinese choice of words such as 'responding to the call from the government' and 'the problem could not be solved':

> Relations with relatives have been so so. Only my older brother has suffered a lot in the last decades and I have been involved in some degree. At the beginning of Liberation he was still young. He was secretary of the Communist Youth League branch in the village. In 1954, responding to the call from the government, he led a group of young people to reclaim land in the mountains. When they reached the mountain land belonging to [an old man called] Can, he disagreed. The problem could not be solved through discussion. In the end my older brother irresponsibly decided to reclaim the mountainland by force. The old man could not bear this and hanged himself My older brother was sentenced to three years in prison. So I took responsibility to support his wife and children. After the three years in prison, he felt too ashamed to come back home. His wife decided to divorce when he did come back in 1962 . . .
>
> Later I found a wife for his son. Two conditions were set [by the bride's family]. One was that she would be my daughter-in-law [not my brother's] and the second was that I must build a house for the couple. I accepted them. I built a new house for them in 1978 and let my older brother live in the old house. The wedding took place in 1979 and the problem was thus eventually solved. My older brother did not spend a penny and I did not ask him for money because we are brothers.

Our project was concerned with rural social support arrangements and the transformation of local traditions. Like all our respondents, this man knew we were interested in tracing the history of the institutions of support in the village, and this must have determined the selection of what he told us. But I do not think it determined the genre.

Like the others, his is a genealogical biography, crossed with the events of land reform and collectivization and some of its duties and responsibilities, including the categories of identity such as 'peasant' and of position, such as 'secretary of the youth league', distinct from those of genealogical fortune and responsibility. The responsibilities and the genealogical subject of the account are both genre and condition. They cannot have been determined by the research agenda, although they are of key interest to the research. They refer more to authoritative registrations which occur to the respondent and to his idea of the Chinese investigator, than to the objectives of our project. Among the authoritative registrations he is used to is genealogical reckoning itself. Others might be citations for being a model of selfless leadership, of socialist civilization, or of hygiene, which are framed and hung on walls at work. Less official is the register of reputation for honour and grace in human relations (*renqing*, an ethic and strategy of reciprocity). Both the official and the unofficial registers of reputation are among the habitual references detectable in his story.

Even though it was told to one who could be taken to represent a Western interest, there is little in his story either of defiance or of deference to a Western power and its discourses. Studies of China come halfway between two Histories. China was never, despite imperialist humiliation, in a fully colonized situation. Subaltern studies are not entirely appropriate to it, even though imperial powers plundered China's coastal and riverine margins. For a European, to learn the language of China is to be humbled and mystified. To master it is a wonderful achievement, never accomplished. I have never achieved more than passing fluency, and now work entirely with Chinese colleagues who do most of the fieldwork and interviewing.

They are trained in the observations of their fellow inhabitants as strangers, and indeed, being more formally educated, more intellectual and urban, they are in many ways themselves other to their own popular culture. But these co-workers are also interruptions in the chain, and not just links. Through them the route from recorded text back to the native language and to the politics and culture of their country is a shorter circuit. Their presence can evoke, in them as well as in our informants, memories of work teams investigating class crimes or checking out models of political advancement and economic development. They are a reminder of ways in which informants may find themselves involved in another history. At the very least they may find themselves placed in a policy-making frame of reference, or being used as an example of a new way of writing local histories.

Certainly, the characters and genres of their narratives, including the registers of authority and recognition to which they have become used, can become subjects of an ethnographic enquiry and figure in a polytextual ethnography. But there is a recalcitrance between the texts and the enquiry. What have they to say to each other? Is there any conversation between their authorities and that of the ethnographic record and commentary? The ethnography can serve a project of policy making or evaluation, and so appear to engage, critically, constructively or cynically in the politics of their or of other states. But it is a service, not the ethnography itself. Could there be a more engaged ethnography? I do not think ethnography makes policy or saints. There is a difference between ethnographic and other authorities.

Some of the strangeness of a text which comes from a literacy which is unrelated to Europe may help settle this question. It is another of the authoritative registers available to Chinese respondents, in another of the provinces in which we worked. It is part of the promotion of a cult.

Among the intermediaries for the establishment of a cult and the name of its place in the past was the local magistrate, agent of the emperor, through whom the local gentry reported miracles as they saw them. They were miracles in service of the order and prosperity of imperial rule. A memorial in 1853, entitled 'Report on the Divine Spirit's manifest responses', was quoted to his superiors by the magistrate of a district in the prefecture of Quanzhou, on the south-eastern coast of mainland China. The text was found and translated by Kenneth Dean:[6]

> In the fourth month of 1853, the local bandit leader Lin Jun rounded up a band of four or five thousand men, and crept into Yongchun City from Dehua. From dawn until noon the government troops battled against the bandits. After they had fought for over four hours, things were at a crisis. Suddenly we saw atop Dapeng Mountain to the north of the city masses of soldiers dressed in armor. There among them were flags and banners with the name 'Guo' [the family name of the god] upon them. When the gentlemen [which is to say the authors referring to themselves in the third person] and soldiers saw this, their courage increased one hundred-fold. They attacked with furious strength. The band of thieves was forced together and decimated. Countless heads were chopped off. The bandit leader Lin Jun was forced to run far away. The town and its moat were thus recovered by the hour of noon . . .

Further episodes of responsiveness are described. Prayer for rain is briefly mentioned. Detailed description, however, is reserved for the defeat of skulking, sneaking, ratlike, hairy bandits. The memorial ends thus: 'Were it not for the resplendent power of the god how could we have annihilated these demons? Now in the entire Datian, Dehua, Yongchun, Nan'an region, all is calm: the villages and households are at peace. We felt deep thanksgiving and so composed this report.' The magistrate adds his endorsement: 'The report has been reworked into a memorial requesting the enhancement of the enfeoffment and bestowal of Imperial plaques [which had already been awarded].' His endorsement is itself endorsed by superior levels of authority through province to imperial capital, and eventually the title Bao'an, Preserver of Peace, is bestowed.

This is Chinese local history, a text set apart as an appendix within Kenneth Dean's ethnography. Its language is that of imperial bureaucracy, as it might be composed for the recommendation of an award for honours to a virtuous magistrate who has achieved 'merit with the people' as this magistrate recommends the god, except that a title like Preserver of the Peace could only be bestowed posthumously. What makes it even less like the context which ethnography supplies to it is a metaphoric crossing which betrays it as a text which doubles earthly with heavenly worlds: the bandits are equated with demons, and the gentry together with the god annihilate them. Demons are not simply a scornful analogy.

The rhetoric of this report is deference to imperial authority, hyperbole in praise, dehumanization in scorn. It is the tone solicited by authority, imperial or divine. Petitions and memorials to gods are composed in similar language for rain or other repairs of fortune and expulsions of demons.

Here the gentry, who were the local elite, sought recognition and increased fame for their most renowned local cult, conscious of an imperial history and its local versions in which their own merit could be inscribed. Commoners were represented in terms chosen for them by the local gentry.

More for themselves but again through an intermediary, this time a Taoist priest, a similarly bureaucratic memorialization was addressed to the god himself by representatives selected directly from the residents of a village. The Taoist's language of deference is similar. But according to Dean's account his representation includes becoming divine through a sacrifice of texts (scriptures and memorials) and through meditation in which he visualizes the cosmos through which he moves, bearing the wishes and needs of the people employing him. His representation also includes commands over minor deities and all demons. His spiritual journey is marked by an invocation of the gods. Its hyperbolic praise turns into mystical poetry in scriptures recited and offered. The Taoist's inner/other journey is undertaken to present a humble petition for the tranquillity and prosperity of the village and its households. The petition is a document described as a memorial and it is despatched by sacrificial burning to the gods. In it the god of the cult is addressed as the key intermediary in a hierarchy of deities described as a cosmography reaching from the village, given its Communist designation 'Seventh Brigade' as well as older administrative suffixes, up ultimately to The Three Pure Ones of the Great Tao. It ends with this prayer:

> That people and their animals shall all be healthy. That rain and wind will be seasonal. That Overseas Chinese and Hong Kong and Macao Compatriots will prosper in their business activities. That scholars, farmers, workers and merchants will all thrive together. That all things will be auspicious and lucky. That the five grains will rise up, the six domesticated animals all flourish, disasters will be averted, disease-carrying miasmas not intrude, and all things will be fortunate and fine. In all this we forever depend upon your divine radiance and protection. We reverently memorialize thus for your information. On the [date]. . . we burn incense, kowtow, and memorialize.[7]

Unlike the imperial bureaucracy and its local elites, this ritual remains and is used today. The memorial was burned in an annual festival of collective thanks in 1987. The language includes the present in the categories and formulations of ancient classics. It is the vocabulary of an archaic past made present. It is also the language of fortune in which the events of individual lives – failures of harvests, gifts from overseas relatives – are couched collectively. These ordinary eventualities are addressed to a god whose biography is the making of a local history and its part in imperial history, through the canonization efforts of a previous elite.

These prayers are one mode, literate and rhetorical, of presenting ordinary Chinese lives in formulas accepted for the description of luck and disaster and the rituals for changing fortune. Something that has happened or might happen is told as a typical or as an extraordinary event.

I say it is a history and a recognition. Dean discusses the burning of the memorial in terms of and as a contribution to anthropological theories of sacrifice. In either case, we have to reinterpret prayers into our discourse; miracles go into quotation marks as categories of fortune and contingencies of history and interpreted as social and psychological process. This is not a criticism. I point to what I think is a necessity. The genre of miracle and fortune, as well as the genre of canonization and of another, imperial authority, have to be placed at an interpretative distance. The address to gods is in the time of revelation, the events of intervention which are the history of a cult, the myths of its hero, its place and its links to other cults. In my own interpretative discourse, they are about the foundation of places, their ancestry and their access to a notional time of merit, mercy and immortality. I turn them into the historical and discursive reality in which I can treat them as evidence.

There are other, more individualized and historically sensitive accounts of lives among our Chinese sources and respondents than those given for divination and petition. They are set in a different temporality. They are stories of fortunate or disastrous events, stories of a suffering, an avoidance or a success in the manipulation of fortune or of the powerful. Historians of China and elsewhere often treat history and lives in terms of generations, in which the generations accord with key events which formed them as a before and an after. There is no limit to their number, to the phasing of continuity and discontinuity. Ordinary Chinese narratives, however, are frequently stories of luck or bad luck.[8] When historical events do impinge, as in the case of 'Liberation' (the establishing of a Communist state in China) there is simply a before in which an indefinite past is conceived. Nationalist and dynastic eras are all part of the same before, not through ignorance, but because they are the prehistory of the present. Historical events, in the sense of a consciousness of their historical significance and of life as a witness of history, are absent. Instead there is a continuous condition in which events appear as minor or major changes of fortune and misfortune. Luck is the history of those caught up in events. The investigator who records them can be treated as a threat or as a rare opportunity to tap the sources of fortune.

An equivalent difference between history and ritual suggests further implications of the difference between the two registers of life stories. History and ethnography are contestable accounts of what happened and what is significant, with evidence of records. Ritual is not contestable as an account, but as a performance it can be blamed as incorrect, causing displeasure and offence, or praised as splendid and reputable. Ritual does mark before from after, and celebrates the before in the after. But ritual is a register of the native, at the furthest remove from our own. Our register is never that of the native. I include myself as a native, since I too experience historical events as destiny or luck. But the discourse in which I am professionally engaged translates it into a history of agency in which those affected are included as the affected, as instruments, subjects or agents which constitute the outcomes of Events. We do not canonize into myth, but we do record the agency of ordinary makers of local history.

*   *   *

To present the record we use the registers of the native. We, China anthropologists, use gazetteers and other local records, and respect the calculations of kinship and generation by which names are given and transmitted. We translate and expound them with as great a precision as we can. They should be translatable back into the language of our materials without much distortion having occurred. But we differentiate them in other juxtapositions than their own. We record but do not feel the dreads of misfortune, such as the ending of a male line of descent or the shame of poverty, which mark their time, compel their silences and disguises, and display their triumphs.

We translate into a temporality and subjectivity which hovers on the outer edges of the times and spaces we record. We create tenses of subjectivity, inhabiting none. You might say that our informants inhabit a minor subjectivity in our texts and in relation to the history against which we seek their accounts. We respect and hear a sense of distance from the forces and activators of fortune or from the events other actors make and render effective. We participate with other intermediaries in revealing the other narratives and giving them significance. We faithfully repeat them in a present tense surrounded by quotation marks, or in a past tense of narrative surrounded by a present of commentary, or in a third person present which becomes a hypothesis about them. But there is no way in which we can avoid the relationships between texts, with all their indentations and quotation marks. We may democratize our presentation and offer the reader a collage of registers and persons singular and plural. We may render them as realities. Even though they are not the seductive apparatus of invention, of characters in fictions, like fiction they can seduce a reader into strange settings. But all the time our typographical frames solicit a look to the argument which contains and renders their reality significant.

We generalize and criticize, addressing other ethnographies, other experts.

Adam Kuper made this point in a recent article.[9] He contrasted two levels of 'conversation'. A metalevel of 'conversation' is beyond the field relationship. At the metalevel are three possible readerships: curious foreigners including ethnographers, the ethnographic subjects themselves again, and locally based experts. If Kuper means to include ethnographic subjects as possible interlocutors in an ethnographic conversation within or between texts, he creates a relativistic illusion. The so-called conversation sets its own terms, it has precedents which are those of a regional ethnographic tradition, as Richard Fardon has already pointed out in such a salutary fashion.[10] These are sequences and networks of texts, problems, concepts and issues which all those working on the region as anthropologists, sociologists or historians, whether native or stranger, take or can be expected to take as points of reference and departure. Even if we address our subjects, we do so from elsewhere. To engage in its conversation demands the removal of the ethnographic subject both as source and as interlocutor to that elsewhere. There is no getting away from the intrinsic hegemony of the fact that we are writing in an empirical genre. The native ethnographers with whom my work is bound up are equally caught in this genre as local experts. We, the foreign and the local experts, may have different agendas, each writing our own tribal biography, but we are engaged in an argumentative strategy in which demands have to be met: we must address certain issues. Challenges of validity and procedure have to be faced. Issues have to be addressed.

What are or have been the burning issues of Chinese anthropology into which we transport our subjects would include, for instance, the work of Maurice Freedman on the segmentation of local lineages and the linking of lineage with imperial state formation and its classes. They would also include work stemming from Morton Fried on webs of reciprocal relations which in another regional anthropology would be discussed as honour and grace. The critique of 'ritual' and 'religion' could also be admitted to general anthropology from the regional anthropology in which Chinese ethnography is written. The fact that neither it nor the others have been admitted is intriguing. Is conversation blocked by China's being so different – because we are so entranced by the peculiarity of 'China' and trapped in endless efforts to describe its singularity, a peculiarly absorbing tribal mission? Or is it that we like to keep China at the furthest remove in order to derange the categories of humanist social science? But I will not attempt any exploration of these possibilities. The point is that these questions and the lack of familiarity of most readers of this chapter with the names and issues I have described do indicate a regional tradition and I assure you that they do constitute an intertextual reality. Moreover, they are regional because they also refer to a larger intertextual reality, that of the profession of academic anthropology. The conventions of that reality are distinctive in ways which are much more general.

Compare ethnography with stories of native or nationalistic history or of

138

miraculous events. Ethnography is by definition a writing which can be checked. It is like historiography. Even if it is not as carefully chronological, it is written without recourse to the archaism of unquestioned truth, or luck, even when that is how we ourselves experience the contingencies of history. Our elsewhere is the authority of scholarship, academic distance, subjection to critical appraisal. In relation to our subjects' agency and involvements, we as ethnographers are passive; in relation to our activity, they are passive. They must become anthropologists to participate.

In its mirror, we identify ourselves professionally. But for those who claim descent from the realities we have reproduced, it is the objectification of memories and identifications. Through local experts who are not ethnographers, through the intelligentsia participating in the great event of 'history' by writing it or teaching it, our authority can be claimed as their authenticity. A biographical narrative, as well as a collective narrative such as one told of a nation or of a local cult, is a story lived and inherited. It is recalled as a collective moment like the myth of the birth of the sacred in Durkheim's theory of solidarity. Such identifications and idealizations and their negative projections are bound in a constant negotiation of protected, home spaces of tribal biography. We participate in these discursive forces, whether we like it or not. But ethnography is another kind of writing.

The persons involved consider themselves or their ancestors to have been important actors. For us, they are all remote. They are not our homes nor our cults; our subjects are not saints. Our identification and immortalization of others' homes are an amplification of the remote. We place the remote in a global context of professional conversation. What we publish can be translated back intrusively, as authentification of favoured identities and against others' claims. We participate through listening, recording and by transmission of our work back to our sources. But we do so from a necessary distance. When we cover ourselves in the glory of quoted texts and recovered agents, our clothes can still be exposed, our identifications arrested by the police of others' evidence and argument. It is a distance and a rigour well worth preserving because it is one from which we can continue to question.

Michael Herzfeld advises that 'anthropology must come to terms with the besetting otherness of ourselves – an *ethnos* as alienated as any it selects for study'.[11] His relativism removes the distance with which he starts and which I am emphasizing. Instead of an *ethnos*, I prefer to use another of his terms: anthropology is not an *ethnos*, it is a quality. It is an aspiration to a critique of ethnocentricity and prejudice; it is an exposure of assumptions, whether they exist in ourselves or in others. That is our usefulness and our profession. Here at last, in the critique of prejudice and ethnocentricity, our elsewhere participates on its own terms, in the questioning of both our own and our subjects' identifications and idealizations.

By piercing 'realities', by rendering them provisional, we reach towards other realities, obscure agencies. Unlike other social sciences, we work through identification. We share with religion, poetry, fiction and philosophy the capacity to create new possibilities. But our realities are historical, not transcendent. Our realities are grounded by arrested identification and evidential contestation.

Santa Zita for me is a name, a story, a papal decree, her worshippers, an epigraph to remind us of our professional discomfiture. We respect her worshippers but must do so in a language of inquiry in which she is not an agency. However they represent her as protector, cause or intercession, she is not. They are. But they are not agents of our enquiry, we are. There is no point in being liberal or balanced about this.

NOTES

1 Paul Atkinson, *The Ethnographic Imagination: Textual Constructions of Reality* (London: Routledge, 1990).

2 I am referring here to the highly influential opposition in neighbouring chapters of *Writing Culture* between advocacy of an aesthetic integration by a multiplicity of texts or voices in a postmodern ethnography by Stephen Tylor, and a reminder by Talal Asad of the dominance, linguistic and political or economic, in which this occurs: Stephen A. Tylor, 'Post-modern ethnography: from document of the occult to occult document', and Talal Asad, 'The concept of cultural translation in British social anthropology', in James Clifford and George E. Marcus (eds), *Writing Culture: The Poetics and Politics of Ethnography* (Berkeley: University of California Press, 1986).

3 This is to rely on Hobart's close criticism of Tylor's assumption of subjects in dialogue within the polyvocal text of his postmodern ethnography: Mark Hobart, 'Who do you think you are? The authorised Balinese', in Richard Fardon (ed.), *Localizing Strategies: Regional Traditions of Ethnographic Writing* (Edinburgh: Scottish Academic Press; Washington: Smithsonian Institution Press, 1990), pp. 306–10. But I am striking off in a different direction. Instead of treating texts as the products of agencies, and writing from them a fascinating and productive exposition which is a new text about agency, as Hobart does, I will turn back to realism, in which I can be accused of naivity as realists often are, but by which I do nevertheless mean a necessary referentiality in which Hobart's and any other ethnographic text themselves participate.

4 Michael M. J. Fischer, 'Working through the other: . . . Dialogue, silences and the mourning of Polish romanticism', in George E. Marcus (ed.), *Late Editions 1. Perilous States: Conversations on Culture, Politics, and Nation* (Chicago and London: University of Chicago Press, 1993), p. 187.

5 The project was funded by the Economic and Social Research Council of the UK, for which I am sincerely grateful.

6 Kenneth Dean, *Taoist Ritual and Popular Cults of Southeast China* (Princeton: Princeton University Press, 1993).

7 Ibid., pp. 160–1. His translation of the accompanying scripture is on pp. 162–8.

8 Amy Tan's fictions have taken up this genre. *The Kitchen God's Wife* (London: Harper-Collins, 1991) is a contrast of two biographies, one a knowing tale of misfortune, the other an unknowing tale of fortune.

9 A. Kuper. 'Culture, identity, and the project of a cosmopolitan anthropology', *Man* 29(3) (Sept. 1994): 549–51.

10 Richard Fardon, 'Localizing strategies: the regionalization of ethnographic accounts', in Fardon, *Localizing Strategies*.

11 Michael Herzfeld, *Anthropology through the Looking-Glass; Critical Ethnography in the Margins of Europe* (Cambridge: Cambridge University Press, 1987), p. 79. Herzfeld mounts a critique of anthropological distance through an analogy with the chimerical certainties of state authority, particularly when it is European. He is able to show that among the cherished habits of anthropology is the celebration of Western Europe's own national diversity while denigrating the messy ethnicism (tribalism) of other diversities. Another telling observation is that habitual dichotomies in anthropological theory between theory and practice, rules and strategies, structure and event, unconscious and conscious models, homogeneous and heterogeneous, simple and complex societies support an overarching dichotomy between a knowing us and a known them. The objects of our knowledge, including the dichotomy of (unconscious) rules and (calculating) strategies of action, need rebalancing. 'In balancing our analyses between rules and strategies, we easily forget that they are *qualities* rather than *things*' (p. 83).

9

THE ORAL HISTORY INTERVIEW IN A CROSS-CULTURAL SETTING

An Analysis of its Linguistic, Social and Ideological Structure

Yvette J. Kopijn

For a long time, oral history methodology was accompanied by an almost total neglect of the problems of language, meaning and context – problems which are critical to understanding how interviews work. Influenced by the movement of 'history from below' and by social-scientific perspectives on interviewing in general, the standard oral history frame was based on the assumption that life stories of the people who had actually experienced past events revealed the past 'as it actually was'. As a consequence, most oral historians were content simply to interview and transcribe, making little effort to comprehend more than the literal meaning of the words. The only methodological problem to be concerned about was the problem of standardization.[1]

Over the years, however, oral historians have come to realize that life stories are not as transparent as they seem. They do not reveal objective truths, but the truths of the interviewee. So it is only through interpretation that we can fully understand life stories, paying careful attention to the contexts that shape their creation.

This insight has led us to recognize the power of life stories as cultural, social and psychological constructions. The shaping of a life story is a complex process which draws upon an array of sources, including historical context and available cultural models. Facts do not exist as free-standing objects, but are produced through grammar and larger conventions of discourse. As such, the creation of life stories reveals the interplay between self and society, the dialectics between the personal and the political/symbolic. This means that if we want to appreciate the full potential of the oral history interview, we have to scrutinize the interview as text, making a close-reading of the transcript while focusing on the flow of social discourse.[2]

However, as fruitful as this insight may be, it has diverted attention away from the creation of the interview *itself*. Since the interview encapsulates our own native theories of communication and reality, most oral historians go on to work on the transcripts without reflecting on the context of the interview situation in which the process of narrating takes place.[3] However, as Tonkin has noted, 'the oral conditions mean that oral accounts or life stories are actively "dialogic": social activities in real time.' Since 'the remembering and the telling are themselves *events*, not only descriptions of events', they will clearly be misunderstood 'if they are treated as texts-in-themselves, detached from the oral conditions of production'.[4]

It is this hiatus that I felt most strongly while interviewing Javanese-Surinamese women in Surinam. Studying the experience of double migration among three generations of Javanese-Surinamese women in the Netherlands, my fieldwork in Surinam centred around interviews with elderly women who had actually experienced migration from Java to Surinam.[5]

Sakinem was one of these women. The basic biographical details furnished by her account are as follows. She had been born on Java on 28 October 1912. Due to the poverty and misery they suffered as landless peasants, her parents had decided to commit themselves to a five-year contract to work on the defaulted Surinamese plantations in 1924. After a boat trip which lasted three months, in which she had to endure the illness of her mother and the death of her smaller brother, Sakinem and her parents were sent to the plantation 'Hasard' in the West of Surinam. Earning less than they were promised, it is likely that her parents – like many other parents – were not able to take care of her properly. In any case, Sakinem was sent to an aunt, who had arrived earlier and had no children of her own. As her aunt decided to return to Java after the termination of her contract, Sakinem was soon sent back to her parents. There she was taken by a Dutch evangelist to a Christian children's home in Nickerie, a nearby village.

From the age of thirteen, Sakinem started doing all kinds of jobs. Her marriage did not put an end to the work. Cultivating her own plot of land, helping her husband with his sewing business and raising four children, all her life Sakinem worked very hard. When I visited her in Nickerie, Sakinem was enjoying the care and company of her granddaughter.

Sakinem's sex, age and cultural background provided a unique interview setting which presented me with many challenges. The meaning of words she uttered to communicate her experiences did not seem to be transparent at all. Moreover, as I wished to create a relationship based on mutual trust, which would be best achieved by respecting her daily routine, I began to wonder if the standard oral history frame equipped me sufficiently to attain this end. As Tannen has noted, cultural homogeneity and transparency of meaning are never fully attained in conversation. Even individuals reared in the 'same culture' exhibit regional, ethnic, age, gender, class and other differences in the way in which they relate. The level on which such differences occur, and the depth of possible misunderstandings, are however far more extreme in the case of broadly cross-cultural communication.[6] Doing my fieldwork, I therefore sensed the seriousness of what Briggs has detected as one of the fundamental contradictions surrounding the interview. On the one hand the interviewer is expected to be able to attend to the communicative norms surrounding the interview; on the other hand, the success of the interview depends on the interviewer's capacity for allowing 'native' communicative routines, drawing on everyday sociolinguistic norms of the interviewee, permitting the interviewee to 'wander' off the point and provide 'irrelevant' information at times.[7]

My point is this: are oral historians sufficiently equipped to prepare and conduct an interview in a cross-cultural setting if they have been trained to work within the standard oral history frame? Such a frame teaches them to view Western communicative patterns as the norm, while others are denied; to regard the individual as more important than the group, and judge views of self which differ from this norm as deviant. It trains them to keep control of the interview: the interviewee is expected to take the floor, yet their contribution to the discussion is kept within the boundaries of the topics selected by the interviewer. These premises are highly problematic, for once they have been uncritically imposed on the interviewee they will transform any oral narrative that is produced in a cross-cultural interview situation into a mirror that simply reflects Western assumptions,[8] which is precisely what Briggs calls 'communicative hegemony'.[9]

As Grele has suggested, the oral history interview should be regarded as a 'conversational narrative' or 'dialogue', a struggle for meaning and interpretation, jointly created by interviewer and interviewee.[10] Since the interviewer's performance and strategies thus seem to be as important as the narrator's in the production of meaning, it has now been acknowledged that analysis of the oral history interview requires an understanding of the subjectivity of both the interviewee and the interviewer.[11] In my opinion, this means that we should take into account not only the cultural baggage the interviewee brings to the interview situation, but also that of the interviewer. Put differently, when crossing cultural boundaries, oral historians should call into question their own methodological and practical vantage point, that is, the Western notions underlying the accepted canons of interview technique.[12] If they do not, they risk becoming trapped in their own Western assumptions about the form an interview should take.

In order to evaluate whether the standard oral history methodology provides an appropriate framework for cross-cultural interviewing, this paper will focus on the oral history interview as a communicative event. I shall scrutinize Sakinem's life story, applying Grele's definition of a conversational narrative in which he discerns the following set of interrelated structures. The first of these is the linguistic structure. The second, the social structure, is the set of relationships established between interviewer and narrator within the interview setting. The third, the ideological structure, emerges during the conversation between interviewer and narrator, and the dialogue of each with the larger cultural or historical traditions through which they are speaking.

LINGUISTIC STRUCTURE

Until now, standard oral history methodology has not paid much attention to the specific cultural patterning of oral narratives. Etter-Lewis is one of the few oral historians to have noted that oral storytelling can take various forms: 'Although styles may vary as widely as individuals, recurring patterns indicate more than a speaker's personal quirks.'[13] Therefore, only if we gain some communicative competence *vis-à-vis* the speech community in which the interviewee is situated are we capable of evaluating the information an oral narrative conveys.

According to the sociolinguist Coulthard, any description of 'ways of speaking' will need to provide data along three interrelated dimensions: the linguistic resources or styles available to the speaker; the different linguistic or speech events available to the speaker; the rules of interpretation and norms that govern different types of social interaction.[14]

When discussing different speech styles, it should be noted that there are several procedural constraints surrounding the interview situation which affect the creation of oral narratives. One of these is the norm of coherence. Following McMahan, for instance, the interviewee is expected (1) to tell a topically coherent story, (2) tell a narratable story, (3) tell a story that begins at the beginning, that is, one in which time moves ahead reasonably smoothly except for flashbacks which seem to serve a justifiable purpose, and (4) to evaluate states and events in such a way that it is possible to retrieve the core of the story and thereby deduce the point being made. For, as McMahan says, 'only if the narrator can accomplish a cooperative, suspenseful, co-herent telling, is the listener willing to wait for the point of the story to be made.'[15] The standard oral history frame therefore seems to be very clear as to how an oral narrative should be told in order to be heard.

Let us now turn to Sakinem's life story. As she was raised by Dutch evangelists, she was able to speak Dutch to me. Yet although we spoke the same language, her utterances sometimes seemed to me to be relatively unrelated. Hence she did not seem to observe the norm of coherence at all; in fact, she talked in a manner which I experienced as highly fragmented.

Still, after transcribing the interview, I discovered that her speech was not as incoherent as it had first appeared: all her digressions eventually combined to form a very coherent story, although it did not meet the norm of coherence defined above. Comparing her speech style with that of the other elderly women I interviewed, it seems to be common to narrate in a circular, associative way, which resembles the segmented style which Etter-Lewis found while analysing black women's narrative texts.[16] Take the following example, when Sakinem had just told me that her parents decided to go to Surinam to escape poverty:

And your parents, they went by boat?
Yes, in the boat. And in the boat, [louder] sailing for three months! . . . So, when I travelled, three months, my mother and father get, they get [sorrowful] oh, oh – she is sick, sea-sick. She was, er, not treat herself and er, I have to get a, a, the wife of the captain, who wants to see her: How is she, how does she look? [desperate] Because she couldn't, because she has to, if – because the boat is too big! There are thousands, more than a thousand people on the ship. [calmly] Then, they slaughter, er, cows, because people have to eat. [excited] So all kinds, I got all kinds of food, I got, eh – [asks her granddaughter the name of a particular fruit in Javanese] – oh yes, grapefruit, I got apples. You get, you get – pear – every person got two or three – then you got – you got nice food, you see, you, you, you mean, on the boat, er, those people didn't have to *pinaren*! [I didn't have to worry]. So if she [her mother] arrives there – she couldn't go to Surinam, the boat was too big. So – but the Princess Juliana and Albina sailed those people to Surinam.

Initially, I did not see the relation between her mother's illness and her discussion of food. However, analysing the interview holistically, I discovered that in Sakinem's view these topics were very much related. Her mother's illness had made the wife of the captain feel sorry for her, so she asked Sakinem to look after her two daughters. In return, Sakinem could enjoy the splendid food which was reserved for the captain's family.

Conceiving of the interview primarily as a communicative event, we soon realize that the interview is a relatively unusual speech event that is patterned by a complex array of communicative features, many of which are not shared by 'ordinary' conversation. The interview is performed for a specific purpose (gaining information from an individual), in a specified place (the interviewee is usually isolated from his or her everyday companions), with particular participants (the interviewer as questioner-listener and the interviewee as speaker). In these respects interviews may differ from many of the other types of speech event available in a particular community. As Tonkin puts it:

Researchers often assume that their work is 'doing an interview' *with* interviewees. They have not been taught to consider that interviews are oral genres, so it is not in these terms that they could recognise interviewing as a genre which tellers may not feel qualified to talk in, although they have command of other genres in which they could speak differently.[17]

Within the Surinamese-Javanese speech community in which Sakinem is partly situated,[18] so-called *slametans* (religious meals where food is shared by the community in order to worship good spirits and protect the individual involved against bad spirits) are held to celebrate 'rites de passage' like birth, marriage and death. The so-called *lèk-lèkan*, in which family and friends gather for a *nyagak melèk* (vigil) to intimidate bad spirits, is another example of a Surinamese-Javanese speech event. In order to prevent those who are present from falling asleep, a *tukang matya* (storyteller) will tell stories.[19]

What these speech events have in common is that they are performed collectively with the common aim of strengthening what they call *rukun* (mutual harmony within the community) and generating shared understandings with respect to themselves and their experiences. As such they contrast with the interview, where the interviewee is asked to reveal his or her beliefs individually, isolated from the group.

It should also be noted that the use of interview techniques imposes a particular model of social interaction in other respects. Typically, the aim of the interview is defined by the interviewer, while the interviewee's primary obligation is to answer questions. This may contrast with the 'local' rules of verbal interaction, and many interviewees may find it hard to accept the suppression of the participant statuses which normally shape their interaction, such as social status or seniority. As Briggs puts it,

> The greater the distance between the cultural and communicative norms of interviewer and interviewee, the more likely it becomes that this hiatus will generate interpersonal tension and misinterpretations in interviews. This will commonly lead to difficulties in inducing the interviewee to answer the question, producing seemingly irrelevant or incomplete replies or even silence.[20]

Some understanding of the non-linguistic rules that inform appropriate modes of verbal interaction thus seems to become crucial.

Within the Surinamese-Javanese speech community of Sakinem's generation, social interaction is accompanied by *explicit* norms governing appropriateness in speech, non-verbal behaviour and permissible actions. These norms require that interactions demonstrate a high degree of awareness of other people's social status. Gender is one factor guiding interaction. There are different expectations of men and women, men being encouraged to talk on all occasions, women to be silent. For example, women are not supposed to join the *slametans*; their task is to take care of preparing the food. Also on the occasion of a *lèk-lèkan*, women recede into the background. If they are among themselves, they tell stories. It is, however, considered improper to do so in the company of men.[21]

Respect for seniors is another determinant of the form of social interaction. Traditionally, a younger person should address an older person in *krama* (polite or high Javanese) in order to show his or her respect; only individuals who share the same social status are allowed to address each other in *ngoko* (everyday or low Javanese).[22]

A final norm of interaction involves avoidance of conflict. In order to keep *rukun* (the maintenance of mutual harmony within the community), conflicts in verbal interaction are to be avoided as much as possible. One way to attain this end is to avoid topics that are provocative (which could upset the listener), or to express disagreement when a provocative subject is brought up in the conversation in guarded terms.[23] In Sakinem's view, for instance, it was inappropriate to discuss her marital life in detail. As I had not understood that her husband had died early, I asked her if she had been married only once:

Have you been married only once?
Yes. It is hard work when you live in a children's home. Especially in the expensive time – cheap time is not so bad as in expensive time. Expensive days, mmm – you have to experience everything, especially these days [refers to the economic crisis in Surinam]. Everything is expensive.

As she considered it improper to discuss private matters with strangers, Sakinem refused to give an answer to my question. Instead, she went back to the central theme of her account, namely poverty.

ORALITY IN LIFE STORIES AS CONTEXTUALIZATION CUES

Although historians have recently focused more and more on the transcript in order to expose the broader social and cultural context surrounding the words spoken, this has not led to an adjustment in the practice of transcribing. As early as 1981 Alessandro Portelli pressed oral historians to consider the paralinguistic features of interview data (intonation, loudness, speed of speech, etc.) on the grounds that these may provide a significant vehicle for conveying the interviewee's attitude.[24] However, most oral historians still urge researchers to smooth the narration by deleting reference to paralinguistic cues. After the tape is transcribed, it is usually put aside, never to be listened to again. Consequently, precisely those paralinguistic elements that give oral sources a surplus value vis-à-vis written sources are neglected: what is left of the tape is simply a reduction and translation into a literate text. This is a serious problem, for, as Portelli has noted, 'expecting the transcript to replace the tape for scientific purposes is equivalent to doing art criticism on reproductions, or doing literary criticism on translations.'[25]

As paralinguistic cues may reflect the interpretative frame in which utterances are to be understood, it seems to be important to include them in the transcript. These cues can be found in any part of the message form, including its visual (gesture, gaze, bodily stance, etc.), prosodic (intonation, loudness, pitch, etc.) and verbal dimensions. Additionally, the interviewer's questions, and all back channel cues, including the interviewer's verbal encouragement and ungrammatical sentences should be included in the transcript, because they reveal the nature of relationship between interviewer and interviewee.[26]

If we turn to Sakinem's narrative, we can learn a lot about her attitude towards the interview by paying attention to her style of speech. Her speech was, for instance, full of pauses. Not only did she fall silent when she had difficulty recalling certain events, she also paused when she had used a word that provoked associations with other important events in her life. Take the following example, in which she just had told me that there were two boats which sailed the contract labourers to Surinam:

Two boats?
Yes, and when she gets there, then the contractants get divided, one half to [the plantation] Waterloo, one half to [the plantation] Hasard and I – my parents got to Hasard, district Nickerie. So, from there we get, how do you call it, in Javanese they call it *ranson* [ration]. You get rice, you get all kinds of food, every, every, every week I guess, I can't remember, you know. How long? That long. I already came here in 1920, 1920 – [pauses for one minute] [excited] And my boat, it is called 'Roti' [called after the Hindustani pancakes], it was called Roti, isn't it? [bursts out laughing] – [another pause for one minute] [calmly] So anything, and, but when they, um, arrived at Hasard, then they get – [short pause] food – [short pause] every two weeks or every week, you get rice *bakkeljauw* [salted fish], oil, anything.

As noted earlier, her pauses and silences also referred to moments in the interview where she had difficulty accepting the interactional norms underlying the interview. As it is a common Surinamese-Javanese belief that disagreement is not expressed openly, but only through mutual avoidance or concealed disobedience, silence was her way of expressing her uneasiness and 'breaking the frame' of the interview without offending me. As another example, knowing that in the past Surinamese-Javanese people who had converted to Christianity were more or less left to their fate by the Surinamese-Javanese community, and that, in general, there were a lot of conflicts in those days, I asked her:

Do you remember how people got along in those days, was it nice?
Ah, it was rather nice, not like – what you have to do, you have to be content [laughs bashfully].

What she actually wanted to communicate to me was that, although in the past relationships had not been harmonious, in the present people are even more unfriendly towards each other. Often people told me that the military coup in 1980 had made people more distrustful towards each other. Moreover, due to the economic crisis, people could no longer afford to be as generous as they used to be. Yet, since it is improper to discuss conflicts within the community openly, in the middle of the sentence she decided to keep her thoughts to herself ('it was rather nice, not like – '). Instead of finishing her sentence she emphasized one of the prominent Surinamese-Javanese values (for which she expected that I would appreciate the Surinamese-Javanese even more), namely: you should not resist your fate, 'you just have to be content.'

Changes in loudness and speed of speech also give us cues to Sakinem's attitudes. When Sakinem slowed down and lowered her voice, this not only indicated that she had greater difficulty recalling a particular event; she also did this when she was talking about an emotional event. In the following example, she had just told me that after having stayed a month at Hasard with her parents, her aunt came to pick her up and take her to the plantation where she was employed. I then asked her:

> *Your aunt, she had left for Surinam earlier?*
> Yes – Then I from there, and my aunt, she goes – back to Indonesia. [sadly] Then I go back to my mother . . . [slowing down] and my parents, they thought, I said: 'Oh daddy, that I have [been] deserted' and that is . . . [softly] I forgot which year – then I was there, I went to children's home, after two weeks, [more softly] when I came to my mother – and there was someone who – who, eh, evangelists come searching and there I stayed.

When she told me that she could neither stay with her aunt nor with her parents, Sakinem got so emotional that she could not speak as loudly as before. Note that she was not able to finish the sentence in which she tried to describe how deserted and disappointed she felt towards her father for having her taken away by the Dutch evangelists.

THE SOCIAL STRUCTURE

As Briggs and Mishler have noted, the social situation created by the interview shapes the form and content of what is being said. The context[27] in which a question is raised affects the way in which the narrator interprets the question and therefore the nature of the answer.[28] For example, when I asked Sakinem if she had had any children, initially she answered, 'No, no children'. However, after a short pause she said, 'four children'. This gave me a hint that maybe she had fostered children who were 'lent' to her, as is a common habit among the Surinamese-Javanese.[29] By further questioning, eventually the story came out:

> *How many children did you raise?*
> No, no children – four children.
> *So you raised four children?*

Yes, yes, four of them. Two I got – whereas I, these, this one is in Wageningen [a village nearby]. And this one, is going to be married in two weeks.
So you raised four children. To whom did those children belong?
That was family. His [her husband's] sisters and sisters-in-law.
They had lent those children to you?
Yes.

Had I not been familiar with the custom of lending children to women who cannot bear children themselves, probably I would simply have misunderstood her initial answer and, consequently, stopped asking further questions. Again, this example shows how important it is to have some competence in the frame of reference of the interviewee.

The orientation of the narrator can also affect the answers that are given. As Patai has noted, narrators more or less consciously select their subjects according to their perception of the interview's purpose, their definition of what it is permissible to say in this context, their play of memory and their relationship with the interviewer.[30] For example, Sakinem, unused to being interviewed, was not able to adhere to the rules of the interview completely. For her, being interviewed meant to have the opportunity to have 'easy talk' with a stranger. Sensing that my goal in the interview was to gather information about her experience of migration, rather than to have a nice conversation, she tried to satisfy both goals by switching between answering my questions and general talk.

As the presence of others can jeopardize the conventional interview hierarchy, the standard oral history frame requires that the interviewee be interviewed in private. Yet the fact that speech events within the Surinamese-Javanese community traditionally take place in a collective setting had its influence on the actual interview situation: it proved to be impossible to interview the elderly women without the presence of neighbours or family members, which could sometimes be quite disturbing.

Given this discrepancy, to hold on to directives given by the standard oral history frame and to interview the women in isolation would have meant a violation of their daily routine. As I eventually realized, interviewing the women in the presence of others also had its rewards. When I interviewed Sakinem, for instance, the presence of her granddaughter turned out to be quite beneficial. Not only did she manage to put her grandmother at ease, she also supplemented Sakinem's narration, allowing her to refresh her memory and continue her story, and translated the Javanese words which Sakinem sometimes uttered when she got overemotional or could not find the right Dutch translation quickly enough. In the following example, Sakinem had just told me that her foster-son helped her a lot in the household. I then asked her if the other children had been that nice to her as well:

Me: And the girls, did they help you as well?

151

Sakinem: Yes.

Me: Yes, what did they do?

Sakinem: Yes, they work. The kitchen, cleaning the house ... those others, those others, [fiercely] they are lazy! [says something in Javanese].

Granddaughter: She says that they always had stomach-ache.

Sakinem: The boy was really strapping. If I said to him: 'Do this and that', then he does so. Everything, washing the floor, cleaning the house, then he does so.

Me: He's really a nice boy then.

Sakinem: But the girls were, look, yes, how do I tell you – [says something in Javanese].

Granddaughter: She says that they had to go to school, whereas her son did not attend school, 'cause he couldn't catch up with them.

As Cornwell and Gearing have argued, the quality of the relationship between interviewer and interviewee affects the quality of the material obtained.[31] I therefore believe that it is essential to create a relationship of mutual trust in which the interviewee feels relatively uninhibited. However, during my interviews with the elderly women, there were occasions when the relationship worked only with great difficulty. Some women even refused to be interviewed as they felt that they simply had nothing to say.

Having gained some communicative competence in the speech community in which Sakinem was situated, I now understand that Sakinem, as a woman, was not accustomed to take the floor for hours. Of course she had told parts of her life story once in a while, but she was seldom encouraged to tell the whole story at once. Minister has pointed out that because the oral interview takes place in a public setting, it may be an appropriate tool for understanding the lives and experiences of women in most cultural settings.[32] However, within the speech community in which Sakinem was situated, self-disclosure proved to be problematic, not so much because of the public nature of the interview as because of the fact that the interview prescribes a way of relating that contrasts with their own way of relating. Within the Surinamese-Javanese speech community, ways of communicating require *sharing* experience and knowledge, whereas the interview situation requires a monologue form of relating.

Still, as Olson and Shopes have warned, I realize that I should not overestimate my own importance in the eyes of Sakinem. If I assert my power by asking for her revelations, she in turn asserts her power by gratifying or denying my request.[33]

In my opinion, it is important to respect the fact that there are certain subjects which it is considered unsuitable to discuss with strangers. Nevertheless, I think it is also important to put at ease those interviewees who are not talkative by nature, or who believe their lives are not worth consideration, especially in cases where class, age and cultural distinctions are likely to inhibit self-disclosure. I agree with Tonkin when she argues that although fluency seems to be an aesthetic skill, there are conditions which inhibit authorial competence.[34]

One of the approaches which proved effective here was my own self-revelation. In the case of Sakinem, for instance, she turned out to be more willing to reveal her own experiences after she had learned that I had a father and grandparents who themselves were half Dutch, half Javanese. During the interview, I talked about the stories my father and grandparents had told me about Java, and what I had learnt from these stories. This gave me the opportunity to show her that I appreciated her, as I did my grandparents, as a wise woman who deserves to be respected. Implicitly, it enabled me to make it clear to her that I wanted to share the control over the interview; in listening to her stories, I could grant her right to be heard.

Additionally, telling her that I had been born in the Caribbean allowed us to share our experience of migration. This made it possible to make it clear to her that I conceived of the interview as an interactive process or dialogue in which we could engage, through speaking and listening, in trying to understand important life experiences.

THE IDEOLOGICAL STRUCTURE

As Grele has noted, personal stories, including interviews, are embedded in ideologies, which not only represent the conflict between the self and the group, but also the (potential) conflict between the interviewee and the dominant discourse within oral history. Where the group is the invisible audience to which the interviewee directs his or her story, it is the dominant discourse which constitutes the unspoken ideological vision of the oral historian. Consequently, the questions asked by the interviewer will also be embedded in this dominant discourse.[35] In order to evaluate his or her suitability for a cross-cultural interview, it therefore seems crucial to explore some of the ideological baggage with which the interviewer enters such a situation.

As a Western literary form, biography is based on certain assumptions about the self. For instance, oral historians expect a biography to present a unified life through anecdotes that reveal unity while, at the same time, demonstrating change and growth. As a consequence, recollection is privatized and seen as personal: readers habitually identify the first person singular 'I' with a single centre or voice, with an autonomous person who directs his or her life individually.[36]

How well do these assumptions hold in the case of the elderly Javanese women in Surinam? An emerging body of anthropological research now allows us to see how the subjective experience of self is contingent on culturally specific norms and socialization practices affecting perception, communication and action. Johnson, for example, has noted that, whereas Western thought tends to accentuate the boundary between the domains of intrapsychic and extrapsychic realities, no such rigorous distinctions can be found within Eastern thought.[37] In Surinam I also found that although the elderly women within the Javanese-Surinam community varied individually, their experience of self was less individual than might be expected. Their selves were inextricably connected with the 'family'[38] to which they belong. In Surinam, the elderly Surinamese-Javanese who live in rural settings have, in particular, developed into a homogeneous group with a strong sense of group identity that is strengthened by marginality, low level of education and a lack of significant class distinctions. Therefore, when Sakinem employs the first person singular, it would be a mistake uncritically to attribute individuation to the 'I' in the narrative.

It has been argued that life stories are important to self-development and self-expression: writing one's life story can prove a great source of satisfaction and even be used as a therapeutic technique for people of all ages, particularly the elderly.[39] However, it is doubtful whether this 'life review' phenomenon works for individuals cross-culturally. It may simply be a construct of Western, Judeo-Christian cultures where the ethos of individualism, and the relative isolation of the elderly, may contribute to experiences of this type. Anthropologists of American life have pointed out that psychology and its therapeutic discourse – in both its academic and popular varieties – can be seen as one of the most important discourses in Western cultures.[40] Johnson, for instance, pointed out that individualism is upheld by a personal fear connected with the cultural belief in ontological separation and alienation from a Judeo-Christian God. For people who are socialized within this tradition of Christian thought, telling one's life story may act as a confession that helps them to find coherence and meaning in their lives and overcome feelings of guilt and self-doubt – feelings that accompany the positive heightened significance given to self-determination.[41]

Within the Surinamese-Javanese community to which Sakinem belongs, the self is more concealed. Whereas in Western societies children tend to be socialized to be obedient and at the same time to develop a progressive independence, the concepts central to the socialization of Javanese children are the concept of respect and the maintenance of harmonious social appearance (*rukun*). What the child mainly learns is how and when to show what measure of respect: in order to avoid conflict within the community, children learn not to express their feelings towards others.[42] As a result, there is more denial of self and less assertiveness, which is antithetical to the mild degrees of narcissism accepted in urban and/or Western(ized) communities.

Since this difference in the experience of self will automatically affect the presentation of self, it may be an ethnocentric assumption to look for psychological depth in Sakinem's narrative and expect to find a confession from the inner core of her intimate and private being. Indeed, Sakinem did not reflect on her life in a revealing or self-confessional manner. In any event, much more scrutiny will be needed before one can really specify the social conditions which promote self-awareness, or clarify the sort of subject which this self is, at any moment. Moreover, as Tonkin has noted,

> an inarticulate interviewee may be so through having had so little authority over the life described that actions and events can only be rendered blurrily and inconsequentially. This 'poor informant' may, however, have a respected skill like cooking, or a private passion for gardening, and in these domains have developed a confident if still not verbally confident self. In such cases, there may be no culturally recognised genre of discourse through which this passion can be expressed: it is after all a form of action, not words.[43]

CONCLUSION

In this chapter I have attempted, in scrutinizing one of the life stories which I collected during my fieldwork in Surinam, to pinpoint those areas in which the conventional oral history interview technique needs to be refined for a cross-cultural interview. It is important to realize, however, that cultural heterogeneity is always present in interview situations. As argued before, even individuals reared in the 'same culture' exhibit regional, ethnic, age, gender, class and other differences in the way they relate.

Once a researcher leaves his or her own 'native' speech community, there is no common body of experience to smooth initial encounters. Therefore, gaining some competence in the speech community of the people we interview, surveying which question can be asked and discovering in advance the most suitable social situation in which to ask these questions seem to be relevant in all events.

It is, however, not enough simply to 'correct' the standard oral history frame through an injection of cultural sensitivity and systematics. As Peacock and Holland have noted, historical-ethnographic interpretations – just like psychological ones – are never sufficient in themselves, because self-narration is only partially responsive to historical events and culturally specific institutions. Paying more attention to the oral narrative should not mean that we exclude the interview. An exclusively culture-oriented approach is similarly limited, in so far as it ignores the interviewee's personal experiences, which are active forces in the narration, and regards the narration simply as a culturally defined script.[44]

As argued in this chapter, a reflexive oral history frame (which takes into account the context of the interview itself) will still be caught in the trappings of Western thought. Hence, what is needed is a thorough rethinking of oral history methodology. In this sense, it might be sensible to evaluate the interview process from time to time and examine our role as interviewer in the creation of interview-narratives more carefully. What ideological baggage do we bring into the interview situation; what are the presuppositions or even prejudices with which we enter the interview? In what way do we affect the interaction and what is being said during the course of the interview? Why do we formulate our questions as we do and why do we get certain answers to these questions?

To evaluate their own functioning thoroughly, it may be wise to make notes during the interview process about the setting, the events that occurred during the interview, the themes that were brought up, the subjects that were kept hidden and the social interaction. In addition, it may be worthwhile to resist standard editorial policies and include contextualization cues such as I have mentioned before. What is needed is a full appraisal of the orality of our data. To end this chapter with Portelli:

> There seems to be a fear that once the floodgates of orality are opened, writing (and rationality along with it) may be swept out as if by a spontaneous uncontrollable mass of fluid, irrational material. But this attitude blinds us to the fact that our awe of writing has distorted our perception of language and communication to the point where we no longer understand either orality or the nature of writing itself. As a matter of fact, written and oral sources are not mutually exclusive. They have common characteristics as well as autonomous and specific functions . . . therefore, they require different and specific interpretative instruments.[45]

NOTES

I am especially grateful for the financial support of the Netherlands Foundation for the Advancement of Tropical Research (WOTRO), and for the practical assistance of Mrs W. Karijopawiro and Mr J. Sarmo during my fieldwork in Surinam.

1 See, for example, Paul Thompson, *The Voice of the Past* (New York, 1988), p. 118.
2 See, for example, Personal Narratives Group, *Interpreting Women's Lives: Feminist Theory and Personal Narratives* (Bloomington, 1989), p. 100; James L. Peacock and Dorothy C. Holland, 'The narrated self: life stories in process', *Ethos, Journal of the Society for Psychological Anthropology* 21(4) (1993): 373; Ronald J. Grele, 'History and the languages of history in the oral history interview: who answers whose questions and why?' in Eva M. McMahan and Kim Lacey Rogers (eds), *Interactive Oral History Interviewing* (Hillsdale, N.J., 1994), p. 15.
3 C. L. Briggs, *Learning How to Ask: A Sociolinguistic Appraisal of the Role of the Interview in Social Science Research* (Cambridge, 1986), pp. 14–15; E. G. Mishler, 'The analysis of interview-narratives', in Theodore R. Sarbin (ed.), *Narrative Psychology: The Storied Nature of Human Conduct* (New York, 1986), pp. 233–4.
4 Elisabeth Tonkin, *Narrating our Pasts: The Social Construction of Oral History* (Cambridge, 1992), pp. 51–2, 67.
5 Javanese-Surinamese women have a history of double migration. Following the abolition of slavery in 1863, the Dutch colonial rulers recruited Javanese contract labourers in order to provide cheap labour on the Surinamese plantations. When

Surinam gained independence in 1975, many Javanese emigrated to the Nether-lands to escape the threat of ethnic conflict. After 1980, when Surinam was temporarily taken over by the military Bouterse, again many Javanese decided to emigrate to the 'mother country'. In 1990, about 15,000 Surinamese-Javanese lived in the Netherlands.

6 Deborah Tannen, 'Involvement in discourse', in D. Tannen, *Talking Voices: Repetition, Dialogue, and Imagery in Conversational Discourse* (Cambridge, 1991), pp. 10–11. See also Tonkin, *Narrating our Pasts*, p. 6.

7 Briggs, *Learning How to Ask*, p. 28; Tonkin, *Narrating our Pasts*, p. 54.

8 For a similar critique see Doris Sommer, 'Not just a personal story: women's *testimonios* and the plural Self', in B. Brodzki and C. Schenck, *Life/Lines: Theoretizing Women's Autobiography* (Ithaca, N.Y., 1988), pp. 107–29; Claudia Salazar, 'A Third World women's text: between the politics of criticism and cultural politics', in Sherna Berger Gluck and Daphne Patai (eds), *Women's Words: The Feminist Practice of Oral History* (London, 1991), pp. 93–107.

9 Briggs, *Learning How to Ask*, p. 28.

10 Grele, 'History and the language of history', pp. 1–19. See for a discussion on the 'dialogical' nature of language, Michael M. Bakhtin, *The Dialogic Imagination: Four Essays*, ed. M. Holquist (Austin, 1981).

11 See, for instance, E. Culpepper Clark, Michael J. Hyde and Eva M. McMahan, 'Communication in the oral history interview: investigating problems of interpret-ing oral data', *International Journal of Oral History* 1(1) (1980): 28–40, and Allen W. Furtrell and Charles S. Willard, 'Intersubjectivity and interviewing', in McMahan and Rogers, *Interactive Oral History Interviewing*, pp. 83–107.

12 The switch in perspective from text to dialogue has been discussed by interpret-ative anthropologists. See, for example, K. Dwyer, *Moroccan Dialogues: Anthropology in Question* (Baltimore and London, 1982), pp. 255–69; L. L. Langness and G. Frank, *Lives: An Anthropological Approach to Biography* (Novato, 1985); George E. Marcus and Michael J. Fischer, *Anthropology as Cultural Critique: An Experimental Moment in the Human Sciences* (Chicago, 1986); M. di Leonardo, 'Oral history as ethnographic encounter', *Oral History Review* 15 (Spring 1987).

13 Gwendolyn Etter-Lewis, 'Black women's life stories: reclaiming self in narrative texts', in Berger Gluck and Patai, *Women's Words*, p. 40. See also Tonkin, *Narrating our Pasts*, p. 3.

14 Michel Coulthard, 'The ethnography of speaking', in Coulthard, *An Introduction to Discourse Analysis* (London and New York, 1985) pp. 33–58.

15 Eva M. McMahan, 'Storytelling in oral history as a collaborative production', in McMahan (ed.), *Elite Oral History Discourse: A Study in Cooperation and Coherence* (Tuscaloosa, 1989), p. 81.

16 Etter-Lewis, 'Black women's life stories', p. 46.

17 Elisabeth Tonkin speaks of *genres* when referring to the different conventions of discourse through which speakers tell history and listeners understand them, see Tonkin, *Narrating our Pasts*, p. 54.

18 I speak of the speech community in which Sakinem was *partly* situated to emphasize the fact that individuals are always situated in different speech com-munities simultaneously. When speaking, they switch between those speech communities. Sakinem, for instance, seems to be situated in both the Javanese and the Christian speech community, which might have made it easier for her to communicate her experiences to me. Moreover, as Tonkin has noted, just as in literacy, practices and traditions in oracy seem to develop and change over time (ibid., p. 4).

19 E. Pawirodirjo, 'Javaanse verhalen uit Suriname: literatuuranalyse en interpretatie',

term paper, Leiden, 1988, p. 13; Hein Vruggink, 'Javaanse volksverhalen', *OSO* 4(5) (1990): 173.

20 Briggs, *Learning How to Ask*, pp. 27–44. See also Mishler, 'The analysis of interview-narratives', pp. 245–7.

21 Vruggink, 'Javaanse volksverhalen', p. 173.

22 Hildred Geertz, *The Religion of Java* (Glencoe, 1964), pp. 19–20; E Pawirodirjo, 'Javaanse verhalen uit Suriname', p. 148.

23 Geertz, *The Religion of Java*, p. 153.

24 Alessandro Portelli, 'The peculiarities of oral history', *History Workshop Journal*, no. 12 (1981): 96–106.

25 Ibid., p. 97; see also Tonkin, *Narrating our Pasts*, p. 75.

26 Briggs, *Learning How to Ask*, pp. 106–11; Tonkin, *Narrating our Pasts*, p. 40.

27 Following Briggs, I consider the context in which the interview takes place to be jointly created by interviewer and interviewee. As Briggs puts it: 'Not only are contexts not simply situational givens, they are continually renegotiated in the course of the interaction. The words of the interviewer and the interviewee do not simply occur within this frame; along with non-verbal components, they are the very stuff of which the context is constructed. Each utterance thus reflects this ongoing process, just as it contributes to it' (Briggs, *Learning How to Ask*, p. 26).

28 Ibid., pp. 22–3; Mishler, 'The analysis of interview-narratives', pp. 233–4.

29 Among Sakinem's generation, it is a common belief that one should have children in the house in every life stage. Children bring you happiness, and in this sense they protect you against sorrow and misery. As a result, women who are barren or whose children have already left home often raise children who are lent (that is, the control of the children remains in the hands of the biological parents) to them by relatives, see Geertz, *The Religion of Java*, pp. 37–41.

30 Daphne Patai, 'Is ethical research possible?', in Berger Gluck and Patai, *Women's Words*, p. 142.

31 Joyce Cornwell and Brian Gearing, 'Biographical interviews with older people', *Oral History* 17(1) (1989): 36–43.

32 Karen Minister, 'A feminist frame for the oral history interview', in Berger Gluck and Patai, *Women's Words*, pp. 27–41.

33 Karen Olson and Linda Shopes, 'Crossing boundaries, building bridges: doing oral history among working-class women and men', in Berger Gluck and Patai, *Women's Words*, p. 96.

34 Tonkin, *Narrating our Pasts*, p. 134.

35 Grele, 'History and the languages of history', p. 5.

36 Tonkin, *Narrating our Pasts*, pp. 48–9; Sommer, 'Not just a personal story', pp. 107–29. For an extensive elaboration on the Western concept of self, see, for instance, Frank Johnson, 'The Western concept of self', in Anthony J. Marsella, Francis L. K. Hsu and George DeVos (eds), *Culture and Self: Asian and Western Perspectives* (New York, 1985), pp. 91–138.

37 Johnson, 'The Western concept of self', p. 114. See also Fred R. Meyers, 'Emotions and the self: a theory of personhood and political order among Pintupi Aborigines', *Ethos* 7(4) (1979): 343–70; Michelle Z. Rosaldo, *Knowledge and Passion: Ilongot Notions of Self and Social Life* (Cambridge, 1980).

38 Within the Javanese-Surinamese community, 'family' refers to a *cultural image* which is constructed not only out of real family members, but also imagined assumed family members; individuals esteemed as 'father', 'mother', 'daughter', 'son', etc., because of their social status within the community are also part of the family.

39 See, for instance, Thompson, *The Voice of the Past*, pp. 116–17.

40 Langness and Frank, *Lives*, p. 103; Peacock and Holland, 'The narrated self', p. 368.

41 Johnson, 'The Western concept of self', p. 115. See also Tonkin, *Narrating our Pasts*, p. 11, when she argues that the different life stories people produce can be related to the different kinds of society of which they are members.
42 Geertz, *The Religion of Java*, pp. 108–13.
43 Tonkin, *Narrating our Pasts*, pp. 133–4.
44 Peacock and Holland, 'The narrated self', p. 375.
45 Portelli, 'The peculiarities of oral history', p. 97.

10

IN THE ARCHIVE, IN THE FIELD

What Kind of Document is an 'Oral History'?

Kathryn Marie Dudley

I begin this chapter with a confession. As a cultural anthropologist who studies contemporary American society, I never used to think of the interviews I do in the course of my fieldwork as 'oral history'. This changed when I discovered that the most promising source of funding for my ethnographic study of a farming community in western Minnesota was not one of the traditional anthropological foundations, but the Minnesota Historical Society. Thus, in my grant application, I wrote of my intent to conduct 'oral history' interviews, choosing to use this term instead of the more familiar 'ethnographic' or 'in-depth' interview. Under the circumstances it seemed wise to appear as historically minded as possible.

As it turned out, the Historical Society was delighted with my project and, in deciding to grant research funds, encouraged me to make use of their oral history collections, and to add my own tapes and transcripts to their archives as well. Grateful for the funding, and eager to get 'into the field' (even when 'the field' is only a six-hour drive from the Mall of America), I told the Historical Society that I would give my informants the option, if anonymity was not an issue for them, of having the tape and transcript of their interview deposited 'in the archive'. Had I known how this seemingly benign agreement would complicate my fieldwork, and had I anticipated the acute discomfort my informants experienced when faced with this option, I would have thought twice about characterizing the kind of interviews I conduct as 'oral history'.

In this chapter, I explore what I have come to see as an uneasy relationship between oral history and ethnography. In contrast to my earlier view that these two modes of interviewing and documentation were virtually interchangeable, I am now aware of a disruptive tension between the two – a tension which highlights the incompatibility of oral history and ethnography rather than their points of convergence. We are accustomed to thinking about interdisciplinary relationships and 'tensions' as productive, particularly when the desired borrowing and cross-fertilization seem to occur without radically altering the central presuppositions of our own disciplines. Thus there tends to be a complacent, if not condescending, attitude on the part of anthropologists who contemplate the role of 'oral history' in their own work. Renato Rosaldo, for example, chides oral historians for assuming that collecting oral source materials is an end in itself, rather than recognizing it as part of a larger effort to reconstruct the past.[1] Nevertheless, he considers the collection of oral testimonies to be an indispensable aspect of historical understanding and the anthropological study of culture; he implies that anthropologists could make better use of the work of oral historians, and that oral historians could do more with the materials they collect.

Micaela di Leonardo also takes up the question of how oral history and ethnography are related.[2] While noting several aspects they have in common – such as the impulse to give voice to lives that our society has rendered voiceless, and the ability to interact, often on intimate terms, with people outside our own social groups – di Leonardo also points to a number of differences which distinguish oral history from ethnography, among them a focus on the individual versus the group, and an emphasis on gathering materials for the public record rather than on protecting the privacy of informants. Nevertheless, she concludes that anthropology in general, and ethnography in particular, have much to offer oral history, namely, an appreciation of the 'intersubjectivity of the interview' and the 'innately theoretical nature of any interview project'.[3]

The idea that anthropologists have something to offer oral historians, that we are in possession of some insight into the nature of oral testimony, springs from the fact that ethnographers have become increasingly concerned with the representation of cross-cultural and interpersonal realities. Representational dilemmas arise for us when we acknowledge the necessarily collaborative dimension of the texts we produce. Thus there has been much debate about who really 'authors' an ethnography: the anthropologist or the native informants on whose lives and words it is based.[4] And there has been much hand-wringing about the claims of authority implicit in our representations of other people's realities.[5] While these are certainly critical issues for ethnographers, it is not at all clear to me that oral historians have anything to gain from our soul-searching. On the contrary, my close encounter with the oral historian's enterprise has led me to conclude that the disciplinary practices associated with oral history neatly side-step many of the politically charged issues that complicate the use of oral testimony in ethnographic texts.

I argue that oral history involves three disciplinary practices that ethnography, with its emphasis on mediated experience and cross-cultural interpretation, necessarily subverts. That is to say that the practices of (1) identifying informants by their real names, (2) building collections around historical events, categories of people, or time periods, and (3) omitting from the final document reference to the character of the interviewer or context of the interview, all set the discipline of oral history apart from that of

161

ethnography. Let me hasten to add that I realize that not all oral historians follow these conventions, and that those who do have reasonable and worthwhile objectives.[6] I focus on these conventions not to privilege one discipline over the other, but to address a larger set of questions about the disciplinary practices involved in the production and representation of oral source materials. What is of interest to me are the ways in which our divergent research practices constitute an understanding of *where* empirical data is to be found or 'discovered', in a spatial and textual sense. How is it, I want to ask, that we think of the domains of history and culture as involving two mutually exclusive sites of discovery – sites we designate, respectively, as 'the archive' and 'the field'?[7]

SITES OF DISCOVERY

Ethnographers, as James Clifford argues, tend to assume that the practice of taking notes is the empirical basis for their descriptions of cultural reality.[8] For us, 'the field' is the place where the meaning of lived experience (that of the natives as well as our own) is first apprehended and expressed in our fieldnotes, which then become the primary material for a formal text, the ethnography. Along similar lines, Edward Bruner argues that oral history also involves crucial distinctions between reality, experience and expression.[9] We assume that people who tell their life stories provide a description of historical reality that expresses their lived experience in the form of a document, which can then be used as a primary source for formal history texts. In certain respects, we might be tempted to say that the transcript of an oral history interview is the same kind of text or document as the ethnographer's fieldnotes. Both represent a social interaction that focuses on the 'discovery' of something about the lived experience of one or more people who are not, by definition, the interviewer or the note-taker.[10]

The appearance of an epistemological equivalence between transcripts and fieldnotes rests on the assumption of a dichotomy between oral and literary traditions. Speaking and writing are shorthand ways of signifying a basic difference between informants and ethnographers – between the site where we collect our materials and the academic environment where we present it. Indeed, the distinction between speaking and writing operates to justify our mission as researchers and our interest in other people's lives. Were our informants able to write their own life stories, they would have no need of us, with our tape recorders, note pads and questions. When speaking is juxtaposed to writing in this way it is marked as the spontaneous, down-to-earth, evanescent expression of lived experience, in contrast to the reflective, analytical and enduring inscription of that experience in a literary text. Thus, in both oral history and ethnography, speaking is coded as a preliterate mode of communication, and the written word is privileged as a diagnostic activity. The business of cultural or historical interpretation only proceeds when 'the facts', as told to us or observed by us, are 'discovered' in the preliterate experience of everyday life and set down in writing, for it is here that they become available for scrutiny and for a presumably more objective type of discovery. 'The archive' as a site of *textual* discovery thus presupposes 'the field' as a site of *pre-textual* discovery.

The three conventions of oral history that I mentioned earlier each contribute to the idea that oral testimony expresses pre-textual experience, and that the transcript is the textual representation of that experience. First, the practice of disclosing the real name of the person who participates in an oral history interview partakes of a literary convention which identifies the 'source' of an orally produced text in the same way we identify the author of a letter, diary or memoir.[11] A link is therefore made between the lived experience of 'a speaker' and the textual expression of 'an author' – the speaker and the author are held to be one-in-the-same, and they are identified by the same name. Second, the practice of building oral history collections around specific events, categories of people or time periods draw on a convention, common to museum displays, which establishes the significance of a collection – its scientific, artistic or historical value – with reference to a system of classification that claims to be indifferent to the political motivations and goals of the researchers or their institutional sponsors. A link is made between the pre-textual experiences shared by many speakers and the textual representation of those experiences as a social phenomenon. Third, the practice of treating the transcript of an interview as a primary document requiring little or no explanation enacts the convention in experimental science which holds that when established guidelines are followed, neither the character of the investigator nor the context of the investigation will significantly influence the content of what is discovered. The identification of the implied speaker and the author of the oral testimony is thus fortified by the textual erasure of the researcher.

Ethnography necessarily subverts each of these practices, in large part because it has, since its inception, drawn its literary conventions from travel writing and the novel.[12] In both genres, the figure of the author (as explorer and novelist) as well as that of the implied author (the ethnographer depicted as a character in the text) occupy the discursive space that is, in oral history, occupied by the speaker and implied author of the documentary transcript. That is, in ethnography, the lived experience and oral testimony of the native informant is presented as intelligible or 'textual' only to the extent that it is mediated in and through the lived experience and literary expressions of the ethnographer. In this sense, the conventions that establish authorship in ethnography are a mirror image of those that establish authorship in oral history: whereas ethnography erases the text-producing activities of the informant, oral history erases the text-producing activities of the interviewer. Herein lies what I take to be the fundamental tension between our two disciplines.

This brings me to the question that preoccupied me while doing my research in Minnesota: why can the ethnographer not adopt the conventions of oral history? Or, to put it another way, why was it not possible to use my fieldnotes, the transcripts of my interviews, as oral history documents?

First, a major stumbling block was the issue of anonymity. Since my interviews were designed to explore the cultural consequences of changes in the rural economy, I was often asking people to talk about experiences that they would not, under normal circumstances, have shared even with their closest neighbours, let alone a relative stranger. Many of the families I interviewed had lost their farm during the financial crisis of the 1980s and they would not have spoken with me if I had not promised them that their real names would never be used in anything I wrote about them. When I offered them the choice of having the transcript of their interview deposited in an archive at the Historical Society or having it remain in my possession where their privacy would be protected, almost all of the more than a hundred people I spoke with chose the latter option. Second, the random, idiosyncratic way in which informants were selected – my rule of thumb as an ethnographer is that I will interview anyone who wants to talk with me – did not fall under the rubric of any single topic or particular category of people or events. To get an understanding of what the contemporary transformation of rural life means to the people who live there, I have interviewed people from every walk of life, inside and outside the local community, young and old, rich and poor, male and female. Indeed, it soon became apparent to me that if one were to rely exclusively on the existing oral history collections which focus on rural issues during the contemporary period, one would discover a history dominated by the voices of political activists – the very people who, in my ethnographic study, tended to be outcasts in their own communities and expressed a point of view that was not widely endorsed at the local level. Finally, to pursue new lines of inquiry that open up during the course of my fieldwork, I often alter the focus of my interviews as I go along. The shifting format of these interviews only makes sense when seen as part of a larger project, which is guided by my own personal and professional interests as well as by current issues within the domain of cultural studies as a whole. Thus the content of the interview is structured both by my own narrative strategies (the story I want to tell) as well as by my informants' narrative strategies (the stories they want to tell). To attend to only one of these stories – by designating one person the narrator and the other the interviewer – is like listening to only one side of a conversation.

To acknowledge the dialogic or intersubjective nature of the interview situation is to introduce the possibility that the ethnographic encounter is not 'pre-textual' at all, but rather one in which each participant steps back and reflects on the meaning of the social practices and historical events under consideration, and in so doing 'textualizes' the phenomena described.

Anthropologists have begun to recognize that oral communication is inherently textual, in the sense that it can express theories about the nature of experience just as readily as it can express that experience directly. As Nigel Rapport observes:

> Orality and literacy do not necessarily define differing habits of thought. Both in communities which depend largely on an oral mode of communication and in those which prefer a written one, there can flourish the practice of scrutinizing and abstracting from experience so as to produce a rationalized and objectified text. . . . Thus, *every community is a textual community.*[13]

CONCLUSION

Breaking down the distinction between orality and literacy, seeing each as a textual mode of communication, forces us to question the epistemological foundations of those institutionalized sites of discovery we call 'the archive' and 'the field'. If there is no pre-textual 'story' to discover, and no way to elicit that story without introducing another story, then what kind of document is an 'oral history'? In this paper, I have suggested that oral history is based on a set of disciplinary practices which endows the speaker who gives oral testimony with what Michel Foucault has called the 'author function'.[14] That is, the textual representation of an oral account of social phenomena has credibility and authenticity only to the extent that it has 'an author'; a presumptively real person to whom the production of the text can be attributed. The same is true in anthropology, although here it is the fieldworker who is endowed with the author function: in the ethnographic representation of oral testimony, the production of the text is attributed to the ethnographer, not the informants.

In conclusion, as we consider the uneasy relationship between oral history and ethnography, the question to bear in mind, it seems to me, is not: Which discipline has it right? Who is *really* the author of an oral history document? For, as our fieldwork experiences remind us over and over again, the production of oral testimony is always a collaborative, dialogic, jointly orchestrated affair. Out of this social interaction emerges a document of which it can rightly be said that the author function is up for grabs. Were the issue at stake merely one of meritocracy or celebrity – of who really deserves the credit or the limelight – this would be a moribund debate. For what gives the author function its critical edge in oral history and ethnography is the fact that no one 'authors' the texts we produce, yet the truth conditions of our discourse require that *someone* step forward to claim that authorship, with all the legal, political and moral ramifications it entails. A bit of the real, then, is always sacrificed to gain the appearance of the true. The crucial question for us to ask, both as oral historians and as ethnographers, is why do we have such a hard time acknowledging and representing the *social* sources of our knowledge?

NOTES

This paper was presented at the annual meeting of the Oral History Association, 19 October 1995, in Milwaukee, Wisconsin.

1 Renato Rosaldo, 'Doing oral history', *Social Analysis* 4 (Sept. 1980): 89–99.
2 Micaela di Leonardo, 'Oral history as ethnographic encounter', *Oral History Review* 15 (Spring 1987): 1–20.
3 Ibid., p. 20.
4 This dilemma has been addressed in a number of ways, leading to a growing body of 'experimental' approaches to the writing of ethnography. See George E. Marcus and Michael J. Fischer, *Anthropology as Cultural Critique: An Experimental Moment in the Human Sciences* (Chicago: University of Chicago Press, 1986); James Clifford and George E. Marcus (eds), *Writing Culture: The Poetics and Politics of Ethnography* (Berkeley: University of California Press, 1986).
5 On the problem of ethnographic authority, see James Clifford, *The Predicament of Culture: Twentieth-Century Ethnography, Literature, and Art* (Cambridge: Harvard University Press, 1988).
6 Valerie Raleigh Yow's *Recording Oral History: A Practical Guide for Social Scientists* (Thousand Oaks, Calif.: Sage, 1994) offers an excellent overview of the ways in which oral history can be used to address substantive and theoretical issues of concern to historians and social scientists.
7 James Clifford has observed that while social and cultural historians have become increasingly interested in ethnography as a literary form, 'as yet no systematic analysis exists concerning the differences and similarities of research practice, juxtaposing "the archive" with "the field"', see 'Notes on (field) notes', in Roger Sanjek (ed.), *Fieldnotes: The Makings of Anthropology* (Ithaca: Cornell University Press, 1990), pp. 47–70.
8 Ibid., p. 56.
9 'Experience and its expressions', in Victor W. Turner and Edward M. Bruner (eds), *The Anthropology of Experience* (Chicago: University of Illinois Press, 1986), pp. 3–30.
10 While a consideration of psychoanalytic practices is beyond the scope of the present chapter, the analysis I develop here could, with little modification, be extended to include 'the couch' as a discursively constructed site of discovery.
11 The recognition that the notion of 'author' is a cultural construction is based on the work of Michel Foucault; see his essay, 'What is an author?', in *The Foucault Reader*, ed. Paul Rabinow (New York: Pantheon Books, 1984), pp. 101–20.
12 For recent work on ethnography's literary precursors, see Clifford, *The Predicament*; Clifford Geertz, *Works and Lives: The Anthropologist as Author* (Stanford: Stanford University Press, 1988); Mary Louise Pratt, *Imperial Eyes: Travel Writing and Transculturation* (London: Routledge, 1992); Edward Said, *Culture and Imperialism* (New York: Alfred Knopf, 1993).
13 Nigel Rapport 'Writing fieldnotes: the conventionalities of note-taking and taking note in the field', *Anthropology Today* 7(1) (Feb. 1991): 10–13. See also Brian Stock, *The Implications of Literacy* (Princeton: Princeton University Press, 1983) and *Listening for the Text* (Baltimore: Johns Hopkins University Press, 1990).
14 Foucault, 'What is an author?'.

SHARING AND RESHAPING LIFE STORIES

Problems and Potential in Archiving Research Narratives

Paul Thompson

In 1995 Ron Grele, in a proposal to the Ninth International Oral History Conference in Göteborg, Sweden,[1] writing from the perspective of the North American oral history movement with 'its origins in archival practice' which gave priority to archiving for the future rather than to immediate research efforts, sought to raise the 'rarely discussed' but 'interesting theoretical and methodological problems' which this posed. 'How useful are documents produced by others?' he asked; 'how does one predict the needs of scholars far into the future?'

The oral history movement in Britain originally strongly rejected the archival approach. It began in the early 1970s, some twenty years after the beginning of oral history work in the United States, as a branch of social history research, and then spread into community history, including work with the social and health services. The American approach to oral history was treated with very strong suspicion because of its then focus on the recording of 'great men', and it was assumed that the prevalence of privately funded archival projects was one reason for this imbalance. By the later 1970s contact had also been made with Scandinavian ethnologists, who had a long-standing commitment to the archival recording of folk culture and ordinary people: originally of peasant culture in the countryside, but by then of urban culture too. Equally important, the written autobiographical competitions in Poland and Scandinavia since the 1920s, with their strong tradition of peasant and worker autobiography, had also become known. Nevertheless the logical conclusion, that there was more than one possible model of archival work, and that its priorities could reflect the needs of the research community as well as the vanities of funders, was not yet drawn.

It has thus only been from the late 1980s that any sustained concern with archival issues has developed among either oral historians or life story sociologists in Europe. The change is indicated by the fact that currently the chairman and secretary of the Oral History Society in Britain both work at the National Sound Archive. And at the same time I myself have moved in the same direction. From beginning as simply a researcher, by 1987 I was setting up the National Life Story Collection at the National Sound Archive, hoping through this to launch a national autobiography in sound. And then in 1994 I became director of a new archival resource unit, Qualidata, set up by the national Economic and Social Research Council at the University of Essex. Qualidata's task is to seek out and rescue valuable qualitative research material, including especially life story interviews and ethnographic fieldwork notes, that has not yet been archived.

The experiences of working with both the National Life Story Collection and Qualidata have raised many of the same questions which Ron Grele posed. Let me explain how my own interest in archiving has developed, and at the same time suggest some of the key issues which this work has presented.

* * *

My first oral history research was the 'Family life and work experience before 1918' project which was carried out in 1970–3 specifically for my book *The Edwardians*,[2] which is a social history of Britain between 1900 and 1918. I drew especially heavily on the interviews for the chapters on childhood and family life. In terms of writing from the research team, the project also resulted in Thea Thompson's *Edwardian Childhoods*, a chapter in my *I Don't Feel Old*, and many of the insights in *The Voice of the Past*.[3] But from the start we recognized that the interviews could be invaluable to others.

The transcripts of the 444 interviews – all on paper, given the date – were organized in two versions: first, the interview as given, and second, cut up versions re-sorted according to the twenty main themes of the interview guide. Once the project was ended, due to the generosity of the Department of Sociology at Essex and the concern of Brenda Corti and Mary Girling, we were able to maintain the transcripts in a special room and – without officially advertising ourselves as an archive – allow access to bona fide researchers who approached us. The collection has proved a very valuable inspiration to many of our own students, and it has also resulted in some notable publications by visiting scholars. These include, for example, Standish Meacham, *A Life Apart* and substantial parts of David Crouch and Colin Ward, *The Allotment* on working-class culture, and Charles More, *Skill and the English Working Class* and Michael Childs, *Labour's Apprentices* on work, and John Gillis, *For Better, For Worse* on marriage, as well as articles on class by Patrick Joyce, on social mobility by David Vincent, on education by Jonathan Rose, on religion by Hugh McLeod, on stepfamilies by Natasha Burchardt, and on women and the family by Ellen Ross.[4] Sometimes rereading the material made us all too aware of issues which we could have easily pursued at the time, for example on stepfamily relationships:[5] and above all made us regret that, just because the interviews were carried out for a book whose span was to end in 1918, we obtained scarcely any information on the last fifty years of the lives of those we interviewed, and indeed too often cut them off from telling us about what had since happened to them. Nevertheless, as time went on it became increasingly clear that this representative set of interviews, now unrepeatable, constitute a priceless historical resource for the future. We also began to feel an increasing concern at the purely informal arrangements on which our 'archive' was based.

In the meantime I had become interested in the possibility of developing an oral history section of the National Sound Archive. Right at the beginning of our research project in 1970 Patrick Saul, director of the British Institute of Recorded Sound (from which the NSA originated), had called a meeting of the nascent group of oral historians and encouraged us to offer our material to him. We indeed did so, but were put off by the experience: we were expected to check all the copying ourselves, there was no prospect of the material being catalogued for years, and on one visit there was not even a functioning tape recorder available in the building. Fortunately by the mid-1980s the Institute had evolved into the National Sound Archive as part of the British Library, and although it still had some basic problems – notably in cataloguing, only now being solved – it had become a much more efficient organization, with outstanding collections, particularly in music. It had not, however, developed any active collecting in oral history.

It was at the end of the 1980s that I launched the National Life Story Collection (NLSC). This time the aim was not to collect material for a single book, but as a wider resource for other researchers, writers and broadcasters. This time too the plan was to carry out full life story interviews, rather than just interview people about their earlier lives. The National Life Story Collection is an independent charity, with a governing body of distinguished trustees, carefully balanced to represent both the principal spheres of oral history activity and the main political parties, but based within the National Sound Archive, which gives it free office facilities and takes in the material which it generates. In some ways the strategy has been very successful: in particular, in making the British Library a national focus for oral history activity. We have also carried out some very worthwhile projects. But so far it has proved impossible to raise funding which remotely approaches the scale needed to fulfil our original aims.

We had envisaged the creation of a national autobiography in sound, which would encompass, on the one hand, any man or woman notable enough to deserve an obituary notice in the daily press, and on the other, a continuing cross-section of ordinary men and women right across Britain. If we could have enthused a generous billionaire we might have succeeded in this, but none of those whom we approached found 'oral history' sufficiently compelling. So we were thrown back on fund-raising for separate projects. We have managed to do some good things: our projects include lives of sculptors and painters (with the Tate Gallery), Jewish Holocaust survivors in

Britain, the financial elite of the City of London, and workers at all levels of British Steel. We have also carried out the first British national competition for written and oral autobiography, for which we received nearly a thousand entries.

I had hoped that private sponsorship would enable us to sustain a more continuous and broader recording programme than is possible through research funding. In practice that has not proved the case. In Britain private sponsorship remains narrow and rather unimaginative in its aims. And while we have certainly raised considerable funding in the City of London, we have also at times been astonished by the sheer meanness of very rich people. From our experience, it remains, despite the cuts in public funding, much more possible to gain substantial financial support, and in one block, from research foundations and councils.

What is the potential historical value of the interviews which we have collected through NLSC, primarily with archival objectives? The proof of course can only come in the longer term, when the interviews have been fruitfully used by other historians, or not. So far only our own publications have emerged: a CD – a collage in sound of steelworkers' memories; a set of tapes with an introduction, for school use, on the Holocaust, which has been much in demand; and just out, *City Lives*, a book of edited testimonies from the City's financial elite, which will provide a crucial new perspective on a very powerful group.[6]

With each project, we have started from a life story interview guide, a simpler version of that used for *The Edwardians* (printed in *The Voice of the Past*), in the hope that this would ensure a baseline of comparable information for the whole set, but encouraged interviewers not only to follow the enthusiasms of interviewees but also to develop fruitful new themes as the project progresses. For the 'City lives' collection, which I have read almost entirely, I have no doubt that the interviews cumulatively provide a highly significant historical resource. But they certainly vary a great deal, depending both on informants and interviewees. Why was this?

It did not turn out to be true, as some had anticipated, that City bankers and financiers would as a whole be extremely reluctant to break their public front and tell us anything incautious. Their openness varied a great deal according to individual personality. Some informants remained cautious throughout, always presenting the kind of public front which would also be available in the written record, while there were others who talked astonishingly freely, even about major scandals in which they and their banks had been involved. Still more important, however, was the varying skill of the different interviewers, with at the one extreme a few who recorded shallow and partial interviews of less than two hours which had little value, and others by contrast going into extraordinary and revealing depth about the culture of day-to-day experience and personal feelings at the same time as covering the basic life story. It is perhaps significant that in this case the best interviewers were not the research historians. My conclusion would be that the problem is not whether the interviewer is an archivist or a researcher, but how far he or she is willing to take the trouble to follow the basic scheme of the interview guide, and equally important, has a sensitivity in choosing which lines to pursue in depth.

The other key question is how the informants are chosen. For the City, since we were recording an elite, a snowball approach working through personal recommendations is precisely what is needed scientifically, as well as being the most effective way of raising the necessary funding. But the more a project seeks to record cross-sections of ordinary men and women, the more there is likely to be an incompatibility between the representativeness of sampling demanded by serious research and the considerations of private funders. I am inclined to feel that this kind of work must remain normally publicly funded.

The National Life Story Collection is primarily a collecting organization, but its existence has proved a catalyst in persuading other researchers to deposit their recorded interviews in the National Sound Archive. We were, however, well aware that such deposits represented the mere tip of a gigantic iceberg. Consequently, from the late 1980s we began to lobby the Economic and Social Research Council (ESRC) about their lack of any policy for ensuring the preservation of worthwhile material, other than survey statistics, from the research projects which they funded.

* * *

From its origins in the eighteenth century, the progress of social science has been essentially cumulative. Knowledge has been built up incrementally, resting on the foundations of earlier findings, and interpretation has always depended upon comparisons: with other social groups, other contexts, other cultures, other times.

Comparison can only be effective when the data is sufficient to allow convincing re-evaluations. Fortunately many social scientists grasped this relatively early. For example, the original returns of the British population census were kept as public records, and have proved an invaluable basis for reanalysis in recent years. And when Beatrice and Sydney Webb had completed their pioneering study of British trade unionism, they archived their notes on their interviews carried out throughout the country in the newly founded London School of Economics, where they remain the principal source of information on late nineteenth-century trade unionism.

It was in this spirit that the ESRC Data Archive was set up in 1967 in order to retain the most significant machine-readable data from the research which it funds. Thus crucial data can be reanalysed by other researchers, so that the money spent on research becomes not only an immediate outlay, but a resource for other researchers in the future.

There was, however, a significant gap in this policy. Although the advances of word processing now mean that most research of any kind is machine-readable, until recently most machine-readable data was statistical, based on surveys. Qualitative (non-statistical) research was paper-based. Thus the Data Archive received only a fraction of the qualitative material collected by research projects funded by ESRC.

There was no intellectual reason for this. Qualitative and quantitative research are equally based on comparison. Classic restudies include not only Seebohm Rowntree's three surveys of poverty in York, and Llewellyn Smiths's repeat of Charles Booth's in London, but also the two successive community studies of Banbury, or, to take an anthropological instance, the controversial restudy and reinterpretation by Oscar Lewis of Redfield's Tepotzlan in Mexico.

Eventually in 1991 the ESRC asked us to carry out a small pilot study of what was happening to qualitative data from projects which it had funded. This revealed that 90 per cent of qualitative research material was either already lost, or at risk, mostly in researchers' homes or offices. Even some of the material which researchers reported as 'archived' turned out to be deposited in so-called archives which had none of the basic requirements of an archive, such as physical security, public access, reasonable catalogues, or with recorded material, listening facilities. In the worst instance of all, generations of distinguished anthropologists had been depositing their life-time's work with the Royal Anthropological Institute in London, which then had no catalogue, no archivist, no access, and not even physical security: the collections appeared to be slowly rotting into oblivion.

We calculated that it would have cost at least £20 million to recreate a resource on the scale of that at risk. For the older material, moreover, the risk was acute, and the need for action especially urgent. This has been subsequently borne out by the fate of the research material on childrearing which John and Elizabeth Newson had been collecting in Nottingham since the early 1960s, consisting of over 3,000 high quality in-depth interviews with parents and children. It need hardly be said that parenting is and will remain a major issue for both research and public debate, and the Newsons were the outstanding pioneers of social science work in the field. Only their earlier series of interviews were fully exploited in their own writing, and the possibilities of drawing on the unused material, and also of carrying out further follow-up studies, would have been immense. Tragically, just weeks before Qualidata opened, the Newsons decided that their lifetime's research data should be destroyed.

As a result of our pilot study report we were invited by ESRC to develop our proposed solution, and the outcome was the founding of Qualidata (the ESRC Qualitative Data Archival Resource Centre), with myself as Director, Louise Corti (a scientist and social scientist by training) as Senior Administrator and Janet Foster (an archivist) as Senior Research Officer. Qualidata has a double purpose. The first is a salvage operation: to rescue the most significant material created by research from previous years. The second is to work with the ESRC and the ESRC Data Archive to ensure that for current and future projects the unnecessary waste of the past does not continue. Thus we are very much concerned not only with oral history projects, but also with more contemporary sociological studies, with anthropology, and indeed with the whole range of social science disciplines.

Qualidata is not an archive itself: it is an action unit. We locate and evaluate research data, we catalogue it, we organize its transfer to suitable archives, and we publicize its existence to researchers. We consult with the ESRC and other funding bodies on qualitative aspects of datasets policy. We provide advice to researchers on the implications of archiving for research, both through organized workshops and through individual consultations.

The first step was to find where we could best deposit the material we traced. We began by visiting a list of potential repositories which we could recommend as having good facilities, such as the British Library and its National Sound Archive, the Modern Records Collection at Warwick University, the Institute of Criminology at Cambridge, and the Mass Observation Archive at Sussex University, and we have worked out with them suitable forms of agreement for the conditions of deposit. Rather to our surprise, however, we found that no library was willing to take large collections on social policy or social change. In the event, we have been able to set up a special new archive for these areas at Essex itself, with initial support from the Joseph Rowntree Foundation.

At the same time we were evolving a model pathway along which any dataset was intended to travel from being traced, evaluated and selected as a priority for archiving, through cataloguing to deposit in a chosen archive. For this we developed forms of agreement for depositors, and produced a set of documents for the guidance of researchers which set out a strategic *practical* path through the key issues, such as confidentiality and copyright, which must be confronted during the process of deposit. They have required a great deal of discussion and we regard them as an important step forward in themselves.

The material we have been currently handling includes my own research interviews: we felt it right that I should be the first guinea-pig for testing out our transfer procedure (and indeed it proved a humiliating process, revealing the extent to which I could not remember what I had done, or why, on earlier research projects). Other early sets of interviews are for pioneering studies of stepfamilies and single parent families, and for Annette Lawson's book on *Adultery*. But the biggest challenge has been presented by our encountering the lifetime's research material of Peter Townsend, Britain's leading investigator of poverty since the 1950s, which was under threat of destruction because he had to leave his university rooms on his retirement. His material includes, for example, a completely unused set of interviews carried out in the East End of London, which were intended to link up with the observations made by Beatrice Webb (herself one of the pioneers of oral history) when she was a rent collector there in the 1880s. There are also richly detailed ethnographic accounts of visits to several hundred old people's homes in every part of the country.

A collection like this will be of obvious value to future historians. Paul Barker, who visited Qualidata recently, described being taken down into the basement to see the archive:

> a room they call the 'coal hole', which is more like a squirrel's cache. It is lined with box files dating back to Townsend's earliest days as an Institute of Community Studies researcher – the basis for *The Family Life of Old People* (1957) and *The Last Refuge* (1962).
>
> Here are the typed-up, but unedited, Bethnal Green diaries of informants such as Mrs Muckley (who became 'Mrs Tucker' in the published text).
>
> Here are notes, also, that Townsend made for a study which was never published. He was comparing Beatrice Webb's extant ledger of the inhabitants of Katherine Buildings, in Whitechapel (where she worked in the 1880s as a rent collector), with the people who lived there in the 1950s. 'On the top floor of Katherine Buildings, Cartwright Street, Stepney,' Townsend wrote on 20 August 1957, 'lives Mrs Matilda Oldfield. At right angles from the balcony at the back of the block runs a short passage, in which there are four doors.' He meets 'a small stocky woman with a mop of reddish hair playing out from an untidy bun. A dirty bedraggled blouse was held together with at least four safety pins.' She mistakes Townsend for a busybody from the YWCA. When he reasures her, she agrees to speak to him.
>
> This is living history. . .[7]

And not just of past revelance. It is also important to emphasize that the sheer scale and depth of Townsend's studies of poverty and old age are unlikely to be repeated in the foreseeable future, and must continue to provide an exceptionally rich quarry of experience to guide contemporary social policy experts who cannot afford to replicate such studies.

One of our most basic challenges has been to get a measure of how much material of comparable significance may survive from earlier research projects. Establishing this is a very substantial task in itself, and has involved setting up three different surveys which together take us back to 1945. We believe that the information which we are gathering will be of considerable intrinsic value for researchers, as well as a foundation for our own activities.

Once we have established the existence of qualitative material and the willingness of the researcher to consider deposit, we seek the advice of specialists in the relevant discipline in deciding which projects should be evaluated. In prioritizing, we take into account both intellectual and practical criteria. In intellectual terms, we ask, is this research recognized as of high quality, influential in its field, or representing the working life of a significant researcher; and does it have a high value of potential for reanalysis or comparative use? Practically, we consider whether it is at high risk of destruction; can be made freely available for research use, with copyright and confidentiality not too restrictive for reasonable access; and whether it is legible or audible and in reasonable physical condition, and sufficiently documented for informed reuse.

However, the mention of confidentiality and copyright leads to the thorniest problem an archiving retrieval programme must face.

We have been well aware from the start that both for researchers and for archivists confidentiality and copyright must be basic issues in considering the archiving of qualitative material. The two are different, but intertangled. The ethical importance of confidentiality has always been important. Whether or not confidentiality has been explicitly promised, all social science researchers have a reponsibility not to expose their informants to potential injury, whether through publicizing confessions of illegal activity, or through the risk of countersuits for libel, or simply the risk of scandal and ridicule. For this reason some research material, such as studies of criminal behaviour or paramilitary groups, may be intrinsically impossible to archive. Others might be accepted, with a timed delay for research access, or with access restricted to bona fide researchers only. Some material can be made anonymous. The alternatives have to be weighed up for each set of material.

Copyright, on the other hand, was not a problem for most British researchers before the 1988 Copyrights, Designs and Patents Act. Until then, an interviewee's willingness to be interviewed was held to imply an oral contract to be interviewed and for the researcher to hold the copyright in the interview. The position has now been reversed in European and in British national law. The interviewee is assumed not to have transferred copyright unless there is a written contract. The position is still worse for researchers, in that in Britain the new law no longer allows short quotations from copyright material without permission as 'fair usage' (as for example is normal in citing other printed works). Since most British social researchers have not adapted their practices to the new legal situation, this means that a high proportion of them are regularly breaching copyright in their publications, and also that it is difficult if not impossible to secure the copyright of their datasets for archiving.

What can be done about this? We believe that it is essential for British social researchers to take the law more seriously. But we also hope that in the long run political pressure may be brought by the ESRC and other European research councils to amend the law, at least to the extent of allowing brief quotations as fair usage.

As for research already carried out, in more recent cases it may be possible to write to informants seeking written copyright agreements, but these will very rarely cover all those interviewed. More usually, in our view we have to weigh the copyright difficulty against the potential value of the particular material, and the knowledge that legal suits against researchers are extremely unlikely, since in most cases their publication value is trivial. It is important to remember that archivists have long been accustomed to accepting and allowing the use of written material whose copyright was held by (often unknown) others, and this has rarely caused serious difficulties.

Thus in our view, while in theory copyright may seem the more difficult issue, in practice this is more likely to prove to be confidentiality.

* * *

To fully realize the aims of Qualidata, we would need not only to succeed in archiving significant qualitative material, but also to influence the culture of this whole school of social science research. In the past, partly because of the absence of a policy for archiving, and also because research material was usually paper-based and in some cases (such as anthropologists' fieldnotes) handwritten and difficult to understand, qualitative researchers rarely thought of archiving, or (except historians) of the reanalysis of earlier data. Now with most transcripts machine-readable, the possibility is opening up for a crucial shift in attitudes among social science researchers and students towards a new culture of secondary analysis, based on the assumption that the creation of in-depth interview material should be for the benefit, not only of the individual investigator, but of the research community as a whole.

In that spirit we should, I believe, look more closely at the practice of ethnographic researchers in Scandinavia. In Stockholm the Nordic Museum Archive, with a staff of 250, provides a national service for museums encompassing libraries, photographs, exhibitions and objects. It has a separate 'Memory' section, led by Stefan Bohman, with a staff of ten. The archive has been collecting material resulting from the researches of academic ethnographers for almost a hundred years: substantial in quantity, well kept and indexed, and regularly used in an attractive reading room. I was told that such research material was useful only when the original words of informants were recorded; when they had merely been summarized, they had been reshaped by the academic preoccupations of the time to such an extent as to be of little research interest to contemporary ethnographers.

Still more strikingly, the archive has been organizing regular autobiographical competitions since 1945, and since 1928 it has been collecting special thematic essays from a panel of 400 correspondents right across Sweden. The themes have gradually shifted from earlier historical preoccupations to encompass all aspects of contemporary everyday life, including even computing. The archive also has a notable collection of diaries. All the basic thematic and autobiographical data are well indexed and have now been computerized, so that very full information on the collection in Stockholm can be available at centres throughout the country. In short, the Nordic Archive provides an impressive example of what can be achieved when research money is put into the creation of general research resources as well as specific projects.

This is one implication of the new technology. But it goes far beyond this. Despite its obvious potential, oral historians and life story sociologists have been strikingly slow in exploring the possibilities of computer programming. I must immediately hasten to plead guilty to being among the most laggardly myself. Until three years ago I persisted in using the typewriter I had bought in the 1950s, a machine I could use fast and confidently and to which I had become very attached. The extent of my technological lag was finally brought home to me when I went to a New York exhibition of Italian post-war design, and saw an identical twin of my own Olivetti lettera 22 exhibited as a museum object! For our research projects, however, we did introduce quantitative analysis by computer in the late 1970s, on which Trevor Lummis wrote in *Listening to History*. And of course we switched to typing transcripts on computers as soon as this was practicable. We have not, however, made much progress in using the numerous programmes which can now assist the analysis of texts: in this I continue to use steam engine technology (or earlier). And I suspect that I am far from alone. It seems highly significant that no international oral history conference has yet featured technical discussions evaluating the various analytic programmes available – let alone the new potential of multimedia for oral history.

In my view, life story social scientists and oral historians face a double technical challenge in the next few years, and the outcome will decide whether a lively life story research movement survives into the twenty-first century. The first is video. At the moment audio recording remains justifiable because it is less disturbing and very much cheaper than video. But when high quality video with equally good sound, simultaneously operable by an interviewer, becomes almost as cheap as audio recording, the arguments against it will vanish. I have already seen a camera-sized handheld Japanese video which can be tucked on to one's shoulder, making it possible to do completely informal outdoor or indoor video interviews: and over the next three years the price of such equipment is likely to fall as fast as its quality rises. Life story and oral history interviews using only sound will obviously be archaic survivals of a past technical era.

Multimedia raises more dramatic possibilities for research, archiving and publishing – but also, for the moment, more doubts. In principle it would be possible to organize an archive so that you could read a transcript, and then at will switch over and hear the sound of the same passage, and see the expressions of the speaker: which would represent an enormous advance in the accuracy and potential interpretative insights of researchers using interviews. But the cost of doing this for a large collection remains prohibitive (and there are also technical problems still in the amount of sound and video which can be included). In practice multimedia has proved commercially viable principally with publications for children (who take more quickly to new media, and are being used as the lead-in for a future adult market) and for reference works such as dictionaries and encyclopaedias.

So far I know of no European social science or oral history project which has brought out its material in multimedia form. I have seen a few North American examples, including one from Berkeley. But so far the most sophisticated to have been produced are the series of multimedia CD-Roms from projects carried out by Karen Worcman and her team at the Museu da Pessoa in São Paulo, Brazil. The most recent are *Memórias do Comércio* on the city's small businessmen and *Memória em Multimídia do SENAC*, on a local firm; the next to follow is about a São Paulo trade union. Whatever the theme, they combine interview texts with shorter extracts of audio and video, along with maps, genealogical trees, old film and other documents. What is novel, and in these CD-Roms beautifully designed, is the way in which all this information is interconnected, so that you can switch easily between one type and another. The elegance of the design and the colours, and the touches of wit such as the faces which ask for a click with a smile or the winking eyes, are all there to help you to enjoy moving around. Multimedia is clearly a new art form.

We have already had to learn how different an interview is on audio tape from a typed transcript with words only. The typed form can never convey more than a hint of the tones, accents and emotions in the spoken word, and the irregular pauses of speech necessarily disappear behind the logical sequence of grammatical punctuation. The testimony will vary yet again if it is to be published in printed form: editing will render it smoother and more condensed, cutting out repetitions and filler-words, helping the reader to focus on what the editor thinks matters most. Each stage requires a reshaping of the original interview. And an interview which is outstanding in one form may not work in another. Some people's words are brilliant on paper but their tone or voice is intolerably boring in sound; add their face and their expressions may captivate you – or put you off altogether. Sooner or later it will become clear that multimedia requires its own kind of reshaping of the recorded life story; and also that a certain type of teller is the best for the medium.

But I am still puzzled by another question. I do not yet understand what the Museu da Pessoa's CD-Roms are meant to do for their audience. With the São Paulo football club project, for example, you can stand in front of the monitor, press your finger on the screen, and opt for the 1930s, then for notable goals, see the goal scored on film and hear the uproar of the crowd, and then switch to the footballer who scored, and discover about his life and memories. In theory, you could use this multimedia design to build up a real historical resource on the club's history, with dozens of testimonies from retired players, managers, patrons and generations of fans. But, in practice, it seems to me that the fascination is in flicking from one sort of information to another, rather than in exploring anything in depth. Ultimately it is another form of reference work; and a dictionary, however fascinating, can never be a novel. Hence, while multimedia can store life stories, it is designed for a form of use which is fundamentally inimical to any sustained narrative, or authorial argument. In other words, it depends on what its users make of it. Karen Worcman argues that – especially in a country like Brazil, where there is little popular interest in history – it can hook in people who would never be attracted to more conventional forms of publication. We shall see. But certainly multimedia *is* a new form of publication. And oral historians are going to be forced to come to terms with it.

The future is all the more challenging, and also more difficult to predict, because of the simultaneous explosion of not only multimedia but also the Internet. Clearly the Internet is now well established as one of the principal means of communication between researchers world-wide. It also provides a new way of sustaining close friendships right across the globe. There is no technical reason why it should not become a principal multimedia form, although this might not come about because of the difficulties of recovering the production costs of commercially produced multimedia packages. There are likely to be crucial battles between the computing and publishing giants over copyright, markets and profits, in which researchers of any kind will be merely marginal. For the same reason we may not see the full flowering of the interactive possibilities of the Internet, through which users might modify the multimedia packages they receive, inserting material of their own, and reshaping them, just as the original sources have already been reshaped to become part of the package. This may be too democratic a possibility for publishers and for academics too.

The kind of life story product we may get from the publishing giants is indicated by recent news of a multimillion dollar deal by Warner Books to publish a multimedia posthumous 'autobiography' of Martin Luther King. Constructed from his speeches, sermons, correspondence and writings, Warner Books envisages multiform autobiography combining an Internet site on King with cassettes and CD-Roms of his speeches and writings, and a book of his sermons. They hope to make a profit of over 10 million dollars a year from the deal with King's family. The King family should do well too.

There can hardly be much room for academic priorities in a project of this kind, but its scale is bound to be exceptional. It is easy enough to see how in a much less grandiose way a family with enough old video and photo albums could compile its own multimedia history. And in principle any oral history project could be used in a similar way. Equally important, in more modest productions based on life stories the quality of the original material will continue to be fundamental, and so will the skill and imagination with which it is presented. Life story researchers will need to develop these new skills and imagination if they are to participate fully in *The Rise of the Network Society*: in that restructured transnational information society which some of the world's leading sociologists apparently see as our common future.[8]

To sum up, then, I have no doubt that research and archiving should work hand in hand. Certainly there will always be knotty problems over the types of interviews conducted, the sampling of informants, the prioritizing of material to be archived, and above all, over confidentiality and copyright. But I do not see any of them as insoluble. I am much more concerned that life story sociologists and anthropologists and oral historians, whether researchers or archivists, will fail to come to terms with the development of new technology, and so leave us stranded, cut off from the mainstreams of historical and social science research: beached specialists of a bygone technical era, like the interpreters of shorthand notebooks, or the guardians of medieval Latin manuscripts. Oral history boomed in the mid-twentieth century because, in an era in which radio was still enormously influential, it could bring the past alive with a contemporary authenticity. If we are to remain communicators, we must move with the technology of communication.

NOTES

1 Ninth International Oral History Conference, 'Communicating experience', 13–16 June 1996: at which an earlier version of this chapter was presented.
2 Paul Thompson, *The Edwardians: The Remaking of British Society* (London, 1975; 3rd edn 1992).
3 Thea Thompson, *Edwardian Childhoods* (London, 1981); Thea Vigne and Alun Howkins, 'The small shopkeeper in industrial and market towns', in G. Crossick (ed.), *The Lower Middle Class in Britain, 1870–1914* (London, 1977); Paul Thompson, Catherine Itzin and Michele Abendstern, *I Don't Feel Old: The Experience of Ageing* (Oxford, 1990), ch. 4, pp. 62–91; Paul Thompson, *The Voice of the Past: Oral History* (Oxford, 1978; 2nd edn 1988).
4 In chronological order: Standish Meacham, *A Life Apart: The English Working Class, 1879–1914* (London, 1980); Charles More, *Skill and the English Working Class* (London, 1980); Patrick Joyce, *Work, Society and Politics: The Culture of the Factory in Late Victorian England* (London, 1982); Ellen Ross, '"Fierce questions and taunts": married life in working-class London, 1870–1914', *Feminist Studies* 8 (1982–3); Ellen Ross, 'Survival networks: women's neighbourhood sharing in London before World War One', *History Workshop* 15 (1983): 4–27; John Gills, *For Better, For Worse: British Marriages 1600 to the Present* (Oxford, 1985); Hugh McLeod, 'Religion: the oral evidence', *Oral History* 14 (1986): 31–49; Natasha Burchardt, 'Stepchildren's memories: myth, understanding and forgiveness', in R. Samuel and P. Thompson (eds), *The Myths We Live By* (London, 1990), pp. 239–51; Michael Childs, *Labour's Apprentices: Working Class Lads in Late Victorian and Edwardian England* (London, 1992); David Crouch and Colin Ward, *The Allotment: Its Landscape and Culture* (London, 1988); Jonathan Rose, 'Willingly to school: the working-class response to elementary education in Britain, 1875–1918', *Journal of British Studies* 32 (1993): 114–38; David Vincent, 'Mobility, bureaucracy and careers in early twentieth century Britain', in A. Miles and D. Vincent (eds), *Building European Society* (Manchester, 1993); David Vincent, 'Shadow and reality in occupational history', in Daniel Bertaux and Paul Thompson, *Pathways to Social Class* (Oxford, 1997), pp. 98–123.

Forthcoming books drawing on the archive include major studies of marriage by James Hammerton and of the British middle class by Richard Trainor.

5 Burchardt, 'Stepchildren's memories'.

6 Publications from the projects include Cathy Courtney and Paul Thompson, *City Lives* (London, 1996); Paul Thompson, 'The Pyrrhic victory of gentlemanly capitalism: the financial elite of the City of London, 1945–90', *Journal of Contemporary History* 32 (1997): 283–304; Alan Dein and Rob Perks, *Lives in Steel*, National Sound Archive C14 tape/CD 03 (London, 1993); Carrie Supple and Rob Perks, *Voices of the Holocaust: A Cross-Curricular Pack*, National Sound Archive C10–13 (London, 1993).

7 Paul Barker, 'Banks for the memories', *Guardian*, 4 Dec. 1996.

8 Manuel Castells, *The Rise of the Network Society* (Oxford, 1996); Anthony Giddens, 'Out of place', *Times Higher Education Supplement*, 13 Dec. 1996, p. 18.

RAPHAEL SAMUEL
An Appreciation
Jerry White

I first met Raphael in June 1975. I had been trying to meet him for some time before that but the letter I sent him received no reply. Probably he was too busy to answer: maybe I'd have got one eventually.

At that time I'd drafted half a book on the redevelopment of the Flower and Dean St area of Spitalfields in the 1870s and 1880s. I had never been to university and, at twenty-six, was keen to prove my intellectual worth by writing a book that would make academics sit up. And I had a subject. I had stumbled upon the Flower and Dean St tenement blocks while taking photographs of worn-out London housing and I'd become fascinated by Charlotte de Rothschild Dwellings, among the biggest and ugliest of the East End's Victorian tenements.

At school I had read George Ewart Evans's *Ask the Fellows Who Cut the Hay*, and it occurred to me to extend its technique to the inner-city setting of Spitalfields. Charlotte de Rothschild Dwellings, bleak as a bomb site in 1975, must have been valued as homes once: I recognized myself as an outsider in time and space, and I wanted to see the buildings through the eyes of insiders, people who'd laughed and loved there when the paint was still fresh.

At first I followed two tracks: I set out to discover and talk to people who'd lived there; and I buried myself in the archives to discover how Rothschild Buildings (as I quickly learned they were known) had been built. But soon this second track grew deeper and wider and I found myself in thrall to the social history of Victorian London. I had enlisted in the ranks of the collectors of footnotes: my half-book tingled with them.

Through a friend, I'd shown my text to a Cambridge historian. He was generous and encouraging. But his subject was the Luftwaffe in the Second World War, not the Victorian East End, and so it would be cruel to name him here. Then I met Raphael.

I've forgotten how I heard of him or found his address. But someone told me that if I was interested in the East End then Raphael Samuel was the man for me. So I wrote, but without success. And then a work colleague, finding himself one day in conversation with a historian, mentioned my work to him, and again I got the message that I must speak to Raphael. This time, though, the historian was Alun Howkins, and as well as the message I got Raphael's telephone number.

When we met, he was preparing Sunday lunch in the Elder St cellar kitchen which so many will associate with him: Raphael's habitat when not alone. House, kitchen, Raphael, seemed to me strange survivals from a London of long ago. The Spitalfields house was early eighteenth-century. Raphael, though younger, wore clothes and handled kitchen implements that looked as though they must have been third-hand in the Year of Jubilee: and the wisdom of ages flashed and sparkled behind his dusty spectacles.

He asked me to read some of the text I'd brought while he sliced vegetables at the sink. As I read, I felt the confidence I'd previously had in my work drain out of me. I knew beyond all doubt that this stuff could not stand up to those eyes, sympathetic and encouraging though they were, and their far-sighted gaze that seemed to penetrate text, sources, me, into unreachable depths beyond.

It didn't take long for Raphael to tell me it wouldn't do. He had a gentle bedside manner that dulled my disappointment, and I knew I was incapable of arguing a corner against his reasoning. Then, like some master mariner rescuing me in a bear hug from a sinking dinghy, Raphael gave me hope: I'd not written up the oral history but that sounded most interesting of all; go back to it, write it up and see him again in three weeks; and there was a book just published that might give me some useful ideas. Raphael sold me a copy of *Village Life and Labour*,[1] inscribing it 'For Jeremy in expectation of your coming work on Flower and Dean Street.' And I was back on the bus to Clapton.

At the time, Raphael's kindness on that Sunday seemed to me extraordinary. It seems so still. In many ways we were such dissimilar characters that I could never quite understand why he showed me the sympathy he did. He was slight, sallow, very Jewish; I was beefy, red-faced, mongrel-English. I was a hired apparatchik of the local state, chained to a monthly salary; he was a free-wheeling intellectual who once told me that he had never in his life done anything that he hadn't really wanted to do. As an aspiring historian I was self-taught, and that was always a virtue in Raphael's eyes; but I could hardly qualify for the lauded title of 'worker-historian'. In these circumstances, his commitment to invest more time in me, his apparent confidence that I could produce something of worth despite a substantial false start, seemed an astonishing act of faith. And my life was not the same after it.

Looking again at 'Quarry roughs' in *Village Life and Labour* has made me relive the excitement I found in it at the time. It's a wonderful essay. Its characters live on the page, their individual voices loud and strong. Their testimony is deeply rooted in soil which Raphael has mulched with apparently bottomless information: gleanings from everywhere, no dusty corner of memory unswept, no possible repository for documents unsearched, no relevant text unthumbed. It is an essay essentially about work – of haggle-cart men, well-diggers, brickmakers, laundresses, totters, woodmen, poachers, traders in Oxford college dripping and dozens more. It situates work in the agricultural economy and class relations of late nineteenth-century England. And it does all of this in the precise and wryly elegant prose that was Raphael Samuel's literary trademark, relishing the opportunities of oral history for colourful contrasts of voice and register.

> When the pig was killed, the woman of the house was involved in a whole series of manufacturing activities. 'Flere', the pig's jacket, was melted for lard ('we used to prefer it to butter'); blood, gathered at the killing, was made into black puddings ('nearly everybody, when they had a pig killed, they used to make black puddings'); chitterlings, the pig's innards, went into faggots ('boiled and fried 'em, didn't you?'), trotters into jelly for soup. The pig's head was preserved as brawn ('still see it now with the whiskers sticking in'): hams and bacon were taken off the body and treated with saltpetre ('they used to chuck it in these brawn baths').[2]

'Quarry roughs' had an enormous influence on me – more, I feel looking back, than I realized at the time. I recognize now much unconscious emulation in my own subsequent treatment of oral history. Thus do the 'self-taught' find themselves taught after all.

As far as I can recall, I met Raphael's three-week deadline. I think I produced some three-dozen pages using the little oral material that I'd then gathered. He read it in silence, and at the end he was critical but optimistic. I was sent away to come back in another three weeks or so with a piece on shopping. He asked, I believe, for ten pages. Secretly I was daunted: how could anyone write ten pages on shopping? Was this an aptitude test I was expected to fail? But now I was interviewing more people and, though it took me beyond the deadline, I returned triumphantly – with thirty pages. I remember this particularly because it was the only piece of work I was ever to show Raphael where he had no suggestions for improvement.

* * *

The recovery of memory was a central strand of the History Workshop project – and of Raphael Samuel's own work within it – through the 1970s and the early 1980s. Memory was a highway for restoring the lived experience of those groups in society – comprising together by far the majority – who had been largely excluded from written history: children, working-class men, women. Reconstituting their history, through memory where possible, became an urgent political task. And Samuel's influence on this reconstitution was vitally important, both through teaching and by example.

I suppose that his teaching, essentially, was: know as much as you can, use every source available to you, situate memory and its unrivalled access to recovering lived experience in the realities which are unknowable to the individual but which the historian can recover. And I suppose that his example was expressed through titanic learning based on inexhaustible note-taking from every imaginable document, artefact or personal experience that he could light upon; a passionate belief in what Arnold Bennett used to call 'the interestingness of ordinary things'; and an unshakeable belief that what he was doing would benefit the cause of humanity against those who claim to run the world on its behalf.

Raphael's main legacy to oral history (there are other legacies to the social significance of memory) is *East End Underworld: Chapters in the Life of Arthur Harding* (1981). Harding, or Arthur Tressenden as he was known in adult life, was born in 1886 in the Nichol (or 'Jago') area of Bethnal Green and he was to die within a year of the book appearing. Raphael interviewed him between 1973 and 1979 and the text is a reconstruction of the mass of transcripts that emerged, heavily edited with explanatory footnotes and a glossary of slang.

Harding's was one of the last families to be put out of the Nichol by the London County Council's slum clearance programme around 1895, and his testimony is a unique recollection of the most notorious district of late Victorian London. Given its reputation (crystallized by Arthur Morrison's *Child of the Jago*, 1896), it comes as a surprise to find the Nichol populated by people and not monsters, even if they did hold some pretty odd opinions:

> The strange legacy that my father's family left to all their offspring was their political beliefs. They were all true-blue Conservatives, quite simple. The Conservatives were rich and powerful and they distributed large gifts to their supporters. The Radicals and Liberals were too poor, they were out to get something for themselves so what was the good of voting for them? These political beliefs have remained with all the offspring of those uncles and aunts from the Nichol. With my family and my brother's and sister's family, I can say that all who hold our name vote Conservative.[3]

Harding's life is told in rich detail, prised out of him by Raphael's desire to get as close as possible to the unobtainable 'whole truth' of a fascinating life. The book will stand as one of the key texts of working-class autobiography published in the last fifty years; and the documentary evidence in the foot-notes gives the testimony a unique authority.

It is important to remember, though, that *East End Underworld* is an unfinished project. In fact it was intended to be the *second* of two volumes on the underworld of south-west Bethnal Green, and the projected contents of the other volume were sketched out in a 'Prefatory note' to the Harding book. Memory was to play a part in the companion volume, too, but essentially it was to be based on written sources. It would have fulfilled Raphael's desire to situate Harding' s life within a reality which no one person could comprehend, where the experience of others, and the subterranean forces of class and history, moulded and helped determine an individual life. Its last chapter was to be called 'The voice of the past?' and we can only lament that Raphael was not able to leave it to us.

That schedule took Raphael down many intellectual highways and byways during the 1980s and early 1990s, and I cannot claim to have tracked his footprints. But I think that his fascination and engagement with popular memory never left him. It is a continuous strand in his work on patriotism that produced three volumes of collected essays by many hands in 1989:[4] and some of his own writing in these volumes was to rematerialize in his *tour de force* of 1994, *Theatres of Memory*. In particular, he had a long fascination with the popular expressions of memory that found their way to the surface of culture through enthusiasms like railway mania and steam engine restoration, metal detecting, the gentrification of Victorian houses, or the resurrectionists who re-enact Civil War battles each year at Marston Moor.

And in particular, too, he overcame a deeply engrained Communist diffidence when he put chapters of his own life on public display – admittedly as elucidation of time, culture and place – in three breathtaking articles on British Communism for *New Left Review* in 1985–7.[5]

This was another uncompleted project, situating his early years within the religion of Communism (complete with creeds, articles of faith, heresies, and sins against the Holy Ghost) and within the culture of metropolitan immigrant Jewry in the 1940s and 1950s. The text is a moving evocation of a 'lost world', part lament but also an exasperated critique of the blindness of faith. Raphael's skills as listener and observer – bringing sympathy, engagement, but also critical detachment – are summed up eloquently in his subheadings: Party-mindedness, Time-thrift, Solemnity of meetings. In his *post mortem* the very nerves and blood vessels of British Communism are teased apart, one by one, and their connections, strengths and fallibilities gently opened for all to see. And there is space, too, for Comrade Samuel to offer himself as surgical specimen:

I was brought up as a true believer. My first film – a show arranged by my mother in the village hall of Aspley Guise – was *Lone White Sail*, a touching story of the 1905 Revolution. . . . Where Christian children might have learned their sacred geography, I had *Soviet Russia in Maps*. It was given to me on, I think, my eighth birthday [Boxing Day, 1942], a book with an orange cover and a bas-relief of a hammer and sickle. Soon I was able to show off my prowess in knowing Russian towns, and then with the aid of the war maps I created what was for some time an obsessional game: encircling the German army. . . . As a child I was an obsessive, being by turns a ticket collector, a gardener, a fanatic footballer and a runner. The war was an early focus, and a worried note in my school report (at the age of six) records an obsession with 'justice and fairness'.[6]

There are three unmissable references to 'obsession' in this short passage. And I suppose one of the obsessions that most possessed Raphael was how the past was reconstituted, understood and given significance in the popular consciousness: how memory, reflected and deflected as it inevitably is, moulds and even transforms the present.

It was an obsession that materialized again in *The Myths We Live By*,[7] which Raphael edited with Paul Thompson in 1990. This collection of essays from the 1987 Oral History Conference at Oxford marked 'a crucial turning point' in the development of oral history. It focused on 'the displacements, omissions, and reinterpretations' in oral history narratives 'through which myths in personal and collective memory take shape'. The book's clarion call for interdisciplinary dialogue, a melding of skills from the worlds of psychoanalysis, anthropology and history, was typical of Raphael's commitment to learning from everyone and everything in order better to understand a reality which has more layers than any one 'school' can count. As he and Thompson wrote in their introduction:

[Life stories] should be seen, not as blurred experience, as disorderly masses of fragments, but as shaped accounts in which some incidents were dramatized, others contextualized, yet others passed over in silence, through a process of narrative shaping in which both conscious and unconscious, myth and reality, played significant parts.

Raphael's own efforts to take this project further – the result of endless consideration, based on evidence-taking from every conceivable 'source' available to him – were to be put together in his monumental *Theatres of Memory*.[8]

This, once more, was to be an 'uncompleted project'. Death intervened to prevent the publication of the two succeeding volumes that Raphael had planned, although I understand that enough material for the second volume exists for it to be published posthumously. And, in case by dwelling on this point I've made Raphael sound a poor finisher, I think, rather, it reflects his selfless dedication to teaching at the expense of his 'own' work on the one hand; and on the other his insatiable inquisitiveness, opening out more and more connections to trace and explore, and making every conclusion contingent and preliminary, hardly ever firm enough to fix on the page.

Theatres of Memory is an extraordinary compendium of learning and personal experience. It offers a thoroughgoing reinterpretation of everyday experience. We are invited literally to see the world differently by focusing on the way in which the past penetrates every pore of the present (and thus the future, too). Reading it is like a slow journey on foot through England, being urged to look again at streets, buildings, people or commodities we thought familiar, and finding we had never really seen them at all till now.

In retro advertising, the past is there to humanize the present, and substitute a personal for a corporate image. In the present series of

187

Levi ads, harking back to 1920s hillbillies, as in the 1974 Hovis 'bike ride' commercial directed by Ridley Scott which helped to make nostalgia a leitmotiv of TV commercials, sepia is there to sentimentalize the image. But period is also widely used for comic, or serio-comic effect, as in those parodies of old masters currently being used by Vodaphone in the cordless communications war. An old film clip from Harold Lloyd's *Safety Last*, showing the comic clinging for dear life to the clockface at the top of the Empire State Building, was for many years a very popular insurance ad. A recent Heineken series contrived to parade Marilyn Monroe (from *Some Like It Hot*), John Wayne from a western, and Humphrey Bogart. A much admired current effort is Mercury's pastiche of a 1950 Pathé newsreel in which words and image are out of synch and a nincompoop of the officer class who tries to rally the other ranks.[9]

The making of 'History' itself becomes part of this reappraising eye: in some fascinating chapters on Victorian photographs, for instance, or on historical drama in the cinema and on stage; but also in an 'Afterword' that provocatively resurrects 'the earliest historians' as 'forgers', and then takes the scalpel to the body of present-day historical practice:

> Historians today don't knowingly forge documents. But by the nature of our trade we are continually having to fabricate contexts. We may not construct imaginary speeches in the manner of Thucydides, but by selective quotation we can make subjects give expression to what we believe to be their innermost being. We make extravagant claims for the importance of our subject, and strain interpretation to secure the maximum effect. Footnotes serve as fetishes and are given as authorities for generalizations which a thousand different instances would not prove. We suppress the authorial 'I' so that the evidence appears to speak for itself. We improve on the original, making connections to cover the gaps in the story, the silences in the evidence. Our pictures, apparently seamless, are so artfully framed and carefully composed, that the historian's gaze imposes itself.[10]

* * *

I saw Raphael for the last time in October 1996. We talked a little of his illness, and a little of the past. But most of all we spoke of the future: of his plans for his new post as Professor of History at the University of East London, and the Centre for East End History he had seeded at the Bishopsgate Institute; and of my plans for a book on London government in the twentieth century. Suddenly we found ourselves working together again. Raphael had already sketched out in his head a series of pamphlets on London between the wars – a critical moment, he thought, when London really worked as a city – and I offered something on the London economy which I'd worked up some time ago but never published. I promised him a text by the end of January 1997: but I knew time was short, and I put what I had in the post to him within a fortnight.

I was left with a strong sense of Raphael returning, rearmed as it were, to London and its history; bringing with him the learning he had gathered across the 1980s and early 1990s to help him and us understand this great city that he loved so much. Bringing with him from *Theatres of Memory*, for instance, the strengthened affirmation that memory, its construction and reconstruction, will always be central to the historian's craft, not least in understanding modern society.

> History has always been a hybrid form of knowledge, syncretizing past and present, memory and myth, the written record and the spoken word. Its subject matter is promiscuous. . . . In popular memory, if not in high scholarship, the great flood or the freak storm may eclipse wars, battles and the rise and fall of governments. As a form of communication, history finds expression not only in chronicle and commentary but also ballad and song, legends and proverbs, riddles and puzzles. . . . A present-day inventory would need to be equally alert to the memory work performed (albeit unintentionally) by the advertisers, and to the influence of tourism, home tourism especially. As a self-conscious art, history begins with monuments and inscriptions, and as the record of the built environment suggests, not the least of the influences changing historical consciousness today is the writing on the walls. The influence of video-games and science-fiction would be no less pertinent in trying to explain why the idea of chronological reversal, or time travelling, has become a normal way of engaging with the idea of the past.[11]

It would probably be wrong to inflate this passage into a manifesto. None the less, it carries within it Raphael's clear conviction that nothing which is of importance to ordinary people is unworthy of serious study and contemplation; and that society cannot be properly comprehended without exploring these infinitely diverse influences on popular consciousness. This exploration was the great task he had set himself, with a renewed focus on twentieth-century London. His untimely death stopped him taking it further. And it has deprived us of one of the great democrats of English historical writing in the twentieth century.

NOTES

1 Raphael Samuel (ed.), *Village Life and Labour* (London: Routledge and Kegan Paul, 1975).
2 Ibid., p. 200.

3 Raphael Samuel, *East End Underworld: Chapters in the Life of Arthur Harding* (London: Routledge, 1981), p. 30.

4 Raphael Samuel (ed.), *Patriotism: the Making and Unmaking of the British Identity*, vol. 1: *History and Politics*; vol. 2: *Minorities and Outsiders*; vol. 3: *National Fictions* (3 vols, London: Routledge, 1989).

5 Raphael Samuel, 'The lost world of British Communism', *New Left Review*, no. 154 (Nov.–Dec. 1985): 3–53; no. 156 (Mar.–Apr. 1986): 63–113; no. 165 (Sept.–Oct. 1987): 52–91.

6 *New Left Review*, no. 154 (1985): 47.

7 Raphael Samuel and Paul Thompson (eds), *The Myths We Live By* (London: Routledge, 1990).

8 Raphael Samuel, *Theatres of Memory*, vol. 1: *Past and Present in Contemporary Culture* (London: Verso, 1994).

9 Ibid., pp. 93–5.

10 Ibid., pp. 433–4.

11 Ibid., pp. 443–4.

RAPHAEL SAMUEL
A Select Bibliography

*** sole authored   ** co-authored   * edited

*** 'A left notebook: politics of town planning', *Universities and Left Review*, no. 2 (1957).

** with Stuart Hall, Peter Sedgwick and Charles Taylor, 'The insiders: a study of the men who rule British industry', *Universities and Left Review*, no. 3 (1957).

** with Michael Segal, 'France in crisis: the authoritarianism of the fifties', *Universities and Left Review*, no. 4 (1958).

*** 'Class and classlessness', *Universities and Left Review*, no. 6 (1959).

*** 'The boss as hero', *Universities and Left Review*, no. 7 (1959).

*** 'The deference voter', *New Left Review*, no. 1 (1960).

*** 'Dr Abrams and the end of politics', *New Left Review*, no. 5 (1960).

*** 'But nothing happens: the long pursuit, studies in the government's slum clearance programme', *New Left Review*, nos 13–14 (1962).

*** 'The perils of the transcript', *Oral History* 1(2) (1971): 19–22.

*** 'Headington Quarry: recording a labouring community', *Oral History* 1(4) (1972): 107–22.

*** 'Comers and goers', in H. J. Dyos and Michael Wolff (eds), *The Victorian City*, London: Routledge, 1973.

* *Village Life and Labour*, London: Routledge, 1975. Includes *** '"Quarry roughs": life and labour in Headington Quarry, 1820–1920: an essay in oral history'.

*** 'Local history and oral history', *History Workshop Journal*, no. 1 (1976).

** with Gareth Stedman Jones, 'Sociology and history', *History Workshop Journal*, no. 1 (1976).

* *Miners, Quarrymen and Saltworkers*, London: Routledge, 1977.

*** 'The workshop of the world: steam power and hand technology in mid-Victorian Britain', *History Workshop Journal*, no. 3 (1977).

*** 'History Workshop methods', *History Workshop Journal*, no. 9 (1980).

*** *East End Underworld: Chapters in the Life of Arthur Harding*, London: Routledge, 1981.

* *People's History and Socialist Theory*, London: Routledge, 1981. Includes *** 'People's History'.

* with Gareth Stedman Jones, *Culture, Ideology and Politics*, London: Routledge, 1982.

*** 'The lost world of British Communism', part 1, *New Left Review*, no. 154 (1985): 3–53.

*** 'The Roman Catholic Church and the Irish poor', in Roger Swift and Sheridan Gilley, *The Irish in the Victorian City*, London: Croom Helm, 1985.

** with Ewan MacColl and Stuart Cosgrove, *Theatres of the Left 1880–1935*, London: Routledge, 1985.

** with Barbara Bloomfield and Guy Boanas, *The Enemy Within: Pit Villages and the Miners' Strike of 1984–5*, London: Routledge, 1986.

*** 'Class politics: the lost world of British Communism', part 3, *New Left Review*, no. 165 (1987): 52–92.

* with James Obolkevich and Lyndal Roper, *Disciplines of Faith: Studies in Religion, Politics and Patriarchy*, London: Routledge, 1987.

*** 'Born-again socialism', in Robin Archer (ed.), *Out of Apathy: Voices of the New Left Thirty Years On*, London: Verso, 1989.

*** 'The pathos of conservation', in Mark Girouard et al. *The Saving of Spitalfields*, London: Spitalfields Trust, 1989.

* *Patriotism: the Making and Unmaking of British National Identity*, 3 vols, London: Routledge, 1989. Includes *** 'Exciting to be English'; ** with Gareth Stedman Jones, 'Pearly kings and queens'; ** with Alison Light, 'Me and my girl'.

*** 'Grand narratives', *History Workshop Journal*, no. 29 (1990).

*** 'History, the nation and the schools', *History Workshop Journal*, no. 30 (1990).

* with Paul Thompson *The Myths We Live By*, London: Routledge, 1990. Includes ** with Paul Thompson, 'Memory and myth'.

* *History Workshop, 1967–71: A Collectanea*, Oxford: History Workshop, 1991.

*** 'Reading the signs, 1–2', *History Workshop Journal*, nos 32–3 (1991–2).

*** 'Mrs Thatcher's return to Victorian values', in T. C. Smout (ed.), *Victorian Values*, Oxford: Oxford University Press, 1992.

*** 'The discovery of puritanism, 1820–1914', in Jane Garnett and Colin Matthew (eds), *Religion and Revival since 1700: Essays for John Walsh*, London: Hambledon Press, 1993.

*** *Theatres of Memory, vol. 1: Past and Present in Contemporary Culture*, London: Verso, 1994.

*** 'British dimensions: four nations' history', *History Workshop Journal*, no. 41 (1995).

*** 'North and south: a year in a mining village', *London Review of Books*, 22 June 1995.

*** 'The people with stars in their eyes: does Britain need its heroes?', *Guardian*, 23 Sept. 1995.

*** 'The lost gardens of Heligan', *New Stateman*, 15 Dec. 1995.

*** 'Making it up: Raymond Williams', *London Review of Books*, 4 July 1996.

A CALL FOR CONTRIBUTIONS

ENVIRONMENTAL CONSCIOUSNESS AND ENVIRONMENTAL MOVEMENTS

The third volume of the international and interdisciplinary series Memory and Narrative is to be on the theme of the environment: of how most people become conscious of it, and how some people fight to save or to improve it.

One of the most fundamental changes in the last fifty years has been the growing realization that nature is not an inexhaustible resource which human beings can safely plunder indefinitely, but a complex and delicately balanced set of systems which can be fundamentally unbalanced or destroyed by human intervention. The entire future of human life depends upon the safeguarding and evolving of environmental systems. Yet viewing nature in this way cuts across both traditional rural attitudes and also the short-term materialism of contemporary urban capitalist life. Thus the basic questions which we intend this volume to address are the following. How is it that people develop and change their attitudes to their environment (childhood, education, trauma, travel, etc.) and what leads a minority further into environmental activism? How does this fit with their other political experiences? How do people rebuild their lives after environmental disasters? What images do they have of environmental good and bad, past and future?

We are interested in contributions from any part of the world: on rural or urban environments; on western/northern or southern/non-western cultures; and from the perspectives of literature, social science, history, environmental activism, or development and aid organizations.

The volume will be published in autumn 1998.

Papers should be sent by 31 January 1998, to both:

Professor Mary Chamberlain, School of Humanities, Oxford Brookes University, Gipsy Lane, Headington, Oxford OX3 0BP, England (tel. 01865-484301/483570);

Professor Kim Lacy Rogers, Department of History, Dickinson College, Box 1773, Carlisle, Pennsylvania 17013-2896, USA (tel. 717-245-1521/fax 245-1479).

WAR, MEMORY AND COMMEMORATION

A forthcoming volume of Memory and Narrative will focus on the theme of 'War, memory and commemoration'. It will explore the many ways in which processes of remembering and forgetting have shaped the significance of war, across personal life stories and public formations of memory. The editors invite the submissions of papers *on any aspect of this broad theme*, but are particularly keen to receive contributions on *three specific areas of work*:

1 The First and Second World War
2 War in colonial, neo-colonial and post-colonial contexts
3 Psychoanalysis and war

Questions to be address by the issue might include:
(a) How is war now remembered, what is forgotten, and what shifts in the forms of themes of public memory have taken place – across a range of different national contexts?
(b) What has been the relationship between 'popular' and 'official' memories and amnesias of war, and in what ways has its commemoration been contested?
(c) How is the war remembered and forgotten within family histories – and what have been its psychic and cultural effects across generations?
(d) What are the strengths and limitations of Paul Fussell's *The Great War and Modern Memory*, and in what ways has critical debate developed beyond it, through, for example, work on gender, on popular, middlebrow and working-class writing, on other national literatures and on media other than writing?
(e) How has war been represented in professional historical writing that attempts to relate to popular/national memory?
(f) How are the two world wars remembered in societies then under some form of colonial or imperial rule (especially, perhaps, in Africa, the Indian subcontinent, South-East Asia, Ireland) and in those states which emerged from the disintegration of an empire (in, for example, the Middle East, the Balkans, Austro-Hungary?)
(g) How are anti-colonial wars of national liberation remembered and commemorated, and what kinds of conflict does this process entail?
(h) In what ways might developments in psychoanalysis be seen as responses to war, and to what extent has psychoanalysis been implicated in the exercise of state power – or offered a critical, anti-state perspective – during wartime?

Contributions are invited from researchers working in and across any of the relevant disciplines in the humanities and social sciences, including anthropology, cultural studies, literary analysis, social history, sociology, psychoanalysis, psychology and visual studies. Memory and Narrative welcomes work on a wide range of cultural forms and practices, from oral reminiscence and life stories, to written history, autobiography and imaginative literature; and from monuments, museums and material artefacts, to film, television, video and CR-Rom.

Short proposals or synopses of papers should be submitted as soon as possible. Full papers for consideration should reach the editors by 31 March 1998. It may be possible to consider papers submitted up to 1 September 1988. Proposals and papers (four copies) should be sent to:

Dr Graham Dawson, School of Historical and Cultural Studies, University of Brighton, 10–11 Pavilion Parade, Brighton BN2 1RA, UK.

INDEX

Note: Where information is found in a note, the note number is given after the page number on which it appears.